Iguanas For Dummies®

Abbreviations

Medicine: Dosages and Routes of Administration

Abbreviation	Meaning
sid	Once a day
bid	Twice a day
tid	Three times a day
qid	Four times a day
q	Per; every (sid q4d = once a day for four days)
IC	Intracoelomically (in the belly)
IP	Interperitoneal (also in the belly)
IM	Intramuscular (in the muscle)
PO	*Per os* (by mouth)
SQ (also SC or SubQ or sub-q)	Subcutaneous (beneath the skin)

Units of Measurement

Abbreviation	Meaning	Abbreviation	Meaning
c	Cup	m	Meter
cc	Cubic centimeter	mg	Milligram
cm	Centimeter	ml	Milliliter
fl	Fluid	mm	Millimeter
ft	Foot	oz	Ounce
g	Gram	pt	Pint
gal	Gallon	qt	Quart
kg	Kilogram	tsp	Teaspoon
l	Liter	tbls, tbsp	Tablespoon
lb	Pound (lbs = pounds)	yd	Yard

Recommended Minimum Enclosure Dimensions

SVL (in inches)	STL (in inches)	Minimum Dimensions (in feet)
2.5–7	9–18	3 x 1 x 1.5
8–10	20–28	3.5 x 1 x 2.3
11–12	28–36	4.5 x 1.5 x 3
12–14	30–42	5.25 x 1.75 x 3.5
14–16	35–54	6.75 x 2.25 x 4.5
18–20	45–60	7.5 x 2.5 x 5
20–22	50–66	8.25 x 2.75 x 5.5
20–24	50–72	9 x 3 x 6

For Dummies™: Bestselling Book Series for Beginners

Iguanas For Dummies®

Cheat Sheet

Conversion of Common Measurements

Temperature Conversions

Do This	To Get This
(Degrees Celsius x 1.8) + 32	Degrees Fahrenheit
(Degrees Fahrenheit - 32) x .555	Degrees Celsius

Weight Conversions

Do This	To Get This
Ounce(s) x 28.349	Grams
Gram(s) x 0.035	Ounces
Kilogram(s) x 2.205	Pounds
Pound(s) x 0.454	Kilograms

Length Conversions

Do This	To Get This
Inch(es) x 25.4	Millimeters
Millimeter(s) x 0.0394	Inches
Inch(es) x 2.54	Centimeters
Centimeter(s) x 0.394	Inches
Feet x 0.305	Meters
Meter(s) x 3.281	Feet
Yard(s) x 0.914	Meters
Meter(s) x 1.094	Yards

Volume Conversions

Do This	To Get This
U.S. fluid gallon(s) x 0.833	UK fluid gallons
UK fluid gallon(s) x 1.201	U.S. fluid gallons
U.S. fluid ounce(s) x 1.041	UK fluid ounces
UK fluid ounce(s) x 0.961	U.S. fluid ounces
U.S. fluid ounce(s) x 29.572	Milliliters
Milliliter(s) x 0.034	U.S. fluid ounces
Liter(s) x 1.056	U.S. fluid quarts
U.S. fluid quart(s) x 0.947	Liters

Weight Equivalents

Amount	Equivalent to	Equivalent to	Equivalent to
1 kg	2.2 lbs	1,000 g	
1 lb	454 g	0.454 kg	16 oz
1 oz	28.349 g		
1 g	1,000 mg		

Liquid Equivalents

Amount	Equivalent to	Equivalent to	Equivalent to
1 oz	30 ml		
1 tsp	5 ml		
1 tbsp	3 tsp	15 ml	
2 tbsp	1 fluid oz		
4 tbsp	1/4 c	2 oz	
1 ml	1 cc		
1 c	8 fluid oz	16 tbsp	1/2 pt
2 c	16 fluid oz	1 pt	1/2 qt
4 qt	1 gal		
1 l	1,000 ml		

Important Numbers to Have

Your vet's number: _____

Local poison control hotline: _____

Poison Control Center: 800-523-2222

National Animal Poison Control Center (NAPCC ($45 per case):

900-680-0000 (billed to your phone)
888-4AN-HELP (billed to your phone)
888-426-4435 (billed to a credit card)

IDG BOOKS WORLDWIDE

For Dummies™: Bestselling Book Series for Beginners

Praise for Iguanas For Dummies:

"Whether you are merely contemplating acquiring an iguana, or already have several, this book will meet your need. . . . It covers just about every aspect of iguanas you might encounter, from the query of whether an iguana is right for you to coping with your iguana's attempts to mate with you. . . . It has a personable writing style that is engagingly coupled with the well-established "Dummies" format that makes information so accessible."

— Kathryn W. Tosney, Professor of Biology,
University of Michigan

"Kaplan understands the complex biology and natural history of iguanas as well as anyone I know. Her expertise is based on both careful research and vast experience treating husbandry and behavioral problems in abandoned, homeless iguanas. This book is extremely thorough and covers every topic that iguana owners need to address, including many that inexperienced owners wouldn't consider without Kaplan's prompting, until problems have arisen."

— Stephen L. Barten, DVM, reptile veterinarian,
speaker, author

"Melissa's trademarks — long experience, extensive research, and humor — make this book an essential for every iguana owner, past, present, and future. Following her guidelines for housing, diet, and taming will vastly increase the probability that your iguana will be happy and healthy."

— Susan L. Solomon, Sacramento Wildlife Care Association

"With humor, intelligence, and an astounding eye for detail, Melissa Kaplan urges her readers "to do right by your iguana." So much more than a "care" book, *Iguanas For Dummies* is a blueprint for compassionate and responsible ownership."

— Tracy Basile, Features Editor, *ASPCA Animal Watch*

Iguanas FOR DUMMIES®

by Melissa Kaplan

Foreword by William K. Hayes, Ph.D.,
Associate Professor of Biology, Loma Linda University

IDG Books Worldwide, Inc.
An International Data Group Company

Foster City, CA ◆ Chicago, IL ◆ Indianapolis, IN ◆ New York, NY

Iguanas For Dummies®

Published by
IDG Books Worldwide, Inc.
An International Data Group Company
919 E. Hillsdale Blvd.
Suite 400
Foster City, CA 94404
www.idgbooks.com (IDG Books Worldwide Web site)
www.dummies.com (Dummies Press Web site)

Library of Congress Control Number: 00-104213

ISBN: 0-7645-5260-0

Printed in the United States of America

10 9 8 7 6 5 4 3 2 1

1O/QZ/QY/QQ/IN

Distributed in the United States by IDG Books Worldwide, Inc.

Distributed by CDG Books Canada Inc. for Canada; by Transworld Publishers Limited in the United Kingdom; by IDG Norge Books for Norway; by IDG Sweden Books for Sweden; by IDG Books Australia Publishing Corporation Pty. Ltd. for Australia and New Zealand; by TransQuest Publishers Pte Ltd. for Singapore, Malaysia, Thailand, Indonesia, and Hong Kong; by Gotop Information Inc. for Taiwan; by ICG Muse, Inc. for Japan; by Intersoft for South Africa; by Eyrolles for France; by International Thomson Publishing for Germany, Austria and Switzerland; by Distribuidora Cuspide for Argentina; by LR International for Brazil; by Galileo Libros for Chile; by Ediciones ZETA S.C.R. Ltda. for Peru; by WS Computer Publishing Corporation, Inc., for the Philippines; by Contemporanea de Ediciones for Venezuela; by Express Computer Distributors for the Caribbean and West Indies; by Micronesia Media Distributor, Inc. for Micronesia; by Chips Computadoras S.A. de C.V. for Mexico; by Editorial Norma de Panama S.A. for Panama; by American Bookshops for Finland.

For general information on IDG Books Worldwide's books in the U.S., please call our Consumer Customer Service department at 800-762-2974. For reseller information, including discounts and premium sales, please call our Reseller Customer Service department at 800-434-3422.

For information on where to purchase IDG Books Worldwide's books outside the U.S., please contact our International Sales department at 317-596-5530 or fax 317-572-4002.

For consumer information on foreign language translations, please contact our Customer Service department at 1-800-434-3422, fax 317-572-4002, or e-mail rights@idgbooks.com.

For information on licensing foreign or domestic rights, please phone +1-650-653-7098.

For sales inquiries and special prices for bulk quantities, please contact our Order Services department at 800-434-3422 or write to the address above.

For information on using IDG Books Worldwide's books in the classroom or for ordering examination copies, please contact our Educational Sales department at 800-434-2086 or fax 317-572-4005.

For press review copies, author interviews, or other publicity information, please contact our Public Relations department at 650-653-7000 or fax 650-653-7500.

For authorization to photocopy items for corporate, personal, or educational use, please contact Copyright Clearance Center, 222 Rosewood Drive, Danvers, MA 01923, or fax 978-750-4470.

is a registered trademark under exclusive license to IDG Books Worldwide, Inc. from International Data Group, Inc.

About the Author

Melissa Kaplan began working with reptiles a decade ago, when she was no longer able to work with birds or mammals, incorporating her reptiles into her work as a wildlife educator and wildlife rehabilitator, building on her interests and training in animal behavior observation and clinical veterinary nursing. As reptiles rapidly increased in popularity without a corresponding increase in quality care information, Melissa focused on reptiles in her research and education efforts.

Co-founder of the Reptile and Amphibian Rescue Network in Los Angeles, and the North Bay Herpetological Society in Sonoma County, California, Melissa has written extensively on reptile care and health for pet, herpetocultural, wildlife rehabilitation, and humane education publications. Her paper, *Reptile Rehabilitation*, is a popular reprint in the International Wildlife Rehabilitation Council's literature list. Melissa wrote the chapters on reptile rehabilitation and the use of reptiles in public education, in herpetocultural compendium, and collaborated with zoologist Adam Britton, Ph.D. on a popular and critically acclaimed iguana care video.

Melissa was able to combine her interest in education and reptiles in her master's thesis when she researched how teachers keep reptiles in their classrooms. This resulted in an extensive teacher's guide on the characteristics and care of the captive reptiles, as well as identifying the special concerns of reptiles kept in a classroom.

For the past seven years, Melissa has been a host in both the Veterinary Information Network's and America Online's Reptile and Amphibian Forums, as well as creating an extensive iguana and herp website at http://anapsid.org.

Melissa is presently owned by a *Cyclura* iguana, several turtles and tortoises, a cuddly blue-tongued skink, a ball python, and seven-year-old Rugwort, a diminutive rescued green iguana who is thrilled to be, for now at least, the alpha male.

ABOUT IDG BOOKS WORLDWIDE

Welcome to the world of IDG Books Worldwide.

IDG Books Worldwide, Inc., is a subsidiary of International Data Group, the world's largest publisher of computer-related information and the leading global provider of information services on information technology. IDG was founded more than 30 years ago by Patrick J. McGovern and now employs more than 9,000 people worldwide. IDG publishes more than 290 computer publications in over 75 countries. More than 90 million people read one or more IDG publications each month.

Launched in 1990, IDG Books Worldwide is today the #1 publisher of best-selling computer books in the United States. We are proud to have received eight awards from the Computer Press Association in recognition of editorial excellence and three from Computer Currents' First Annual Readers' Choice Awards. Our best-selling ...*For Dummies*® series has more than 50 million copies in print with translations in 31 languages. IDG Books Worldwide, through a joint venture with IDG's Hi-Tech Beijing, became the first U.S. publisher to publish a computer book in the People's Republic of China. In record time, IDG Books Worldwide has become the first choice for millions of readers around the world who want to learn how to better manage their businesses.

Our mission is simple: Every one of our books is designed to bring extra value and skill-building instructions to the reader. Our books are written by experts who understand and care about our readers. The knowledge base of our editorial staff comes from years of experience in publishing, education, and journalism — experience we use to produce books to carry us into the new millennium. In short, we care about books, so we attract the best people. We devote special attention to details such as audience, interior design, use of icons, and illustrations. And because we use an efficient process of authoring, editing, and desktop publishing our books electronically, we can spend more time ensuring superior content and less time on the technicalities of making books.

You can count on our commitment to deliver high-quality books at competitive prices on topics you want to read about. At IDG Books Worldwide, we continue in the IDG tradition of delivering quality for more than 30 years. You'll find no better book on a subject than one from IDG Books Worldwide.

John Kilcullen
Chairman and CEO
IDG Books Worldwide, Inc.

Eighth Annual
Computer Press
Awards 1992

Ninth Annual
Computer Press
Awards 1993

Tenth Annual
Computer Press
Awards 1994

Eleventh Annual
Computer Press
Awards 1995

Dedication

American Trader
February 1990

Wally
1990-1998

One set me upon the path to the other, ultimately leading to this book. May all the mistakes I made while learning how to do it right be amended by helping others to do it right from the start.

Author's Acknowledgments

This book has, in a way, been ten years in the making, the starting point marked by a life change that enabled me to start studying animal behavior and medicine. That, in turn, brought Wally, my first iguana, into my life, leading me down the green path to what iguana knowledge I have acquired and insights I have gleaned.

A number of people have been supportive of this effort. One in particular is Alta Brewer, who read and commented on the manuscript from the time it was fertilized, through gestation and incubation — of both the book and her own human hatchling, Adam. Adam's namesake, Adam Britton, a zoologist who is torn between the attraction of two powerful lizards, green iguanas and crocodiles, has provided a knowledgeable and insightful ear through the years. Any errors of commission or omission in this book are mine alone.

This book would not have been possible without the thousands of iguanas — and those humans kept by their iguanas — who have shared their sorrows, joys, and other stories with me. Also instrumental in my journey has been the reptile veterinarians and biologists who so generously gave of their time and expertise to help me get where I am today: surrounded by pieces of iguana shed and flung-about leafy greens. Of particular note are Stephen Barten, Stephen Divers, Kenneth Harkewicz, and Robert Jereb.

The *Luv Sock*, described in Chapter 20, was developed by Jamie Wang. The full description and instructions can be found at her Web site at www. geocities.com/Petsburgh/Zoo/4954/luvsock.html.

Publisher's Acknowledgments

We're proud of this book; please register your comments through our IDG Books Worldwide Online Registration Form located at `http://my2cents.dummies.com`.

Some of the people who helped bring this book to market include the following:

Acquisitions, Editorial, and Media Development

Project Editor: Tracy Barr

Acquisitions Editors: Scott Prentzas

Copy Editor: Sandra Blackthorn

Technical Editor: Bonnie J. Key

Editorial Manager: Pamela Mourouzis

Editorial Assistant: Michelle Hacker

Production

Project Coordinator: Maridee V. Ennis

Layout and Graphics: Tracy K. Oliver, Brent Savage, Jacque Schneider, Brian Torwelle, Erin Zeltner

Proofreaders: Laura Albert, Corey Bowen, Susan Moritz, Jeannie Smith

Indexer: Liz Cunningham

General and Administrative

IDG Books Worldwide, Inc.: John Kilcullen, CEO

IDG Books Technology Publishing Group: Richard Swadley, Senior Vice President and Publisher; Walter R. Bruce III, Vice President and Publisher; Joseph Wikert, Vice President and Publisher; Mary Bednarek, Vice President and Director, Product Development; Andy Cummings, Publishing Director, General User Group; Mary C. Corder, Editorial Director; Barry Pruett, Publishing Director

IDG Books Consumer Publishing Group: Roland Elgey, Senior Vice President and Publisher; Kathleen A. Welton, Vice President and Publisher; Kevin Thornton, Acquisitions Manager; Kristin A. Cocks, Editorial Director

IDG Books Internet Publishing Group: Brenda McLaughlin, Senior Vice President and Publisher; Sofia Marchant, Online Marketing Manager

IDG Books Production for Branded Press: Debbie Stailey, Director of Production; Cindy L. Phipps, Manager of Project Coordination, Production Proofreading, and Indexing; Tony Augsburger, Manager of Prepress, Reprints, and Systems; Laura Carpenter, Production Control Manager; Shelley Lea, Supervisor of Graphics and Design; Debbie J. Gates, Production Systems Specialist; Robert Springer, Supervisor of Proofreading; Trudy Coler, Page Layout Manager; Troy Barnes, Page Layout Supervisor, Kathie Schutte, Senior Page Layout Supervisor; Michael Sullivan, Production Supervisor

Packaging and Book Design: Patty Page, Manager, Promotions Marketing

◆

The publisher would like to give special thanks to Patrick J. McGovern, without whom this book would not have been possible.

◆

Contents at a Glance

Cartoons at a Glance

By Rich Tennant

"Hey! I think you've found a friend!"

page 7

"Don't worry- Dr. Payton is one of the finest reptile veterinarians in the country."

page 197

"His diet consists of a lot of greens and vegetables, which he eats sporadically all day long in short feeding bursts. Fortunately, the iguana does too, so we can time their meals together."

page 127

ROBERT LOSES ANOTHER FRIDAY NIGHT STARING MATCH WITH HIS IGUANA, LOU

page 247

EXOTIC PETS

AMERICA | SOUTH AMERICA

page 47

"I built the iguana cage myself. He seems to like the chandelier over his food bowl, but we're replacing the sconces over the fireplace with recessed mood lights."

page 81

"Which one looks better with this shoulder bag, the Black Spiny-tailed or the Desert iguana?"

page 291

FAMOUS IGUANA MOVIES

PREHISTORIC PLANET
CREATURE FROM THE HAUNTED GLIMAR
THE BEAST FROM OUTER SPACE
The Life of Lincoln

page 277

TANNING BEDS
TANFAST TANNING SALON

"Darlene! I said you could bring your iguana to work as long as you check the tanning beds BEFORE you send a customer in there."

page 171

Fax: 978-546-7747
E-mail: richtennant@the5thwave.com
World Wide Web: www.the5thwave.com

Table of Contents

Foreword

∙ ∙

*I*t is late at night. All is quiet in the house. The iguanas have long since nodded off. A large male Burmese python, however, is wide awake as it explores the cozy confines of his cage. He can't help but notice the bluish glow emanating from a small room across the hall. However, without external ears, he is deaf to the faint clicking sounds that can be heard. For in that room is a woman who is typing on a computer. A woman with a vision. A woman who has a passion for his cold-blooded kind. A woman who is focused intently on her work. Several of her fingers bear the scars from encounters with his four-legged kin. Her mind, nevertheless, is filled with fond memories and a wealth of knowledge about his kind.

The book that you have in your hands is a testimony to the years of dedicated work and experience that have made Melissa Kaplan a widely recognized expert on the captive care of iguanas. With her unbridled enthusiasm for things cold-blooded, her work has been a labor of love. After building a friendship with her over years of correspondence and phone calls, I have come to admire this woman that I have never met. When I think of her and her impressive list of accomplishments, I can't help but imagine the scene that I have described above.

Melissa's captivation with wild things began at an early age, but it was not until later in life that it was able to flourish. Her compassionate devotion to helping animals in need, however, would eventually demand a high price. While laboring with seabirds soiled by a southern California oil spill in 1990, she became stricken by a severe case of chronic fatigue syndrome that would render her homebound for the remainder of her life.

Despite the difficulties she faces on a daily basis — you can read about these on her famous home page on the Internet — she has become a remarkably prolific writer and a highly regarded presence on the Internet. She has authored countless articles about reptiles that have appeared in society journals and newsletters all over the world. Many are reproduced at her Web site and at other Web sites on the Internet. For several years, she co-hosted America Online's Reptile and Amphibian forum and still serves on the staff of Veterinary Information Network's Pet Care Forum. Currently she is co-moderator of the Iguanas Mailing List. She coauthored the text for a video on care and breeding of green iguanas that was hailed by International Iguana Society reviewers as the best video on the topic. Many of her articles have been reproduced by veterinarians as handouts for their clients. In addition to her ambitious desire to share basic biology and husbandry advice to thousands of reptile lovers all over the world, she also returned to college a few years ago to earn a Master's degree in education.

Although I have studied the behavioral ecology of iguanas in the wild for a number of years, I found myself consulting Melissa on many occasions when I was editor of *Iguana Times*. She is always eager to share tidbits on iguana care gleaned from years of keeping them as companions in her home, but her wealth of knowledge extends far beyond the confines of captivity. While she has never seen a green iguana in the wild, I am personally convinced she knows them well enough that she could befriend the largest, most aggressive male in Costa Rica in a matter of minutes. I have often wished that her health would permit me to bring her along to my study site in the Bahamas, where I'm certain I could not find a more enthusiastic coworker to help us better understand and preserve the rock iguanas that are rapidly disappearing from that part of the world.

I have found the book in your hands to be an exceptionally well-written, informative and comprehensive guide to the care of green iguanas in captivity. True to her character, Melissa has also taken the high road when preparing the text. She is adamant that acquisition of an iguana is not something to be done lightly or impulsively. A would-be owner bears the serious responsibility for becoming informed on how to care for the wild creature, for providing an appropriate physical environment conducive to its health and behavioral adjustment to captivity, and for seeking appropriate veterinary care when needed. Proper ownership of an iguana is neither a simple nor inexpensive task.

I could write much myself about iguanas, because I share Melissa's love and passion for these fascinating creatures. However, this book does more than an adequate job, and I will let her tell the rest.

William K. Hayes, Ph.D.
Associate Professor of Biology
Loma Linda University
Loma Linda, California

Introduction

1 have been told on many occasions that iguanas aren't rocket science. That's right. They're not. Rockets have much better documentation and are far easier to launch.

Iguanas are incredible, edible lizards, though the majority of those reading this book would never consider eating their Iguanas (or any other iguanas, for that matter). Incredible iguanas require incredible commitments from the humans who have chosen to keep them. The commitments — lifestyle, spatial, and financial — can't be made lightly because they affect your life and your family's life, as well as the life of your iguana. I thought I knew it all when I got my first iguana. After all, I had been working with them and other reptiles before I got him, so what else was there to learn? You'll find, as I did, that there's far more to your iguana than you ever imagined, just waiting for you to tap into the growing body of knowledge and resources now available to you. My hope is that this book and your commitment will lead you and your iguana to a life rich with experience, learning, and the absolute minimum of Iguana Stink Eye.

This book provides the essential info — the straight scoop in plain, everyday English — that you need to know in order to raise a healthy, well-adjusted iguana.

About This Book

For those of you who don't yet keep iguanas, this book gives you the information you need to decide whether an iguana is really the right pet for you. If you recently bought or adopted an iguana without first having done much in the way of research, this book gets you up to speed on what you need to do to help ensure a healthy iguana and a rich, rewarding relationship with him or her.

For those of you who have kept iguanas successfully for many years, there are most likely some new things for you in here. Keeping iguanas — or, more accurately, being kept by them — is anything but a static experience. There's always more to learn.

This book isn't meant to be read from cover to cover, although you can read it that way if you want. Instead, this book is a reference, meaning that if you have a particular topic in mind, you can turn straight to the chapter that covers the topic and get the info you need.

Each chapter is divided into sections, and each section contains a piece of info about some part of iguana keeping — things like this:

- Is a green iguana right for you?
- Picking a healthy iguana
- Iguana-proofing your home
- Making a roost
- Should you let your iguanas mate?
- If things don't work out

Conventions Used in This Book

As a reference book, _Iguanas For Dummies_ is designed to make information easy to find and use. To help you make sense of the information and instructions in this book, we've used certain conventions:

- _Italic_ is used for emphasis and to highlight new words or terms that are defined.
- **Boldfaced** text is used to indicate the action part of numbered steps.
- `Monofont` is used for Web addresses.

Foolish Assumptions

People who buy this book will do so for many reasons but ultimately because they want to find out more about green iguanas. In writing this book, I made some assumptions about you and what you want to get out of this book:

- You may be considering getting an iguana but want to be sure that you have what it takes to keep one _before_ you make the commitment.
- If you already have an iguana, you're interested in finding out how you can keep it healthy and happy.
- Your children have been bugging you for an iguana so you thought you would try to find out more about iguanas before getting your kids one.
- You're a veterinarian who is starting to see an increasing number of iguanas in your practice and want to go over some things they may not have covered in vet school.

✔ You found an iguana — or rescued one — and now want to find out how to take care of it.

✔ Your kids, their teacher, or your friends have an iguana and you suspect that the iguana isn't being cared for as well as it should be.

How This Book Is Organized

To help you find the information you're looking for, this book is divided into nine parts. Each part includes several chapters relating to that part.

Part I: So, You Wanna Iguana?

This part gives you the lowdown on what it takes to keep an iguana so that you can decide whether an iguana is the pet for you. If you do decide to take the plunge, you can also find information on picking an iguana — how to tell a healthy iguana from a sick one and where to get an iguana — and getting your iguana home. And just in case you were wondering whether your iguana needs an iguana buddy, this part covers that, too.

Part II: Iguana: The Species and the Lizard

This part explains where iguanas fit into the big picture and why farmed iguanas need as much care and troubleshooting as wild-caught iguanas. This part also covers the basics of iguana anatomy — information that's useful in understanding the care and dietary requirements of green iguanas and when you need to talk to your vet or other iguana keepers. Here you also find info on thermoregulation, movement, and communication — an essential part in understanding your iguana and making sure that he does what he needs to do safely.

Part III: Setting Up the Environment

This part deals with the fine points of iguana housing, including choosing (or building) an enclosure and setting it up. Here you find info on arranging the climbing and roosting apparatus, appropriate substrates, what plants to use (or not to use), and how to create a safe environment for cageless (free-roaming) iguanas. And because you'll probably want to let your iguana spend some time outside, this part explains how you can do that safely, too.

Part IV: Basic Iguana Care

This part gives you everything you need to know about caring for your iguana: what and how to feed him, how (and how often) to bathe him and clean out his enclosure, and what steps you can take when you're not going to be there to care for him yourself.

Part V: Socializing Your Iguana

Key to taming and socializing your iguana, this part introduces iguana social structure and behavior and your role in the iguana's society. It also explains how you can build trust with your iguana, how to approach him, and how to pick him up. Finally, this part discusses the best way to socialize your iguana — by making him a part of your daily routine — and gives you tips on how you can do that.

Part VI: Health and Well-Being

The chapters in this part deal with normal and expected behavioral abnormalities, such as the crankiness that precedes the monthly shed. This part also deals with the most common diseases, disorders, and other health issues that are bound to occur in the life of an active iguana. Finally, this part addresses the human health concerns associated with keeping iguanas and gives you tips on how you can protect yourself and others.

Part VII: Breeding and Reproduction

Want to know how two iguanas become dozens of iguanas? This part tells you. Because iguanas go into breeding season even if they're the only iguana for miles around, you need to know and be able to recognize the behaviors and physiological changes that accompany this annual event. And, because single, unmated female iguanas can and often do become gravid, carrying as many as 60 or more unfertilized eggs, all keepers of female iguanas need to know what to expect, what signs to watch for, and the health problems associated with being gravid.

Part VIII: The Part of Tens

This part is the place to go for quick, useful chunks of information. Here you can discover ten Web sites that give you lots of good information about plants, ten tips for socializing your iguana, and ten situations when you should take your iguana to the vet.

Part IX: Appendixes

The appendixes contain information such as a list of toxic and edible ornamental plants, where to find reptile-related associations and veterinarians, and books and periodicals. You will also find information on reptile equipment suppliers, a handy resource if you can't find what you need locally.

Icons Used in This Book

To help you find the information you want and to highlight information that is particularly helpful or interesting, these icons appear in the left-hand margins throughout the book:

This icon points out terms that may be new to you but that you need to know as an iguana keeper (they'll come in handy when you want to talk to your vet or other iguana keepers).

When certain products, activities, or events pose a danger or health risk to you or your iguana, you'll see it highlighted with this icon. Skip this information at your own — or your iguana's — risk.

You find this icon beside important information that you'll want to remember.

Ranging from serious to fun, the information accompanying this icon may not address actual care issues but illustrates some of the reasons why iguanas are the way they are and the lengths to which some iguana keepers go for them. Consider this information interesting but nonessential. You can skip it without feeling too guilty.

This icon points out advice, suggestions, and pointers that you'll find particularly helpful as you find, raise, and care for your iguana.

Where to Go from Here

If you're thinking about getting an iguana, or have one but aren't sure why he is the way he is, start at the beginning with Parts I and II. If you decide not to get one, well, you could still finish reading the book and become the life of the party with your incredible knowledge about iguanas. Otherwise, if you later decide to get one, be sure to read Part III first; that way, you'll be well ahead of the game and your iguana will be off to a good start.

If you already have an iguana and have been toddling along for a while, you can delve in wherever you want, hopping around as issues or problems arise or time permits.

Part I
So, You
Wanna Iguana?

The 5th Wave   By Rich Tennant

"Hey! I think you've found a friend!"

In this part . . .

In this first part, you will read about why iguanas are not suitable as pets for everyone, where they come from, and a bit about anatomy. The more you know about these aspects of iguanas, the better you will be able to make the decision to get an iguana, and to better care for the ones you already have. If you make up your mind that an iguana is the right pet for you, you need to know how to pick out a healthy one and where to look for them. This part also explains why having more than one may not be the best thing to do for you or your iguana.

Chapter 1

Is an Iguana the Pet for You?

*I*guanas can be the best of pets. They can also be the worst of pets. How they turn out depends largely on how much time you spend with them, how well you work with and understand them, the individual iguana's temperament, and what your expectations are of iguanas in general.

A green iguana can be a wonderful companion. Regarding its demands and needs for attention and space, a well-adjusted iguana is a combination of a friendly large dog (with a sharp, active tail) and an independent cat (with a sharp, active tail). And regarding its ability to destroy household goods, an iguana that's given the time and space it needs is somewhere between a two-year-old child and a cockatoo (with an active beak and feet).

Because the owner has to pay such close attention to detail and learn about animal behavior and the physics of lighting and nutrition, iguanas are unlike any pet you have ever owned or are likely to own. Iguanas are more complex and difficult to care for than any of the more "normal" pets. Some iguana-keeping parents consider them on par with raising a human child — except you can't send an iguana off to boarding school or summer camp, and they never leave home to go to college.

If you're willing to make the commitment necessary to do right by your iguana, you'll be well rewarded. If you honestly can't make such a commitment, select a reptile or other pet that won't demand as much from you physically and financially. In the long run, making such a decision before you get the iguana is better for both you and the iguana.

The first thing to know when considering an iguana for a pet is that several different types of related lizards have the word *iguana* in their name, including the helmeted and casque-headed iguanas *(Corytophanes* and *Laemanctus),* the desert iguana *(Dipsosaurus),* the Madagascar iguana *(Chalarodon* and *Oplurus),* the spiny-tailed iguana *(Ctenosaura),* the rock and rhinoceros iguanas *(Cyclura),* and the green iguana *(Iguana).* Because green iguanas are the most widely sold of all the iguanas and the ones most likely to be in animal shelters and rescues, this book focuses on them.

Things to Know about Iguanas

Some of the information about iguanas is just plain fun, but most of it is critical to you as you make your decision to get — or not get — a green iguana as a pet. Before you decide to get an iguana, you need to know as much as you can about them — how to care for one, what to expect in terms of temperament, and other stuff — so that you don't join the ranks of those who discover too late that a green iguana isn't the pet for them.

Many people think that the modern-day lizard we call *iguana* was named after the dinosaur called *iguanodon.* Fact is, it's the other way around: Paleontologists named the dinosaur because its fossilized teeth look very much like the modern-day iguana's teeth. The name *iguanodon* comes from the Spanish word *iguana* and the Greek word for tooth, *odont.*

They are herbivores

Iguanas are *herbivores,* animals who eat only plant matter — the vegans of the animal world. There aren't many herbivorous lizards in the world, but they all share a couple of traits: They all need lots of heat, and they all get *big.* Herbivorous reptiles also require good, *nutritious* plant matter, not just a head of lettuce now and then. In fact, most conscientious iguana owners come to realize that their iguanas eat better than their human family members.

Putting together a nutritious plant-based diet can be quite complicated, especially if you can't find a steady, year-round source of all the leafy greens and vegetables that your iguana needs. Head to Chapters 13 and 14 for information on meeting a green iguana's dietary requirements.

They get big

Iguanas reach a total length of 5–6 feet within three to four years (often making them longer than their owners). The body itself only reaches 22–24 inches in length. The rest of the length is in the tail. And that tail is a vital part of the iguana — used in *thermoregulation* (how they regulate their body temperature), balance, and defense.

Want to know one of the biggest mistakes iguana owners make? They think that because the iguana's body is only 2 feet long, they only need to provide an enclosure that's 2–3 feet long. Wrong. An iguana needs an enclosure 1.5–2 times its total length, so an iguana that's 6 feet long needs an enclosure that's at least 9 feet long. Many people realize too late just why so many experienced iguana keepers call these lizards giant green iguanas (see Figure 1-1). For information on getting an enclosure that's the right size, head to Chapter 8.

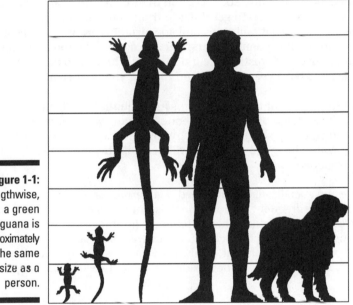

Figure 1-1: Lengthwise, a green iguana is approximately the same size as a person.

Granted, at 15–20 pounds, iguanas may not weigh as much as 6-foot-tall humans, but they can be just as cumbersome to hold. And consider this: They have sandpapery rough, scaly skin, a knife-like ridge on their tail, and 20 claws. They eat like a herd of horses and poop like medium-sized dogs, too. Oh, and have I mentioned the 116–120 razor-sharp teeth attached to strong, tenacious jaws?

They need tropical temps

Green iguanas are tropical lizards. They need the same tropical temperatures all year long, even when temperatures outside your house drop below freezing during the winter. Iguana owners from cold winter climates need to have lots of spare heating equipment for their iguanas in order to provide the necessary 88- to 95-degree Fahrenheit basking temperatures every day of the year. Many iguana owners find that their electric, gas, or propane bills more than double once they have a green iguana in residence.

If you live off the grid or where frequent power failures occur during cold winters, a tropical or desert pet is not a good choice.

They require taming and socialization

Iguanas rarely become tame and socialized on their own. You need to work with them daily for a year or so to get them to trust you and to get them to appreciate the pleasures that tameness and socialization bring — things like head, neck, and body rubs; yummy treats; free reign around a room (or, more often, the entire house); interesting excursions; and a human to cater to their every whim. Yes, it takes a year or so — and that's if you do it right.

Do it wrong, or don't do it at all, and chances are high that you'll end up with a fiercely (literally and figuratively) independent iguana who barely allows you to provide fresh food, a bath, a clean environment, and the occasional yummy treat. If you're lucky, your reward will be a tail thwack rather than a lunge, nip, or crocodile roll.

To remain tame and socialized, iguanas need regular reinforcement. Some iguanas may need less frequent reinforcement as time goes on, but others may never become completely comfortable with human interaction. And, unfortunately, there's no way to predict which hatchlings will tame easily, become affectionate, become merely tolerant, or always be aggressive to some degree toward humans. Head to Part V for details on taming and socializing an iguana.

They pose certain health risks

All reptiles present potential health risks to humans. One of the most highly publicized *zoonoses* (diseases that can be passed, directly or indirectly, from animals to humans) in recent years has been salmonella. The reason salmonella is a problem with reptiles is that the strains or types of salmonella that typically infect them are different from those we normally encounter in our food. These strains can cause symptoms ranging from very mild to potentially lethal. Even mild strains can be deadly to humans who have compromised or immature immune systems: infants, toddlers, the elderly, anyone with a suppressed immune system due to illness, organ donors receiving anti-rejection drugs, or cancer patients receiving chemotherapy.

Most instances of salmonella transmission from pets to humans take place because humans don't know that a risk exists. Knowing about it and taking proper precautions can greatly reduce, but not completely eliminate, the risk. Fortunately, you can take precautions. Chapter 23 tells you how.

All kinds of animals carry diseases that can be passed to humans. Reptiles are no exception. Most, if not all, reptiles carry salmonella, which can cause serious illness, hospitalization, even death, in humans, despite the reptile appearing to be perfectly healthy. If you have or are planning to have babies or have or work with young children or other at-risk humans, you may want to rethink getting an iguana.

Iguanas Are a Family Affair

An iguana can't belong to just one family member. An iguana can't sink into a family unit without ripples like a rock tossed into a pond. Properly cared for, an iguana will alter the existing patterns for as long as it is a part of your family.

Kids and iguanas

Initially, kids are fascinated by iguanas. They're also the reason that most parents end up having iguanas as pets. Then one, two, or three dead iguanas later, or $500 or so sunk into vet bills and proper caging and supplies, the parents begin to realize that they, not their children, have an iguana. Iguanas can be a great learning experience for children, but only when the parent realizes that he or she is the primary caretaker, not the child, even if the child is in high school or college.

Iguanas hatch from their shells already equipped with a mouthful of sharp little teeth, ready to cut leaves, and sharp little claws, ready to scale tall trees. So even though that munchkin iguana looks harmless, it's still capable of scratching, poking, and nipping. Young children typically react by crying out and throwing the iguana away from them, without thinking of the harm they can cause the iguana. Older children, including teenagers, also often react unhappily when the iguana tastes their finger or clings to their hand or arm — or runs up their face to sit on their head. My motto? When it comes to kids and igs, advise and supervise.

Sharing caretaking responsibilities

At some point, the primary caretaker in the family isn't going to be able to take care of the iguana for a day or more. So at least one other person in the family (or a really good friend) must be trained to be the primary caretaker's backup and must hone his or her skills through practice. This person needs to know how to shop for food, prepare and serve the food, clean the enclosure, handle and groom the iguana, and spend regular quality time with the iguana. The backup also needs to be someone who won't get scared off by an iguana who's less than pleased at the absence of its regular caretaker and the disruption of its daily routine.

Iguanas and Other Pets

Iguanas may or may not mix well with other pets, so you need to carefully consider four things about them: their living arrangements, their size, their temperament, and the food chain. *Each* of these things must be considered, regardless of whether you envision combining some or all of your reptiles together in one enclosure or room or plan to allow your iguana to be out where there are birds, mammals, and fish.

Living arrangements

Iguanas are tropical arboreal lizards (they live in trees). They like to be up high, and they need to be able to bask for prolonged periods every day in temperatures ranging from 88–95 degrees Fahrenheit.

Iguanas can't be kept with reptiles from the deserts, savannas, or temperate woodlands. Reptiles like desert iguanas, bearded dragons, skinks, and savanna monitors can't be housed with green iguanas, and neither can tortoises or turtles. One or the other of the species suffers if you don't provide what the individual species needs. If you try to compromise, all pay the price in poor health and failure to thrive as they should. So, if you already have a lizard from another type of habitat, you need to get another enclosure to house the new one. If you don't have the money or the space for another enclosure, don't get another reptile.

Size considerations

Iguanas live in social groups in the wild, generally hanging around with other iguanas the same size they are. Depending on size, they may bask and sleep in piles together — but not necessarily because they're all such good friends. Instead, it's a matter of safety in numbers: Staying in groups when less attentive to surrounding dangers reduces the individual's risk that it will become some other animal's lunch or midnight snack.

Iguanas like to lounge about or sleep with their head, and often their body, resting on something. This isn't a problem if that something is a pillow made of a rolled-up towel or gym socks. But it can be a problem if that something is a baby iguana or another small lizard or frog who could be severely injured by being used as a cushion or stepping-stone.

Temperament

Iguanas, like humans, vary in their individual temperaments. They may not tolerate any other animal in their environment, or they may tolerate or even befriend one or two of them. Tempers flare and temperaments change, so you can never predict or assume who'll get along with whom or that a relationship will last (or not have ups and downs).

Adult iguanas have been known to attack large animals, such as humans and, in one instance that I know of, an 80-pound pit bull. When an iguana attacks a human or dog or grabs a cockatiel, it doesn't necessarily mean that the iguana wants to eat the human, dog, or bird. The iguana may have decided it doesn't want the thing in its area anymore. Or it may have decided that it'd be fun to try to intimidate the thing, the way iguanas do with each other. Iguanas are very successful at intimidating larger animals, especially humans. As humorous as it may sound, it happens frequently enough to be a major reason that iguanas are given away.

A few territorial iguanas have been known to kill, even eat, their small cage mates. It's best for all concerned to assume that iguanas need their own environment, and if you can't provide separate environments for more than one iguana, or an iguana and other animals, choose to have one or the other but not both.

Food chain

It's a dog-eat-dog world out there. Or, in this case, a snake-eat-lizard, lizard-eat-lizard, dog-eat-lizard, cat-eat-lizard, lizard-bite-dog, hedgehog-skewer-lizard, ferret-eat-lizard, lizard-pounce-on-small-bird, big-bird-bite-off lizard's-tail, lizard-crush-small-mammal, and any-other-combination-you-can-think-of world.

When bored or feeling a bit peckish, green iguanas look around for anything that might be considered food. Or, simply bored, they may explore their environment to see what's new. Because iguanas smell as well as taste with their tongues, they tend to taste-smell everything with their sensitive, *bifurcated* (notched) tongue tip. If it's green or brightly colored like their favorite food or flower, they may chomp on it. *It* may be that pretty green anole, day gecko, tree frog, or cute baby water dragon you decided needed an iguana for company, or that exotic, toxic, flowering plant you thought would perk up your iguana's enclosure.

Is a Green Iguana Right for You?

What iguanas are, and will always remain to be no matter how tame and socialized they become, are wild animals with the instincts of wild animals. While green iguanas are being captive-bred on iguana farms, they are not domesticated the same way as dogs and house cats. Dogs and cats and other domestic animals (farm livestock as well as pets) have been bred for thousands of years for specific traits found useful or attractive to humans. Green iguanas are just being bred for export to countries where they are popular for pets and for food. They are not being selectively bred for traits such as docility, dulled teeth, no claws, or limp tails, all traits that would make them easier to handle as pets.

So *don't* get an iguana if

- You're looking for an always sweet-tempered, gentle pet to cuddle with and who will seek you out for affection.
- You do a lot of traveling or have a busy schedule and want a pet who'll be fine with minimal care during the week and a couple of hours on the weekend.
- You want a pet you can walk on a leash or let roam off-leash when you go on day hikes.
- You want a hardy pet your youngsters can play with while you're busy elsewhere.
- You want an iguana because it'll look cool in your living room or office.

Do get an iguana if

- You are interested and willing to spend the next decade or two — and a hefty chunk of your paycheck and living space — with a demanding, rough-scaled lizard who may not always appreciate the time and money you lavish on him.
- You are interested and willing to learn about the complexities of iguana diet, environment, and behavior, all in the effort to make you a better iguana keeper and your iguana a healthier lizard.
- You don't mind your hands and arms and possibly other parts of your body being decorated with a variety of interesting scars from claw scratches, tail lashes, and bites.
- You will treasure those brief moments of communion — when your iguana holds on to you and doesn't want to get down, or sneezes gently in your ear, or lays quietly beside you as you watch television or read — knowing how rare these moments may be.

Chapter 2

Picking an Iguana

*O*kay, you've made the big decision. You're going to commit the next (hopefully) 15–20 plus years, considerable financial resources, a significant chunk of space in your home, your presently scar-free arms, and your sound mind to a teeny green iguana who'll no doubt act like you're trying to make his life miserable for quite some time to come. Congratulations! You've now joined a very select group of iguana owners who find themselves thoroughly enslaved.

The questions now facing you are how to go about finding and selecting a healthy iguana and how to get him home. The answers may not be as easy as you think. You may see a number of places selling iguanas that look pretty much alike to you, but are they? Should you buy the iguana, tank, and furnishings all at the same time? Read on to find out.

Here an Ig, There an Ig

Buying or adopting an iguana is a bit like buying a car or a house. Just as you probably wouldn't buy the first car or house you see, you probably won't get the first iguana you see at the first place you see them. Buying an iguana is an investment in the future, so take your time with the looking and final decision-making. Go to several stores and spend the weekend driving to more distant stores if they have a good reputation among knowledgeable *herpers* (reptile and amphibian keepers). Besides pet stores, you may also find iguanas for sale or adoption at reptile expos and herp society meetings.

Pet stores

Iguanas are shipped from Central and South America to importers in the United States and other countries. The importers in turn sell them to whole-salers, pet stores, swap meet and herp expo vendors, and carnival operators.

- ✔ Be aware that some stores keep sick and injured animals, putting them in the display enclosures along with the healthy ones for sale.

- ✔ Some stores are picky about the animals they receive and return to the wholesaler those that are unhealthy or injured. (Note that the whole-saler, though, generally turns around and sends them to other stores or retailers who may not be so picky.)

- ✔ Other stores check every animal very carefully, treating minor wounds, worming or rehydrating them, and keeping the sick iguanas out of the display enclosures until they're healthier. Some even call in a reptile vet-erinarian to treat those who are injured, dehydrated, or sick, or they have a reptile vet on call who comes in, checks, and treats the animals that arrive in every new shipment.

The problem is that you can't always tell what goes on behind the scenes, and you may be dealing with store employees who don't know a great deal about the animals they sell — especially exotics. To pick the best of the best, you need to use your judgment, backed up by the knowledge you've gained by reading about how to select iguanas, and look for the following when you go to a pet store:

- ✔ **Ask questions about the care of iguanas.** You want to see whether they know the answers. If they just keep telling you how fun or interesting or easy iguanas are, they're more interested in making a sale than they are in making sure you're prepared for an iguana.

- ✔ **Look at the enclosures.** If they're dirty or ill-kept, chances are the igua-nas aren't cared for any better. Look elsewhere.

- ✔ **Look at what the iguanas are being fed.** If the main part of their diet consists of dry pellets, powder, or "junk" food like iceberg lettuce, they're probably malnourished.

- ✔ **Ask to hold the iguana.** To evaluate the health of the iguana, you must be able to hold it and look at it (see the section "Picking a Healthy Iguana" for details on what exactly you're looking for). If the store won't let you hold the iguana, look elsewhere.

- ✔ **Look at the other reptiles in the store.** How are they being cared for? If their enclosures are dirty or the reptiles are sickly looking (thin, caked with feces, crawling with mites), look elsewhere.

- ✔ **Ask what they do with any sick or injured iguanas they receive.** If they tell you they don't get any or there is no indication that they have sick animals cared for under a veterinarian's supervision, look elsewhere.

Iguanas in the pet trade
(or why your new iguana needs to see a vet)

Iguanas in the United States wholesale to pet stores for around $2–$3 per iguana, in lots of 100 or more (less for "imperfect" ones). So exporters and importers aren't going to spend their small profits ensuring clean, safe, and humane shipping and storage. When unpacked at the importers, the iguanas are stressed, cold, and covered with feces; many are dead. They're uncrated and piled into large enclosures to await repackaging and shipment to regional distributors or pet stores. All in all, it's not a pretty picture.

On the whole, conditions are abysmal for imported green iguanas and other reptiles. But some bright light shines through the darkness. If you're lucky, a nearby pet store owner is knowledgeable about the animals he or she sells and ensures that they're all housed and cared for properly — examined and treated as necessary by a reptile vet as well as cared for daily, with enclosures cleaned, water replaced, and proper foods offered in sizes that the iguanas can get their little mouths around.

If you find such a pet store, thank the folks who work there and patronize it. This store may be more expensive than the competition, but quality care costs.

You don't *have* to have an iguana *today*. Tomorrow, next week, or even next month is just fine. Take the time necessary to look at all the iguanas in your area and to make sure that you're selecting the best one for you.

Reptile expos

Reptile expos are like all expos: A bunch of people (vendors) with related products get together in a big room and try to sell their products to the general public, which pays an admission fee to get in the door. In the case of reptile expos, the product is, for the most part, living reptiles, amphibians, and invertebrates such as tarantulas, walking sticks, and assorted beetles (yes, people keep these as pets, too . . . and you thought keeping an iguana was weird!).

Unfortunately, many, many expo organizers do not prohibit the vendors from displaying and selling obviously sick animals. If you notice any of the following, get your iguana elsewhere.

- ✔ Sick, dead, dying, or lethargic iguanas in the enclosure.
- ✔ Iguanas in overcrowded pens, showing signs of caked-on urates or feces, scratches, or other injuries.

Also, if the vendor won't let you hold any of the iguanas, you're better off looking elsewhere. (True, a crowded, bustling expo is not really the place for a vendor to pull out iguana after iguana for you while trying to answer other people's questions, but a good vendor should invite you off to the side to give you the opportunity to handle several iguanas of your choice.) You can find expos in herp magazines (see Appendix C if you can't find these magazines in your local pet stores, bookstores, or newsstands). You may also see expos advertised in local newspapers or herp society newsletters during the month before the expo's appearance in your area.

Herp society meetings

Volunteer-run nonprofit herp societies are organizations founded by people who have an interest in reptiles and amphibians. The experience and backgrounds of the members may range from biologists studying herps in the field and lab, to youngsters with their first pet snake or lizard. Most societies meet once a month and publish a newsletter. Some societies permit members to bring herps to sell before or after meetings, while others have an annual exhibition at which some sales may be allowed. All societies allow members to run sale and adoption ads in their newsletters.

Generally speaking, when looking at animals for sale at herp societies, the sellers are going to be more knowledgeable than pet store staff and, because the sellers are society members who will be seeing the other members month after month, they are less likely to bring sick animals to sell. Nonetheless, you still need to be just as careful picking out an iguana here as you would anywhere else.

Unlike reptile expos and pet stores, herp societies rarely advertise in any publication. Since there is no permanent society office, you won't find them in the phone book, either. Appendix B gives you some ways to look for a society in your area.

Finding an iguana to adopt

Thousands of iguanas are given away every year by owners who no longer want them or who can't keep them. Most of these iguanas are no longer babies. Some may be sick, and some may be untamed. Some iguanas get passed around to many owners over time, never getting a chance to adjust to their new surroundings. As a result, some can be downright testy about yet another new home and human.

Adopting an iguana means giving a needy lizard a second (or third or fifth) chance at a healthy life surrounded by humans who care about him and who strive to meets his needs instead of neglecting him. Know that it isn't unusual for adopted lizards, even ones who were not tame when taken in, to become highly tamed and socialized, even when they're five or more years of age.

To find iguanas up for adoption, contact your local herp society, reptile veterinarians, humane society, and animal shelter. If they don't have any iguanas available, they may be able to give you contact information on the people doing iguana rescue in your area. Appendix B contains information on how to find societies and rescues on the World Wide Web.

If you're adopting an iguana from a private party, shelter, or rescue, take your time. By doing so, you have a better chance of finding one you feel a connection with — and one who may respond positively to you when you first meet. The better you and your iguana get along in the beginning, the easier the transition will be for both of you.

Picking a Healthy Iguana

You *must* check out each iguana that catches your eye. The only way to do so properly is to spend some time looking at the iguanas and then holding the ones you're interested in.

Don't feel rushed by the salespeople. After all, you're the one buying a long-term companion, not them. They may think you're crazy or walk off to help other customers or go off to do some other work. That's okay; take as long as you need to check the igs out.

Look before you leap

Before you start holding every baby iguana in the enclosure, watch them for a while first. Pay attention not only to the iguanas but to the enclosure as well. The condition of the enclosure gives some idea of the additional stresses and potential health problems you'll have to deal with.

Watching the iguanas

A healthy iguana is going to look alert when you come around. He may be sitting on the ground, on a branch, or on top of another iguana. He'll look at you and follow you with his eyes as you move from one side to another. He may flick his tongue as if trying to smell you. A healthy iguana may also ignore you after awhile and go about his business of basking, eating, or walking around the enclosure.

Is one of the iguanas listless — just lying on the bottom of the tank, eyes half-opened or completely closed? Does the iguana react when any of the other iguanas move around or come into contact with him? If you tap on the glass, does he react by lifting his head or getting to his feet? If the iguana remains listless, not reacting to other iguanas or you, he is very likely sick.

Paying attention to the enclosure

While you're looking at the iguanas, look around the enclosure, too. Does it have proper food? Clean water? Is the *substrate* (the floor covering) safe for green iguanas? (Artificial grass, reptile mat, and alfalfa pellets are okay; bark, shavings, and other litters are not.) Is the enclosure clean? What about heating and lighting? If a thermometer is in the tank, check to see what the temperature is. (It should be 88–95 degrees Fahrenheit in the basking area and range from 75–85 degrees Fahrenheit in the rest of the enclosure.) If there's no thermometer, check the heat source to see if you can find out the number of watts it puts out. If it is anything less than a 60–100 watt bulb in a 50–60 gallon enclosure, the iguanas are being kept too cold.

If the enclosure isn't being kept warm enough, you need to take that into consideration when holding iguanas from that enclosure. Cold iguanas are too stiff to hold on to you and unable to put up much in the way of resistance. If the enclosure is littered with feces, well, it's a good idea to carry a bottle of waterless disinfectant to clean your hands with afterwards.

Leaping lizards! Holding an iguana

After you observe the iguanas for a while, identify those that you want to hold and examine up close. Ask the store staff to pull them out, one at a time. (Many pet store employees are afraid to pick up iguanas, so you may have to reach in and pick them up yourself. Just be sure to ask the employees first.)

If the store won't let you hold the iguanas, look somewhere else. Two of the things you need to assess are muscle tone and strength, and you also need to inspect the belly surface and vent — things that can only be done when you hold the iguana.

Picking up an iguana

Holding a hatchling green iguana isn't that different from holding any other small, nervous animal . . . other than the fact that an iguana can detach part of its tail. To pick up and hold an iguana:

1. **Move your hand in from the side (don't swoop down from above) and place your fingers under the iguana's belly.**

2. **Cup gently and lift, letting the body rest on your palm.**

   The head should be looking through the V that's formed by the space between your thumb and index finger, and the tail should be hanging down alongside your wrist (see Figure 2-1).

3. **With your other hand, you can touch the iguana and carefully restrain him if he tries to jump off.**

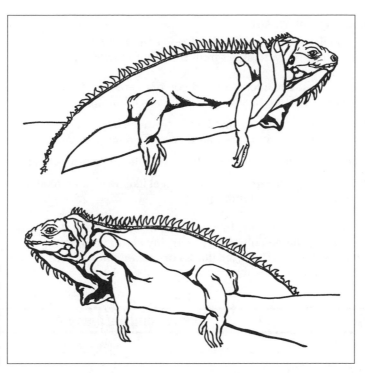

Figure 2-1:
The proper
way to hold
a young
iguana.

If he squirms, talk softly to him while letting him move within your hand or move from one hand to the other. If he tries to walk or run away from you, keep "feeding" him your hands: Place your free hand in front of him; then, once he walks onto it, place your newly freed hand in front; continue rotating hand after hand. To calm a nervous iguana, hold him in one hand and raise that hand straight up in the air over your head for a couple of moments. Just make sure first that there aren't any tanks of snakes, lizards, or other predatory animals up there where he can see them.

If you have never held a baby iguana before and are worried that you may accidentally let it go, consider taking someone with you who knows about iguanas and who can hold the iguanas for you for inspection and show you how to hold them properly.

When handling or even just looking at iguanas, remember to try to keep your movements slow and deliberate and your voice soft. Rapid movements, approaching from over his head (like a predator), and loud voices can increase the already high levels of stress, produce a flight response in the iguana, and cause panic within the enclosure as the other iguanas try to flee.

Examining the iguana

Once you have the iguana in hand, you can check for problems that may not be visible just by watching it from the other side of the glass.

- ✔ Does his muscle tone remind you of overcooked spaghetti, or can you feel some strength and resistance when holding him?
- ✔ Is he flopped in your hand, or is his head up, beady eyes staring at you, tongue flicking out now and then as he checks you out?
- ✔ Does he walk steadily around on your hand or arm, or is he wobbly?
- ✔ Can you feel his grip, or does he feel like he's going to slide right off if you don't protect him?

Healthy iguanas are going to have good muscle tone in their scrawny little legs, and you will be able to feel their tiny claws hold on to you. A weak iguana may be suffering from illness or malnutrition. Table 2-1 lists specific things you should look for.

Table 2-1	Examining the Iguana
What to Look For	*Potential Problems*
The body and tail:	
Dirty skin	Smeared or ground-in feces indicates overcrowding, an unhealthful environment, and a higher risk of skin and systemic infections.
Scratches, bites, scabs, or lesions	Such skin defects may have already caused or may lead to infections later as the stressed iguana adjusts to new surroundings.
Burns on the belly, tail, body, or head	Burns may heal, but the skin in the burned area will always be sensitive to high heat.
Dried feces or urates in or around the vent	Failure to fully expel feces and urates indicates a sick, highly parasitized lizard.
Lumps, bumps, or swellings you can see or feel in or under the skin of the body, legs, dewlap, or tail	Although the joints may appear to be bumps in a skinny iguana, other growths or lumps indicate abscesses or broken bones.

What to Look For	*Potential Problems*
Black, reddish, or bright orange dots moving around on the body or lodged around the neck, dorsal crest, or armpits	These dots are mites, which can severely weaken an already weak iguana. You can get rid of them before the iguana is put into its new enclosure, and you may need to treat everything you buy at this store for mites.
Both thighs swollen, or "buff" looking, or the lower jaw swollen out on both sides	The iguana has an advanced case of metabolic bone disease. A single swollen front or back leg, or one side of the jaw, is likely to be a broken bone or abscess.
Limbs like skin-covered twigs	The causes may be a severe case of parasites, starvation, and/or dehydration. Although healthy baby iguanas are very skinny, they should not look starved.
Skin dull or heavily wrinkled	The causes may be starvation, dehydration, severe parasite infection, or a systemic infection.
Can easily see or feel the vertebrae and hip bones sharply prominent	Prominent bones in these areas indicate little to no fat stores and wasted muscles due to starvation caused by poor environment, parasites, and/or illness.
The head, eyes, ears, nose and mouth:	
Eyes bleary, watery, weepy, or crusty	This is a sign of a respiratory or eye infection.
Mucous (wet or dry) or bubbling fluid coming from the nose (other than the normal salty deposits)	Mucous and fluids, especially when accompanied by a wheezing or clicking sound when breathing and excess saliva, indicates a respiratory infection.
Inside of the mouth pink or pale or grayish pink	Pale tissue may be due to stress but is often due to dehydration or systemic infection.

(continued)

Table 2-1 *(continued)*

What to Look For	Potential Problems
Saliva in the mouth forms a sheet when you open the mouth or looks ropy or stringy	You are looking at a respiratory infection or *stomatitis* (mouth rot), a sign of a more serious systemic infection.
Small yellowish, whitish, or greenish patches in the mouth or patches of burst capillaries	That's stomatitis, a local infection in the mouth that accompanies a system-wide infection, or abscesses.
Bruising or open sores on or around the rostrum or nostrils	This is usually due to bashing or rubbing the snout on the side of the tank, trying to get out. The injuries may become infected.

Generally speaking, healthy baby iguanas are feisty and alert. They may try to run away from you. Sick iguanas, on the other hand, are more likely to just lie in your hand, barely moving, resigned to your attentions. Exceptions exist, of course. Some healthy baby igs who have already decided that humans can be pretty entertaining happily sit in your hand, waiting to see what you're going to do next. Some sick ones figure that they have nothing to lose and will try to escape.

Should you rescue a sick iguana?

It's hard to not feel sorry for many of the iguanas you see in stores or people's homes. Sick, emaciated, or dehydrated; in dirty, cold, and dark enclosures; or intimidated by cage mates, family pets, or children . . . they seem to cry out for you to take them with you.

Many experienced iguana keepers take home such iguanas, and after lots of veterinary intervention and intensive care at their new home, many of these iguanas end up healthy and hearty. But consider this: Most first-time iguana

keepers find themselves with so much to learn and deal with as it is that they end up overwhelmed by the additional care, follow-through, and funding required for a sick iguana.

If you are new to iguana-keeping, starting with a healthier one gives you and the iguana the best chance of learning how to do it right the first time. There's plenty enough time — and needy iguanas — in your future if you decide to start rescuing them once you're experienced enough and ready.

Chapter 3

Bringing Home Baby

. . . .

In This Chapter

▶ Getting your home ready for your new pet

▶ Gathering all the necessary supplies

▶ Setting up the enclosures and performing all the necessary checks

▶ Bringing your new iguana home

. . . .

*I*f you're tempted to bring your new iguana home right away and then work on getting his enclosure set up, resist! A lot goes into creating the proper iguana home. You have a lot to buy, a lot to set up, and a lot to do before you bring your new pet home. (Of course, if you wanted "easy" in a pet, you wouldn't have decided on a green iguana, right?) Read on to find out what goes into making a proper iguana home and the kinds of choices and decisions facing you as you begin to prepare yourself and your soon-to-be iguana for his new life with you.

Setting Up House

One very common mistake first-time iguana keepers make is to get the iguana and his new enclosure and furnishings all on the same day . . . only to find that they can't get things set up properly. The result is a stressed and often cold or cramped iguana. To make things as stress-free as possible for the both of you, first create the iguana's home — as explained in the following section — and make sure everything is working properly *before* you bring your new iguana home.

Gathering your supplies

To start with, make a list of all the equipment and supplies you need. You will need the same equipment for iguanas of all ages. The older (and bigger) the iguana is, the larger the enclosure and furnishings will be and the more heating and lighting equipment you'll need. Assuming that you're starting out from scratch, your list should include the items in the following checklist (head to Part III for more information on these supplies):

The enclosure

___ 1 55–100-gallon enclosure

___ 1 reptile under-tank heat pad or human heating pad

___ 1–2 daytime overhead heat sources (white basking lights, a basking light and ceramic heating element [CHE], or an incandescent household light bulb)

___ 1–2 nighttime overhead heat sources (nocturnal heat light and/or CHE)

___ 1 light fixture for each overhead heat source (porcelain sockets are required for CHEs)

___ 1 UVB-producing fluorescent tube long enough to stretch across the width of the enclosure

___ 1 fluorescent light fixture

___ 2–5 appliance timers to automate the heat and fluorescent lights

___ 1–2 table lamp dimmer switches (or *rheostats*) or a hard-wired thermostat to regulate the heat source output

___ 1–2 power strips (6–8 outlets each)

___ 3 thermometers to be placed in the enclosure to monitor temperatures

___ 2–3 units of suitable substrate, including extras to rotate in and out as they become soiled

___ 1 hide box (a box your iguana can hide in)

___ 1 branch or shelf for basking

Food, vitamins, and supplements

___ Fresh supply of iguana-friendly food

___ Multivitamin

___ Calcium supplement

First-aid supplies

___ 1 container of blood-stop powder or a box of cornstarch

___ 1 bottle of Betadine (povidone-iodine)

___ 1 tube of triple antibiotic ointment

___ 1 reptile veterinarian

Other stuff

___ 1 water bowl

___ 1 food plate

___ 1–2 food storage containers for salads and greens

___ 1 set of cleaning and disinfecting supplies (sponges, paper towels, gloves, cleaner, disinfectant, etc.)

___ 1 pair of claw trimmers

___ 1 room humidifier

___ 1 cloth sack, cardboard box, or animal carrier to transport your iguana home and to the vet

First, pick yourself up off the floor. Okay, it's quite a list, huh? And this is just the minimum start-up equipment and supplies you need. Now you understand why getting all the supplies and equipment home and assembled before you bring the iguana home is so important.

Setting up the enclosure

Setting up your iguana's enclosure takes quite a bit of thought. It's not like setting up a gerbil cage, where the most strenuous thing you have to do is pick it up by its little handle if you discover that you placed it too near the cat dish. An iguana enclosure is large; it needs to be close to power outlets; and it needs to be somewhere where you can enjoy your iguana (that *is* why you want one, isn't it?) and where your iguana can enjoy his new home — both his enclosure and that often entertaining new creature in his world: you.

Finding the right location

You need to figure out where to place the enclosure so that you have easy access to electrical outlets, so that you can get in and service the enclosure without being a danger to yourself or the iguana, and so that the iguana won't be subjected to additional stresses (see Figure 3-1).

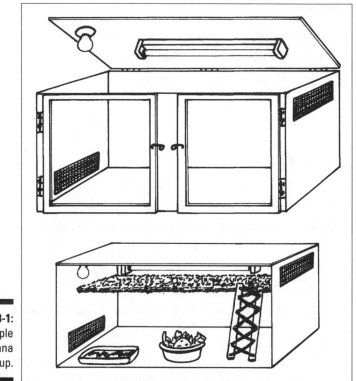

Figure 3-1:
A simple
iguana
setup.

Loud noise and wild activity delays the settling-in process and may lead to a chronically nervous lizard, so here are some things to keep in mind as you decide on a location for the enclosure:

- Iguanas need some visual stimuli to watch, but the stimuli shouldn't include a natural or perceived predator staring at them for hours on end.

- Iguanas like to observe humans, which helps them learn about us and probably provides some degree of entertainment. But it's not a good idea to put them in the family rumpus room or right in the middle of the busiest, noisiest family traffic area.

- Iguanas seem to enjoy looking out windows. They like watching gardens that are periodically visited by birds and butterflies, and they like watching the street and looking at the traffic and pedestrians.

- In some positions, the afternoon sunlight or nighttime room lighting may create a reflection of the iguana on the glass of his enclosure. Having this "other" iguana suddenly appear in *his* home is very stressful to your iguana and may result in his bashing his face against the glass trying to attack or scare his reflection away. Check for these reflections during your equipment setup and testing.

Because iguanas are interested in the environment outside their enclosure, it's particularly cruel to put the enclosure in a garage or rarely visited back room if you spend most of your day away from home (at work or school). If the garage or a back room without a view is your only option for an iguana enclosure, this is a good time to rethink your choice of having an iguana as a pet.

Hooking everything up

After you find the perfect place for your enclosure, you need to set it up. First, clean and disinfect it. Chapter 12 has all the information you need to adequately clean and disinfect your iguana's enclosure and the items inside it. Next, plug in your power strips and set them to one side; then put your new enclosure in its place. When that's done, arrange your thermometers, lights, and heat sources:

✔ Cluster the heat sources, both overhead and undertank, at one end of the enclosure so that one section of the enclosure is warmer than the other (this range of warmer-to-cooler is called *a thermal gradient*).

You don't want to uniformly heat the entire enclosure. Your iguana needs to be able to move from hot to warmer and cooler (but not cold!) areas of his enclosure to regulate his own body temperature.

✔ Place one thermometer at the level the iguana will be at in the basking area, one an inch above the floor of the warm end, and the last one an inch above the floor at the cool end.

✔ Make sure the lights are set up securely so that the iguana (and other free-roaming pets or children) can't come into contact with them or knock them down.

✔ Arrange your heating pad. If you're using a reptile undertank heat pad, don't stick it on the bottom of the enclosure, just set it underneath it. You're going to need to move the heat pad to a larger enclosure by the end of the year, and reptile undertank heat pads are very difficult (and possibly unsafe) to peel off and reuse.

Use shims or other pieces of wood to raise the bottom of the enclosure up so that it doesn't sit directly on the undertank or human heat pad. And place a towel or piece of scrap linoleum under the pad to protect the surface it's sitting on.

If you're using a wooden enclosure, you can place the heating pad *inside* the enclosure. (If you go this route, use a human heating pad.)

When your enclosure's clean and in place, put on your interior decorator hat and start playing around with the equipment and furnishings. Here are a few pointers:

✔ Put the basking branch under the overhead heat source.

✔ Place the food plate and water bowl at the coolest end of the enclosure.

✔ Make sure that the hide box is long enough to span part of the warm end, the middle of the enclosure, and part of the cool end of the thermal gradient.

Check the enclosure door or lid to make sure it fits snugly and locks into place so that the iguana can't squeeze or push its way out — and other inquisitive pets and youngsters can't push their way in.

Testing your lights and heat sources

After everything's set up the way you want, you still have a little more work to do. You need to make sure that all the lights and heat sources are working and that they're providing the temperature ranges your iguana needs both day and night.

During the day, the thermal gradient needs to range from 75 degrees Fahrenheit (24 degrees Celsius) on the cool side to 85°F (29°C) on the warm side, with the basking area kept at 88–95°F (31–35°C). At night, the range for babies should be kept at 73–84°F (23–29°C); adults prefer temps to be a little cooler at the low end, between 70–84°F (21–29°C) at night. Always turn off the basking light and UVB fluorescents at night.

First test everything individually to make sure that each element works. When you're assured that everything is working separately, you're ready to test everything together.

When testing the lighting and heating equipment, keep these things in mind:

✔ Test them at the right time of day and night: Test the nighttime equipment at night and the daytime equipment during the day — starting at about 6–7 a.m., the same time you'll turn it all on in the morning for your iguana.

✔ Be sure to install CHEs *only* into porcelain sockets. They get hot enough to melt the plastic ones.

✔ Providing the required day and nighttime temperatures isn't an option. It's a requirement. You do it, or you don't keep a tropical lizard.

Set up all the fixtures if you haven't done so already, plug everything in, and do the following:

1. **Turn on the nighttime overhead heat sources and the heating pad.**

2. **Monitor the temperatures at the three areas overnight to make sure that they meet and maintain the nighttime gradient.**

3. **Once they do, turn off the nighttime overhead heat light at about the same time you'll turn it off in the morning for the iguana.**

Leave the ceramic heating element (CHE) on if you're going to be using it for day and night heating.

4. **Turn on the daytime overhead heat lights and the UVB fluorescent.**

The enclosure should reach the required daytime temperature gradient within the next hour or two. If it takes longer, or doesn't reach the necessary temperatures within a couple of hours, you need to either lower the heat lights closer to the basking area, change the bulbs to ones with higher wattage, or add additional heat sources. Then test everything again.

If adding fixtures or boosting the wattage still doesn't work or works during the summer but not the winter (something you will find out about since you'll be monitoring the temperatures daily for the next 15+ years), you may need to find a warmer place in your house to place the enclosure during the colder months.

The testing-everything-together phase is also a very good time to see if your circuitry can handle the additional load. While your daytime lights and heat are running in the enclosure, turn on the other lights, appliances, and so on, that run off the same circuit.

Iguana-proofing your home

Because accidents do happen, plan for the eventuality that the iguana *will* escape from your hands or out of the enclosure when you open it. Look at the room from the iguana's point of view: way down low and way up high. Check under any upholstered furniture to make sure no holes will tempt an iguana looking for the perfect hiding place. Make sure a tiny, squishable iguana can't squeeze under the closed door (self-adhesive weather stripping from your hardware store is perfect for closing up such spaces). If you plan on opening the windows for fresh air and sunshine, make sure that no holes or rips are in the screens and that every screen is securely fastened to the sill and window frame. If there are any heavy objects you can't move, block around them so that your iguana can't get under or behind them.

The Homecoming

Finally. The enclosure is set up perfectly, the lighting and heating equipment are functioning just right, you've done the grocery shopping and have a week's worth of salad and greens prepared, you've got a reptile vet lined up, and you have everything else you need to take care of your new baby. Now is the time you've been working so hard for — the homecoming.

Just before you leave for the store, pour some water in the water bowl and place it in the enclosure, and fill up the humidifier and turn it on. Doing so starts to boost the humidity and means you won't have to startle the iguana by doing it later.

Making travel arrangements

Most stores have boxes or paper bags they can stick the iguana in so you can get him home, but you may want to come prepared with your own paraphernalia. A sturdy cardboard box padded with several layers of towels on the bottom makes a nice carrier. To carry your iguana from the store to your car and box, you can use a pillowcase with a couple of rubber bands or masking tape wrapped around the end, to keep it securely sealed during transit. You can put a small towel inside the pillowcase to give the iguana something to hold onto and lie on while the bag is being carried in your arms or hand.

If you're getting your iguana on a very cold day, you have to do a little more than just bring a box. You have to find a way to keep your iguana warm inside the box. See the sidebar "Baby, it's cold outside" for ideas.

The safest way to transport the iguana in your car, whether you are alone or have a human companion, is to set the boxed iguana on a seat and fasten the seatbelt around it. This way, if the driver has to stop the car suddenly or swerve, the box won't go flying off the seat or out of someone's lap.

While you're driving, talk softly to the iguana. If you already have a name picked out, start using it. If you don't, that's okay, too. The main thing is that you start to familiarize your iguana with the sound of your voice. Doing so will give him some sort of connection with you as the strange and frightening events of the next several days transpire. If you play the radio in the car, keep the volume down.

Home, sweet what?

When you arrive home, bring the box with your iguana into his new room and set him down near the enclosure. Close the doors, keep the children and other pets out of the room, and open the box and unpack the iguana: Use scissors to remove the tape or rubber bands securing the top of the pillowcase — *after* making sure that the iguana is at the other end. Fold back the cloth a bit and then reach in for the iguana. If he allows himself to be picked up, lift him gently and move him to the enclosure, placing him carefully inside. If he isn't cooperative, you can place the pillowcase in the enclosure, peeling back more of the fabric to expose the iguana. Or you can leave him sitting on the towel in the pillowcase, looking out at his new home, letting him come out on his own as he feels a little more secure.

TIP

Baby, it's cold outside

If the weather is very cold, you can line the box with sheets of rigid foam; then put a hot-water bottle in the box to one side under a layer of towel, or use a foam or insulated cooler of the right size.

If you don't have (or don't want to buy) a good, old-fashioned hot-water bottle, you can make one. Get out a plastic food storage bag that zips up securely and fill it three-quarters full with hot water. Then bag the water-filled bag inside one or two other plastic zipper bags. Or you can get some pocket/hand warmers from a camping store, activate one or two of them (depending on the size of the box), and tape them to the inside top of the box when you go into the store. Keeping the box closed lets the heat build up inside. If you have a long trip home, make sure that you've poked some ventilation holes in the box top, or open the box occasionally during the trip home to make sure everything is okay. If it gets too hot, let some heat out. Keeping an iguana too hot is just as dangerous as keeping him too cold. Better for him to be a little on the cool side rather than roasted on the trip home.

Close the door or lid of the enclosure and leave the iguana alone for a while. You can move around the room and continue to talk to the iguana. An hour or so later, put some food in his food plate, approach the enclosure, and open it, placing the food plate near the water dish. Let the iguana see you coming and talk to him as you go through the motions.

Staying patient while he adjusts

Many new iguanas are seemingly very calm the first several days or weeks after being installed in their new home and introduced to their new family; then later they become feisty and thrashy and do their darndest to get away from you. Others, from the get-go, view you as their worst nightmare come true; they run wildly away from you the moment they see you and try to scrabble through the far side of the enclosure when you insert your hand to service the enclosure.

Both reactions are normal. Just know that the fear responses will slowly stop as the iguana becomes more comfortable with you and his daily routines, and as you work with him every day over the next several months to tame and socialize him.

Taking Him to a Vet

Take your new iguana to a reptile vet soon after you bring him home. Having a basic checkup, a testing and treatment for parasites, and an opportunity to meet and talk with the veterinarian accomplishes several things.

✔ First, it helps ensure that your iguana is, or becomes, as healthy as possible as soon as possible. You want to make sure that you get the diet and environment right. You want to make sure that your iguana is well hydrated and free of harmful loads of internal parasites. And you want to have any other problems identified and promptly dealt with.

✔ Second, it gives your vet a *baseline assessment*, a picture of what your iguana looks like at the time. A year later, when you bring him for a routine checkup, you and your vet can compare what your iguana is like now to what he was like during the baseline assessment. Going in for regular checkups, compiling notes from physical exams, and making sure that parasite tests and blood tests are done will cause small abnormalities to jump out and be dealt with before they become major problems.

✔ Finally, it helps let the vet get to know you. By paying your bills on time, you will establish a credit history with the vet. If the time comes when your iguana needs major surgery, you may be able to negotiate a payment plan instead of being forced to put your iguana's life (or your next month's rent) on the line. This is unlikely to happen if you have already established a good, working relationship with your vet.

Chapter 4

If One Iguana Is Good, Are More Iguanas Better?

They're cute, they're cheap, and the kids love 'em, so why not get a couple of iguanas instead of just one? Do iguanas do better in pairs or groups? Should I get my iguana a buddy? How many iguanas can live in a 50-gallon tank?

New iguana keepers often ask these questions, or they just go ahead and get two or more hatchling iguanas. After all, they are all kept together in the pet store, so it must be okay. Right? Well . . . .

Although it's okay to keep some hatchling iguanas together in a large enough enclosure, the problem is that they don't stay hatchling size for very long. As they grow, their temperaments and space requirements change, as does their tolerance for one another. So, before getting that second iguana, look ahead to what potential problems lay in your future.

A Society of Iguanas

In the wild, green iguanas are often found in groups (called *aggregations*). They may gather to take advantage of a lush food source, exposed basking areas, or comfortable sleeping areas. Despite being found in aggregations and companionably hanging out with other iguanas, iguanas are not noted for being social animals in the way we usually think of social animals — like primates, who often live in extended, cooperative social groups, and wolves, who interact and function in a pack made up primarily of immediate family members.

Iguanas group together only during certain times and for certain reasons. They are not, by nature, social animals in the same way dogs or house cats are social animals.

One's company, two's a crowd?

Iguanas are independent lizards, preferring to spend a lot of their time alone. That said, they also do seek out or accept other iguanas for interaction or cohabitation (see Figure 4-1). The reason may just be for companionship with a fellow species member. Or, for smaller iguanas, the reason is for safety. The more lizards there are together in a group, the less chance there is that one particular individual will be preyed on.

Figure 4-1:
In some cases, iguanas do seek out other iguanas. Here, a group of iguanas is sleeping in captivity.

Male iguanas have another reason for getting together with other iguanas. Males seek out females during breeding season, which, of course, is how two iguanas become 50 or more iguanas. Mature males may seek out other males to see if they can carve out a little of the other male's territory for their own — or to try to take the territory over. The encounters may involve facing off with another iguana (see Figure 4-2), ritualized posturing and physical contact, or serious fighting that results in one or both becoming seriously injured.

This is stressing me out!

In the wild, a single, large male iguana has a 130-foot (or more) multilevel area to occupy. Iguanas *can* do well in a smaller, confined area, though, if you give them enough room for comfort (which, by the by, rules out commercially available reptile and iguana enclosures). But giving an iguana enough room for comfort means that someday you'll need to supply an enclosure that's more than 10 feet long and 6 feet tall. Overwhelming, yes. But necessary.

Now for an iguana, there's a certain amount of chronic stress involved just being in captivity. Add to that the stress of being confined in an enclosure that's too small. Compound these stresses by forcing the iguana to live in close proximity with another iguana, especially one that your iguana may be incompatible with during some part (or all) of the year, and you have a stress-related illness, injury, or behavioral problem just waiting to happen.

Figure 4-2: A face-off between two male iguanas seeking to carve out (or take over completely) a little territory of their own.

Environmental stress relates to problems with the diet, lighting, heating, photoperiods (the daylight and dark night periods), space, and furnishings. *Behavioral stress* relates to alterations in the iguana's daily routine, which lead to unhealthy behavioral changes. *Social stress* relates to stresses in the social structure, which includes humans as well as any other iguanas the iguana interacts with.

"Iguanas don't hang out with humans in the wild, so why should they in captivity? It's just not natural!"

Let's be honest with ourselves: If we really wanted our iguanas to be "natural," we wouldn't have acquired them to begin with. The only place an iguana can be truly natural is in the wild. No matter how naturalistic we make their environment and no matter how many iguanas we put together in hopes that they'll form a relatively peaceful cohabitation structure as in the wild, captivity is still captivity.

The light is different, the food is different, the very air is different, and iguanas realize all of this at one or more biochemical levels. In captivity, they don't

have the ability to just pick up and leave a stressful environment and move on to a more suitable area a significant distance away. Confining an iguana with walls — whether they're enclosure, room, house, large greenhouse, or mesh cage walls — is still sentencing the iguana to live in a vastly smaller area in a significantly different environment than it evolved to expect and needs in order to be comfortable and function at optimum levels. These realizations — the impact of the conditions experienced in captivity — cause the chronic stress in captive wild animals.

Do iguanas need iguana company?

Yes . . . and no. Iguanas seem to do better in captivity when they are part of a social group. That group can, under the right conditions, be another iguana. Here are the right conditions:

✔ An enclosure or space at east 1.5–2 times the area required by the largest iguana in the group, *per iguana*. If the iguanas are still growing, even more space is required.

✔ At least two to three additional basking areas, feeding areas, water bowls, hiding places, lounging areas, and sleeping areas.

✔ Whatever your iguana says is the right condition. What may look like enough space to you may not be enough space for your iguana to feel comfortable with a new iguana "forced" into "his" territory. (Remember: Females can be as fiercely territorial as males.)

✔ With whatever iguana that *your* iguana says is an acceptable companion. Just because you may consider that nice, sweet, little iguana the perfect companion doesn't mean that your iguana will feel the same way. Put the two together, and they may never come to accept one another, or one may completely — and aggressively — reject the other by terrorizing it, attacking it, or keeping it away from food, water, and heat. (A smaller iguana can effectively dominate a larger one to the point of causing it to starve to death or die of acute stress, so size can't be used to predict acceptance or rejection.)

 If you get two or more iguanas, be prepared to set each of them up in their own fully outfitted enclosure. And because iguanas can smell each other even when they cannot see each other, keeping them in separate enclosures in the same room may not be "separate" enough — you may have to keep them in separate rooms. If your incompatible iguanas are free-roaming, you will have to make sure that there is no chance that they can get to one another. Finally, two iguanas who get along together today may not get along together next month or next year and may need to be housed completely separately.

If the iguana is tamed and socialized, the iguana's social group can be his humans. If you interact on a daily basis with your iguana, including him as part of your daily routine, spending time with him during the day and before the iguana's bedtime, taking the iguana for excursions, petting him, holding him, feeding him treats by hand, and engaging in regular close physical contact, the iguana will come to consider you — a human — as part of his social group.

Should You or Shouldn't You?

If you're just starting out with iguanas, do you have the time, energy, and skill with iguanas to tame and socialize more than one at a time? If you already have an iguana who is tame and socialized, do you have the time to tame and social-ize a new one *and* spend enough time with the established iguana so that it doesn't become stressed and jealous of the time you spend concentrating on the new one? As you consider these questions, keep these things in mind:

- ✔ Whether you have one iguana or a dozen, you need to tame each of them to ensure that you can move among them to care for them without stressing them to the point of illness and injury. Head to Part V for info on how to tame and socialize your iguana.

  Getting a second iguana to avoid the difficulty of taming the first iguana is *not* an option. You'll just make everyone — yourself and your two iguanas — miserable.

- ✔ Taming and socialization take a great deal of time each day, and it may take a year for an iguana to be tame and on his way to becoming social-ized. If you've ever watched the harried parents of human twins or triplets (or more) trying to cope with the basics of cleaning, feeding, and changing infants and toddlers, as well as trying to help them learn social communication skills and learn about their environment, you have some idea of what it's like trying to earn a living, have a life outside of your job, and tame two or more iguanas at the same time.

- ✔ Do you have the space for more than one iguana? Can you fit two or more enclosures of the same size into *your* house? Also think about your iguana's house — his enclosure. Is *it* big enough for two?

An adult iguana needs an enclosure 1.5–2 times its total length, at least 6 feet tall and 2.5 feet deep. Since iguanas average from 5–6 feet in total length, you're looking at two or more enclosures that are each 7.5–12 feet long. Each enclosure needs to be fully outfitted with necessary furnishings and heating and lighting equipment, and each needs daily maintenance. If you plan to keep the iguanas together, you need an even larger enclosure, adding another 3–4 feet in length and 2–3 feet in depth, or 270–528 cubic feet! (By comparison, a 55-gallon tank is approximately 7.5 cubic feet, and a 125-gallon is approximately 19 cubic feet.)

Bottom line: If you can't afford the space and equipment — or the problems (and veterinary bills) when one iguana goes a-hunting the other ones — or you don't have the time and patience to tame and socialize your iguanas (and keep them socialized), don't get more than one iguana.

Introducing a New Iguana

If you cave in to taking in another iguana, you need to know how to introduce it to your established iguana, who will consider his enclosure, room, or house (depending on how much out-time a caged iguana gets and how much freedom a free-roamer has) to be his and his alone, and he'll consider new iguanas to be interlopers. Here are some tips:

✔ Introduce the new iguana to the established one in a neutral territory. Don't just deposit the new iguana directly into your iguana's enclosure. Your iguana will consider that to be a direct threat and may go on the attack.

✔ With both iguanas in a neutral area, hold, pet, and talk to both of them. If the enclosure you plan to house them in is big enough for both of them and their anticipated growth, you can try, after a half hour or so, to put the new iguana into the enclosure and give him an hour or so to familiarize himself with the new environment. Keep the established iguana out of the room.

✔ If the enclosure has different levels, physically put the iguana on the different shelves and show him the way to get up and down. Show him the food and water bowls, climbers, and so on. Once the new iguana has been settled in for a while, reintroduce your original iguana into the enclosure. Watch them closely for the next several hours.

✔ Spend a lot of quality time with your original iguana. If you've ever introduced a human baby into a house with a long-term cat or dog resident, or a newborn sibling to an older child, you're familiar with the feelings of displacement that can affect overall behavior of the established pet or child. It's no different with iguanas. Try not to flaunt the time you spend with the new one in front of the original one for the same reasons. The original iguana does need to see you interacting with, petting, treating, and cuddling the other iguana, but you don't want to rub his face in it.

✔ Don't introduce a new male iguana into the household during breeding season. Even if they can't see each other, the established iguana will know that the new one is there. Both iguanas will be able to smell the other iguana on your skin and clothes, and the original iguana, especially a territorial male, may take his displeasure with the new iguana's presence out on you.

If all goes well, you still need to keep a close watch on them for the next several weeks. You also need to make sure that both of the iguanas are feeding adequately and have unimpeded access to the basking and hiding areas.

When you have more than two iguanas, the dynamics become even more complicated. Figuring out which ones are bullying the new one may be difficult. You also need to watch for signs of stress. See the sidebar "Cohabitation stress (or 'My new roommate is killing me!')."

Sometimes the new iguana — *not* the established one — takes umbrage at the situation. A male or female who's introduced into a new environment where there's one or more established iguanas may become the aggressor or intimidator. So watching for signs of active aggression, intimidation, injury, and stress in *all* the iguanas is important. Don't assume who'll be the dominant/aggressor and who'll be the subordinate/victim. You may be abruptly and unpleasantly surprised to find that your assumption was wrong.

Does gender matter if I get another iguana?

Not really. Established males can still be obnoxious to new females, so don't assume that having a male and female means you aren't going to have conflicts. And, because females can be just as territorial and unaccepting of any other iguana in their home, getting two females is not necessarily the answer.

Also, remember that you can't tell whether an iguana is a male or a female (by looking at them, anyway) until they're at least one year old or 8 inches long (from the snout to the vent).

If Things Don't Work Out

Nature being nature, and iguanas being iguanas, sometimes your iguanas just won't get along. You've got a few options: You can try separating them to see if that makes a difference. You can try giving them even more room for the activities they require. Or you can decide that you've got to find one (or more) of them a new home.

Separating your iguanas

You've tried a new, bigger enclosure, or you've set your iguanas up as free-roamers, but either they fight with each other or one picks mercilessly on the other, often with bloody results. The iguanas need to be separated.

If you have more than two iguanas, and only one is being the dominant, or *alpha,* iguana, or only one is being picked on, you have to choose which one to isolate. If the dominant iguana gets along with any of the other iguanas, you may want to keep the dominant and compatible ones together and separate the subordinate ones (the *omegas*) who are having the most problem with the alpha. Because of their keen sense of smell and hearing, you need to house the omegas in another room.

You need to set up a second enclosure or free-roaming area, one big enough for the number of iguanas to be housed within it. You need to take into account the future growth of the iguanas, especially the omegas, and expect that the growth will be faster than it has been because the omegas will begin eating better now that the stress has been greatly reduced. Of course, as these iguanas settle in and start working out their own social system, you may again have an omega or alpha that needs to be separated.

Cohabitation stress (or "My new roommate is killing me!")

An iguana's social environment can affect his overall health. The longer the period of social stress goes on, the increased chance there is of bacterial infections in the body and increased parasites in the gut. The bacterial infections can cause respiratory infections or *abscesses* — infected lumps — anywhere on the body or in the mouth. The best way to prevent this is to watch carefully for signs of stress and make the necessary changes *before* the stress levels progress to the point of illness.

Signs of cohabitation stress include the skin color turning to dark gray or brown, loss of appetite, failure to bask, lethargy, and alternation or deviation from normal daily behavioral patterns. Prolonged stress results in weight loss and dehydration, malnutrition, and/or systemic infection. All new iguanas should routinely have fecal exams done. All iguanas who show signs of stress in excess of a couple of weeks should also be tested. It's a good idea to have your established iguana's feces tested, too, within a month or two of introducing the new iguana into the mix.

More room means a better chance for peace

Territory, especially for males, is the biggest point of contention between any individual male and any other iguana. If they're given enough room, however, you have a better chance that two or more iguanas will get along together. Enough room is approximately equivalent in size to a room in your house — and not a small one, either. The more basking spots, sleeping places, and feeding stations you can set up over a widely dispersed area, the more the individual iguanas can carve out their own area within the larger area. Having a place to retreat to when an iguana needs time alone is beneficial. It gives the iguana a sense of being able to control what's going on.

Some iguanas do best spending their days in one room, in an area set up for them, and returning at night to a main iguana room to sleep. With this arrangement, the alpha often accepts the other iguanas as the group beds down for the night, sleeping companionably together, and allows them to depart in peace the next day to do their routine over again.

If partial separation and multiple-room free-roaming don't work, then you need to further separate them, incorporating one or more of the iguanas into still more of your own living areas. Or you need to find them a new home.

Finding a new home

Finding your iguana a new home is one of the most difficult things to do. Not only is the decision a hard one to make, but finding a new home usually isn't as easy as it sounds. As you have probably come to realize yourself, many of the people interested in having an iguana don't really understand what it takes to keep one properly. Following are some ideas on where you can start:

- ✔ **Put an advertisement in the newspaper.** Keep in mind, though, that doing so usually draws people who know little about iguanas. You can easily test the caller's knowledge with a few questions.

- ✔ **Contact your local reptile veterinarians** to see if they know of anyone looking for an iguana. Depending on where you live, you may be one of many iguana keepers who've called the vets with the very same question.

- ✔ **Contact the local herpetological society and reptile rescue individuals or groups.** They may know of people who are qualified to take in iguanas or have foster homes set up to take them until a permanent home is found. These groups are nonprofit organizations, so consider making a donation of reptile equipment and supplies or cash; such donations may even be tax deductible.

One option that isn't open is zoos and wildlife parks. They already have all the iguanas they want. Because they generally refer callers to the local herp society or reptile rescue, you may as well save yourself a call and frustration.

Finding a home for the iguana rarely happens overnight. You may end up keeping him for several months until you find someone who knows how to care for iguanas properly.

JARGON ALERT

Oh, give me a home, where the iguanas roam . . .

The term *free-roaming* describes a situation where the iguana doesn't live in an enclosure that's placed within a room. It doesn't mean that the iguana is just left to roam the whole house, like a dog or cat does. Instead, one or more rooms are set up with the necessary lighting, heating, and roosts, with appropriate climbers or other access the iguana needs to ascend to the roosts. The temperatures in the room and roosts are maintained to ensure that the iguana always has the thermal gradient he needs. Chapter 9 provides more information on free-roaming.

Setting him free and other non-options

Releasing the iguana into your yard or nearby park or wilderness area is *not* an option. Not only is it illegal to release nonnative wildlife and considered animal abandonment (which may be subject to heavy fines), releasing an iguana in most areas is a sure death sentence. Furthermore, releasing any long-term captive, especially a nonnative species, puts the local native wildlife at risk. Many iguana keepers who are trying to get rid of their unwanted iguanas assume that there are "iguana parks" out there, a sort of wildlife park set up just for unwanted iguanas. Others think that they can find someone who ships unwanted iguanas back to their country of origin so they can "live free."

Unfortunately, life just doesn't work that way. Some rescuers have been able to set up extensive enclosures and take in lots of iguanas, but it isn't their job to do so, and they aren't funded to do so. As for returning iguanas to the wild, the countries that exported them don't particularly want them back, and it would cost far more in time, money, health inspections, federal permits, shipping, and so on, even if they would accept them. Once the iguanas got "home," however, there is no iguana refuge set up for them and, for the reasons stated earlier, they cannot simply be released into the wild. Sending them back to the farms isn't an option, either.

Be sure the person who adopts your iguana is someone the iguana likes. Make sure your iguana spends time being held and talked to by the prospective new keeper. If the iguana turns dark or brown and doesn't lighten up again until he is in the hands of someone you know he likes, and this happens repeatedly during the meeting, consider it a bad match and try to find someone else for the iguana.

If you absolutely can't find a home for your iguana — either locally or more distantly by researching the Internet for other groups and rescues (refer to Appendix B for a list of resources) — and you absolutely can't keep it, do the right thing and have the iguana humanely euthanized by lethal injection by a reptile veterinarian. Euthanasia sounds harsh and doesn't sit well with many animal lovers, regardless of species. Unfortunately, in the case of iguanas, it seems particularly heart-wrenching because they never asked to be here to begin with.

Part II

Iguana: The Species and the Lizard

The 5th Wave   By Rich Tennant

©RICHTENNANT

EXOTIC PETS

AMERICA   SOUTH AMERICA

In this part . . .

Green iguanas are an interesting species, no matter how you look at them. They are large, intelligent, arboreal herbivores. While that may sound like nothing special, each part of that description affects how they are cared for and treated in captivity.

This part covers structural part of your iguana's insides, as well as the physiological reasons why he behaves the way he does, from his daily schedule of thermoregulating and feeding, to how he moves around his environment. You'll also find the basics of iguana communication and social structure — important info whether you have one or a dozen iguanas.

Chapter 5

Cat-ig-orizing Iguanas

*W*ho are these green lizards, and where do they come from? Now that you have one — or are thinking about getting one — you probably want to know.

Getting info about iguanas in the wild, and who your iguana is related to, can help you understand why your iguana is doing what it's doing. Knowing something about the classification scheme, at least as it relates to iguanas and their relatives, gives you a better opportunity to find material and make sense of it.

Green Iguanas: What Are They?

Green iguanas are part of a group of related lizards, called *iguanids,* native to the New World. Ranging from the southwestern United States far into South America, iguanid lizards leap, run, swim, and climb through a wide range of sizes, diets, habitats, and temperaments.

Green iguanas come from a more limited area, found mostly around the rainforests and in some drier coastal regions. They're the biggest group of the mainland iguanas. Their coloring and markings reflect the environment they live in: in and around trees, with lots of sun, lots of dappled shade, and lots of other animals eyeing them for lunch.

The scientific stuff: Where iguanas fit in

Green iguanas have a place in the grand scheme of things. Their place, as defined by the people who classify all living organisms, is this:

Kingdom: Animalia

Phylum: Chordata

Class: Reptilia

Subclass: Lepidosauria

Order: Squamata

Suborder: Sauria

Infraorder: Iguania

Family: Iguanidae

Genus: *Iguana*

Species: *iguana*

What the heck does all this mean? Simply that an iguana is an animal (a reptile, to be specific) with a backbone. (Don't you just love people who make their life's work finding ways to use Greek and Latin?)

A green iguana is, therefore, officially called an *Iguana iguana.* Some people refer to them as the "common green iguana." You can call yours whatever you like.

The study of reptiles and amphibians is often lumped together under the name *herpetology,* a word coming from the Greek *herpeton,* meaning things that creep or crawl.

The other iguanas: That's some family tree

The green iguana's closest relatives are the other species grouped together in the iguana family:

Chuckawallas (also spelled *chuckwalla*)

Cycluras

Desert iguanas

Fiji banded iguanas

Galapagos land and marine iguanas

Spiny-tailed (also called Black) iguanas

These iguanas range in size from small to large and in habitat from desert to humid tropical forest. With the exception of the heavily protected Fiji and Galapagos iguanas, these iguanas can be kept as pets, though finding them is often difficult. Most are more expensive than green iguanas. Some of the *Cyclura* species sell for $500–$1,100 and require special permits when they're transported across state lines.

The iguana family has other members, as well (consider these the green iguanas' cousins):

Various spiny-tailed iguanas

Curly-tailed and other swifts (a group of lizards in Central and South America)

The so-called Madagascar iguana, which looks more like a swift than an iguana

Collared and leopard lizards

Basilisks

Cone-headed lizards (sometimes called *cone-headed iguanas*)

Helmeted iguanas (sometimes called *forest chameleons*)

Horned lizards (also called *horny toads*)

Fence, crevice, and blue-belly lizards

Earless, sand, and blotched lizards

Anole lizards, sometimes called *chameleons* for their color-changing abilities.

It would take quite a park to accommodate this family reunion.

Humans and iguanas through the ages

Humans have interacted with iguanas for as long as humans and iguanas have coexisted in the same environment. Some people ate iguanas merely for the protein the iguanas added to the human diet, while others believed that eating iguanas gave them extra strength. Iguana eggs have long been considered a delicacy.

Carvings of iguanas have been found on burial artifacts of Mayan kings who chose them as guides to accompany them to the next world. More recently, many new iguana owners have fallen under the spell of their new iguanas, felled by a single glint in their intelligent eyes.

Chicken of the trees

Iguanas raised on farms are power-fed to grow quickly so they get big enough to evade most predators. Such power-feeding generally includes the addition of animal protein to their diet, which makes them grow faster than an iguana on a proper plant-only diet. When relocated by the humans who will eventually eat them, they're released into the trees around the human habitation. There, they continue to eat and grow until they themselves are big enough to eat. The humans often provide some feeding stations with tasty treats to encourage the iguanas to hang around for the next couple of years until . . . . Well, in Spanish, iguanas are sometimes referred to as *pollo de los arboles* ("chicken of the trees"). This has led some iguana owners to chastise their misbehaving iguanas by reminding them, "Tastes like chicken!"

Where Do They Come From?

All the Iguanidae lizards live in very warm climates, from tropical Central and South American forests, to the Caribbean islands, to the deserts of the American Southwest and Mexico. The largest of these lizards, with very few exceptions, are completely *herbivorous* (that is, they eat plants).

Green iguanas are native to many countries in Central and South America (see Figure 5-1). They live in the areas bordering rainforests. Through the years, iguanas sold in the pet trade have generally come from Mexico; Central American countries like El Salvador, Guatemala, Honduras, and Panama; and South American countries like Columbia, Guyana, Peru, and Surinam. Due to various changes in the status of green iguanas within each country, the actual countries may vary from year to year.

Farmed or Caught: How They Get to You

The iguanas in the pet trade are wild-caught, farmed, captive hatched, or captive bred: *Wild-caught* iguanas are just that: captured in the wild and shipped overseas. *Captive hatched* reptiles are hatched from eggs collected in the wild or eggs laid by wild-caught *gravid* (pregnant) females. *Captive bred* reptiles are born or hatched from eggs produced by reptiles who have been cared for in captivity for some time and who bred while in captivity. *Farmed* iguanas may be either captive hatched or captive bred. There's no way for anyone to tell by looking at them whether your iguana was captive bred, captive hatched, farmed, or wild-caught.

The reason imports feed the pet trade is because captive breeding of iguanas in North America and Europe (and elsewhere in the world where iguanas are kept as pets) isn't successful enough yet to compete price-wise with the pet trade's current sources. Unfortunately, as iguana prices dropped over the past decade, more people who bought iguanas began to treat them as if they were without value; they considered them cheap enough that they could let them die and just buy another instead of spending the money required to provide for them properly (including necessary veterinary care).

Where, o where is my little ig from?

All baby green iguanas look alike, so during their infancy, there's no easy way to tell what country they're from. Since pet stores buy from distributors or wholesalers, and the distributors and wholesalers may buy from different suppliers, the pet stores and distributors generally don't know the origin of their iguanas. In the long run, it doesn't matter because all iguanas have the capacity to grow into majestic lizards — each with unique differences that make it special to its keepers.

As iguanas grow older and begin to attain their adult coloration, we can make better guesses about where they — or at least their parents — came from. Generally speaking, the regional physcial characteristics of iguanas are as follows:

- **From Mexico:** Very long dorsal crests and longer snouts. Sexually mature males and females have brownish-rusty orange arms and legs under a predominantly green body. Some may have rostral horns or nubs.

- **From Central America:** Pale green, with silvery-light blue-white heads (when excited or contented) and bold brown-black belly stripes. Sexually mature iguanas generally display varying amounts of orange year round, especially the dominant males. Some of the iguanas may have a network of fine black lines on their bodies, which is actually their skin color showing between their scales. Some may have rostral horns or nubs.

- **From South America:** Blue color retained to their skin. The blue iguanas' heads are shaped a bit differently, with a shorter snout and slight convex hump between the nostrils and eye area on top of the face (as opposed to the flat head of the Mexican and Central American iguana). Many are striking due to their deep reddish eyes, black lacing around the scales on their face, and black skin and scales on their eyelids and dewlaps. The dorsal crests are shorter, and sexually mature lizards rarely display the orange coloring of their Central American cousins.

I've had iguanas from all across the range. All were beautiful lizards, though the ones from Central America seemed to get tamer faster than Mexican and South American iguanas. The blue iguanas from South America were the cuddliest of them all, often soliciting to be picked up and petted. (One of them was also the only iguana who ever decided that I was his perfect mate. He aggressively and persistently tried to mate with me during his annual breeding season.) Green iguanas are not always green — or blue. Many are shades of brown, cream, and black with touches of green. Getting a baby iguana is like having a baby in the days before ultrasound technology: What you end up with is always a surprise.

Chapter 6

Iguana Anatomy

· ·

· ·

*O*n the surface and under the skin, green iguanas are much like other four-legged, tailed animals. They're also much like other lizards. But some things make green iguanas unique, different even from other iguanas in their family.

Knowing about the different bits that make up a green iguana may not seem important, but you'll find it vital when talking with your vet or comparing notes with other iguana keepers. Knowing what's going on inside your iguana can also help you figure out what's going on outside your iguana — you can identify small problems before they become big ones.

The Outside

Like most other lizards, green iguanas have a head (with ears), a neck, four legs (or two legs and two arms, as many iguana keepers refer to them), a tail, and the place (opening) where they do all kinds of stuff — void wastes, mate, and lay eggs (see Figure 6-1). Lizards are structured the way they are because they evolved to take advantage of their habitat.

The head and neck

The green iguana's head and neck have the usual complement of accessories for the well-dressed lizard (see Figure 6-2): two eyes, two nostrils, two ears, one mouth with lots of sharp teeth, and the opalescent parietal "eye" on the top of the head. In addition, the green iguana has two large, decorative scales on its jowls and a soft dewlap.

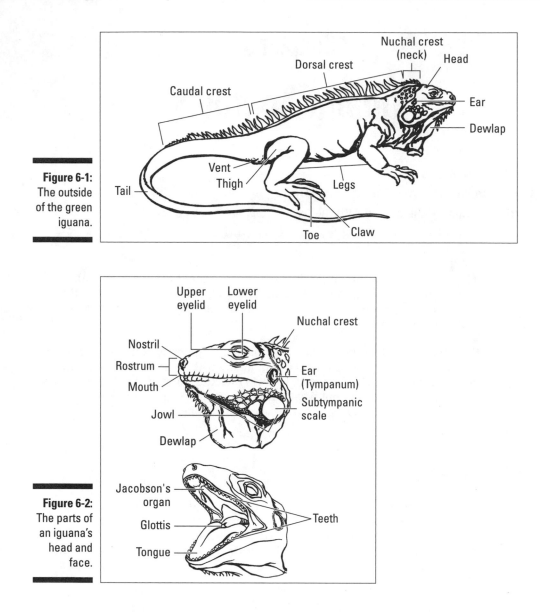

Figure 6-1:
The outside of the green iguana.

Figure 6-2:
The parts of an iguana's head and face.

Toward the back of the head, just before the head becomes neck, are two different-looking scales. The smaller, flat scale that's recessed a bit below the surface of the surrounding skin is the ear. The pearlescent "scale" covering the ear hole is the *tympanum* (tympanic membrane). It is usually greenish or yellowish in color and becomes increasingly yellow as the layer of skin covering it gets ready to shed. On some iguanas, the tympanum gets an orange or rusty tint to it during breeding season.

The large, opalescent scale farther down on the head is essentially just a decoration. Only the green iguanas have this scale, referred to as *sub-tympanic scale,* or "that big thing under the ear." When an iguana is in full defensive mode, it laterally compresses its body (so that it looks taller) and turns sideways so that the perceived threat sees a bigger lizard. The illusion of size is augmented by the extended legs, which add still more height, and the flared-out dewlap, which makes the head look double (or more) its usual size. When seen from a distance, the sub-tympanic scale looks like a wide, staring eye in a big green head.

The body and legs

Depending on where they come from, some iguanas are long and lean, while others are more powerfully and broadly built. Females tend to be a bit broader across the abdominal area, possibly to give them room to carry 60 or more eggs when they are gravid.

A healthy iguana has a chubby chest and smooth body, occasionally with a mild *lateral* fold running down the sides, from behind the arms to the hips. When the gut is full of food, there may be a bulge along one side of the abdomen. The bulge is normal and disappears once the ingested food moves along as it's digested.

The *nuchal* (refers to the neck area) and *dorsal* (the back) crests stand straight up on most iguanas (refer to Figure 6-1), though on some healthy iguanas, the crests naturally sort of flops over to one side. The spikes may be long or short, flat or conical. The spikes on the nuchal crest are generally longer than the spikes on the dorsal crest. The muscles under the crests can be tightened, causing the spikes to stand up higher and the iguana to look taller.

Iguana legs and toes are pretty amazing. The thighs and forelegs are quite muscular, and the toes are surprisingly delicate for such a large lizard. Each toe is tipped by a claw. The main part of the claw looks like most animal claws, but iguanas grow extremely sharp extensions on each claw — to help them climb in the wild. In captivity, these extensions easily shred human skin and clothing (and little things like your antique upholstered love seat and expensive lace curtains). Most iguana keepers clip these points off. Doing so doesn't impair the iguana's ability to climb in captivity but does make handling the iguana a vastly more pleasurable experience.

The skinny on scales

The scales on the iguana body vary, depending largely on where the iguana's from. Some adult iguanas have soft, smooth scales; others have rough, pokey scales that leave clear indentations in your bare arm when you hold them for a while. Still others have scales with a slightly gritty feel, like the fine side of an emery board.

I feel your pain

Iguanas, like other reptiles, do feel your touch. They also feel the surfaces they lay on, though sometimes their choice of surface surprises their humans. Iguanas also feel pain when hit, pinched, or slapped with an object. Although their pain tolerance may be higher, or different, than ours, and they may not react to painful stimuli the way we would in similar circumstances, we must acknowledge that they do feel pain and that they may be in pain even if they don't act like they are.

On baby iguanas, all scales look and feel uniformly smooth and closely fitted. But once an iguana starts to mature, you can begin to see and feel the difference. The belly scales are thick, giving the belly added protection from scrapes and punctures. Tail scales have sharp points that project out, which, when combined with the hard, razor-sharp dorsal crest, easily discourage rubbing an iguana the wrong way. Face and dewlap scales are soft, but the neck has raised, pointy scales that help protect against bites from most other iguanas and some predators. The scales on the back of the legs and toes often stick out, like the tail scales, possibly giving the iguanas more traction when they climb (presuming, of course, that they didn't evolve as a way to help humans accelerate their own rate of shedding when holding a large iguana).

The tail end

One of the most, er, striking features of a green iguana is its tail. Typically two to three times the body length, the tail is a well-muscled, heavily armored appendage. Its length and vivid striping helps the iguana blend into the trees and dappled sunshine. Its powerful slap helps discourage would-be predators and over-eager humans from messing with the tail or with the iguana. Finally, with smaller iguanas, the tail is the original in stealth technology. When a predator is close on the trail of a green iguana meal, the iguana disconnects and drops its tail. The tail lays wriggling on the ground, the strong muscle contractions moving it along. While the predator is engaged in capturing and killing the tail, the iguana continues its run to safety. Of particular dismay to lizard keepers, however, is that a lizard may drop its tail when the keeper goes to pick it up, or to grab it as it's fleeing across the room, or when extracting it from under a particularly heavy piece of furniture. The end result is a lizard peering with interest at its keeper, who's standing there shrieking while holding onto the still-thrashing tail. Needless to say, the keeper in question doesn't find the situation as interesting or bemusing as the iguana does.

The tail is made up of several muscle bundles with special attachments to the vertebrae that run the length of the tail. These attachments connect to the vertebrae in a way that enables the tail to drop, a process called *autotomy*. Many lizards can autotomize (drop) their tails.

Iguanas also use their tails to help balance themselves and find them especially useful when climbing up or down steep surfaces. If your iguana experiences a tail drop, expect to see some clumsiness over the next couple of weeks until it finds its new center of gravity.

If a small iguana (under 8–10 inches) drops its tail, the tail will most likely regenerate, with the new growth starting from the stump of the original tail. Larger iguanas who drop their tails (generally as a result of an accident instead of defense) may not generate new growth.

During the past decade, some sellers of baby iguanas have been intentionally breaking off iguanas' tails so that they'll "grow faster" and "be strong." Not only is this practice cruel, but it also doesn't force faster growth in hatchlings, nor does it make them stronger. Quite the opposite, in fact. The body diverts energy into healing the stump, fighting off possible infections because the tissues are exposed to the environment, and then into growing a new tail. Iguanas grow fast enough when cared for and fed properly. No tail removal is needed.

The Inside

Ewwww, gross! Why would anyone want to learn about the insides of an iguana? Because learning about what goes on inside your iguana helps you understand why iguanas do some of the things they do, why you need to do some of the things you need to do, and why some things go wrong. And things are bound to go wrong at least once in a while. Understanding some basics helps ease things along for you, if not for your iguana.

Measuring up

The tail drop reflex is the primary reason that iguana keepers refer to their iguana's length by using its *SVL*, or snout-vent length, instead of its overall, or *STL* (snout-tail length), size. Remember that original iguana tails vary in length from two to three times the iguana's body length (from snout to the vent, or just in back of the hind legs).

With the dropping and regeneration that's possible, using an iguana's overall length can be very misleading. An iguana 3 feet long may be a typical two-year-old with a 10- to 11-inch body and original tail, or it may be a much older 15-pound iguana with an 18- to 20-inch body and the stumpy remnant of its original tail.

The foundation: The musculoskeletal system

Iguanas have something in common with the rest of us vertebrates: a bony skeleton that forms the basis of support for all the muscles, organs, vessels, and things, all wrapped up in skin. The ligaments, tendons, and muscles provide the iguanas flexibility, agility, and strength. The attachments to the vertebrae in the tail enable the iguana to move it, to a limited degree, in all directions — as well as temporarily help support the iguana when it tries to imitate a kangaroo and bounce on the thick part of its tail while trying to climb up slick surfaces.

Around and around we go: The circulatory system

In reptiles, the blood not only circulates nutrients and oxygen throughout the body, it also acts as an internal temperature control. As the blood in the vessels near the surface is warmed up, it circulates to the center of the body, where the heart pumps it throughout the body — spreading the warmth. The flip side is true, too: As the blood near the surface cools, the coolness is spread to the rest of the body through the circulating blood.

Many iguana keepers freak out when their iguanas submerge themselves for prolonged periods of time. Don't fret about it, though. Iguanas can stay underwater without taking a breath for 20 minutes or so. When they're not breathing, their heart — instead of pumping blood to the lungs — pumps blood out to the tissues. The tissues make efficient use of the oxygen that's still in the blood, keeping vital oxygen-dependent organs and bodily functions going until freshly oxygenated blood arrives, which happens once the iguana takes a breath again.

Take a deep breath: The respiratory system

Iguanas are masters at holding their breath. Like a toddler throwing a tantrum, an upset iguana may hold its breath for several minutes before letting it out — often in an explosive *whoosh*. This breath-holding is also a defensive tactic. Holding perfectly still helps an iguana blend into its background. Needless to say, this tactic is more effective when done in a tree or brush than, say, your living room, but as frustrated keepers will tell you, iguanas can hide in plain sight — disappearing in places like your kitchen, living room, and bedroom. When you finally find your iguana, you may find that it's either holding its breath or beginning to breathe rapidly and heavily. Both are normal responses.

The heavy, rapid breathing can also be a fear response, a result of the iguana seeing something that has frightened it. Iguanas may also pant with their mouths open (*gaping*) when they're overheated or when they have a respiratory infection. Iguanas don't get colds like we do, but they can develop bacterial infections that settle in their lungs, requiring antibiotics and, usually, environmental improvements to recover (see Part VI for more info on your iguana's health).

You may see heaving sides, or closed-mouth panting, when iguanas are comfortable and at rest. Because iguanas use their rib cage muscles to compress and release their lungs, there can be significant movement of the ribs. This may be more noticeable if the iguana has recently defecated and has regained a bit of an hour-glass shape to his figure. Injuries to the ribs or muscles attached to the rib cage may cause problems in breathing by impairing the muscles' ability to compress as hard as they would normally.

What goes in must come out: The digestive system

The mouth is where the first stage of digestion takes place. The very sharp, pointed teeth tear leaves that the fleshy, mobile tongue has pulled into the mouth. Iguanas don't chew their food before swallowing. Sometimes they may manipulate the food in their mouth with their tongue to work it into a more comfortable position before swallowing. Most often, they just gulp food down like a dog.

An iguana's digestive system works pretty much like every other animal's. Once the food is swallowed, it's digested. In an iguana, the food goes from the stomach to the small intestine to the *hindgut,* the place where the majority of the breakdown of food takes place. From there, it goes to the large intestine, where the good stuff is absorbed and the rest is, well, directed into the rectum, where it stays until it's eliminated.

A potty-trained or otherwise conscientious iguana will poop (the scientific term preferred by most iguana keepers) in a designated or appropriate (easily cleaned) place. Iguanas who aren't so conscientious are more likely to pick inappropriate places. Iguanas who have a bone to pick with you will pick a spot designed to convey their displeasure. Iguana keepers have reported finding poop in their most expensive shoes, under the bedcovers (where they don't discover it until it's too late), and on important papers brought home from the office. Call it a sixth sense or just good timing, but some iguanas will poop right on you as you're rushing around, already late for work.

If an iguana is too cold, the stomach and intestines can't do their job of breaking down food into nutrients. In the best-case scenario, the iguana is just warm enough to allow some digestion to occur, which enables the iguana to stay alive and even grow a little but remain highly susceptible to nutritional and other diseases, with growth and development retarded. In the worst-case scenario, food gets stuck in the gut and begins to decompose, producing enough gas to eventually rip apart the intestine, killing the iguana.

My! What a pretty smile you have

Iguanas may sit with a partially open mouth. Called a grin by some iguana keepers, it may be more a showing of the teeth, an indication of annoyance. A grin may also take place when the iguana has just eaten something and stopped in midgulp or when it's thinking about eating something or when it isn't sure whether it likes what you're doing. With the mouth widely opened (gaping), the iguana may be cooling off if it's too hot. A gape may also be an open-mouth threat.

Some iguanas in the process of being tamed are downright passive-aggressive; while clearly enjoying being petted, they will gape or "grin" when they remember that they aren't supposed to like it.

'S Amoré: The reproductive system

The birds do it, the bees do it, and the iguanas in the trees (and on the ground) do it, too. The problem with iguanas is that you can't visually determine their gender until they reach at least 8 inches SVL (snout-vent length), which happens when they're around 1 year of age. You must wait to see whether you have a boy or a girl. At about 1 year of age, certain external physical changes occur that differentiate males from females.

With few exceptions, males have bigger, broader heads and they develop jowls in the area around the sub-tympanic scales. Their dorsal and nuchal spikes get longer than the females native to their area. All the femoral pores on males begin to get larger, with off-white, waxy centers appearing inside them. As males attain sexual maturity, their *hemipenes* (copulatory organ) grow larger, causing gentle swellings on either side of the underside of the tail, just below the vent. Male iguanas are fully equipped with two testes and the hemipenes. The testes are inside the body. The bi-lobed hemipenes are elongated and fleshy, with a groove that runs up one side.

Sexually mature females don't develop the jowls, their heads tend to be thinner and more delicate, and their dorsal and nuchal crests tend to be shorter than the males'. The female's first four or five femoral pores become somewhat bigger when they reach sexual maturity, but the other pores remain virtual pinpoints. The first several pores can be quite large on older females. The female ovaries also reside high up in the body cavity.

When mating, the male inserts one of his hemipenes into the vent of the female. Semen flows along the groove in the hemipenes into the female. Here are some other interesting tidbits of information:

- ✔ Iguanas have the largest testes for their body size of all reptiles. (Some keepers of sexually mature adult males don't doubt this for a second, given how their sweet Dr. Jekyll lizard becomes a raging Mr. Hyde once breeding season hits.)

- Males may *evert* (stick out) their hemipenes when pooping or "flashing" a human or other iguana during breeding season.

- Females can develop and lay infertile eggs without having been mated or even in the presence of male iguanas. (For information on a gravid female and her eggs, fertilized or not, head to Chapters 24 and 25.)

Igs in wonderland: The endocrine system

Iguanas have the same glands we do, and these glands perform the same functions in iguanas that they do in us. Whether regulating growth, empowering rapid flight from a perceived threat, aiding in calcium metabolism, or keeping the metabolism going at the proper rate, the glands all contribute to keeping the iguana up and running.

- The *adrenal gland* produces adrenaline. When the iguana is threatened or stressed, increased amounts of adrenaline are delivered to the body, speeding up the reflexes needed to maintain alertness to the surroundings and to flee danger. If an iguana is under a prolonged period of stress, the ultimate result can be malnutrition and illness because the adrenals keep pumping out adrenaline and interfering with normal body functions.

- The *parathyroid gland* produces two hormones, calcitonin and parathormone, that are critical to the control and metabolism of calcium and phosphorous in the body. If one or the other hormone is off, metabolic bone disease (MBD) occurs, causing impaired systems function and loss of bone density. Metabolic bone disease, one of the most common — and preventable — health problems of iguanas in captivity is discussed at length in Chapter 21.

- The *pituitary gland* produces hormones that affect a variety of bodily functions, including thermal regulation, growth, and reproduction.

- The *thymus* plays an important role in the immune system by helping your iguana fight infection.

WARNING!

No spit!

No digestive enzymes are in iguana saliva. The small amount of saliva produced keeps mouth tissues moist and helps provide some moisture to coat the food to help it slide down, but there isn't enough saliva to soften dry food, like commercial iguana food pellets. This situation presents a potential danger when you feed your iguana those commercial pellets (even the healthier brands) without first moistening them thoroughly.

But, because wetting the pellets can lead to the rapid growth of fungus on such food products, most manufacturers' labels warn users against wetting them. This, along with the questionable nutritional quality of most commercial foods, is a very good reason to stick to a healthy fresh food diet, using the better commerical products as just a small part of the overall diet.

From stomach to hindgut to . . . well . . . you get the picture

When iguanas swallow food, it pretty much follows the route you'd expect as it gets pushed along through the gut. Sometimes they eat faster than they should, so you will see a leafy green or other food sticking up in the back of the mouth, waiting its turn to be passed along. Once the food hits the stomach, digestive enzymes go to work breaking down the food. From here, the food is passed along to the small intestine. Here, further breakdown occurs, mostly in the many folds of the *hindgut* (colon). Living in the hindgut and doing the work of converting the hard-to-digest plants into nutrients are lots of beneficial organisms — *nematodes* (worms) and bacteria. After several hours of processing in the hindgut,

the contents are moved to the large intestine where the nutrients are absorbed by the body. What's left after all this is converted to waste that ends up in the rectum.

During digestion other organs are hard at work, including the kidneys, which filter blood, recover fluids, and produce waste that is passed along to the bladder. One of the kidneys' products is uric acid. When the iguana eliminates wastes, it combines the uric acid from the bladder and the feces from the rectum in a cavity called the *cloaca*. Contractions shove the mixed wastes out of the cloaca, through the vent, to the outside of the iguana's body.

The In-Between Side

Iguanas have an outside and an inside, but a lot also goes on in between. The senses — smell, sight, taste, hearing, and touch — are all finely developed in green iguanas. Because their behavior is often driven by these senses, knowing what they are and how your iguana uses them is important.

Eyes and vision

Like most reptiles that are prey for other animals, the green iguanas' eyes are oriented to the sides, with some rearward vision. Although they have some stereoscopic vision (meaning they can see in front of them, which gives them depth perception), their sideways-oriented eyes enable them to keep track of what's going on around them. Their eyes are quite mobile in their sockets, allowing iguanas to easily see behind, above, and below them. One of the most unforgettable expressions iguana keepers come to know well is when their iguana cocks an eye down at them, looking amazed or annoyed at the foolish things we humans do. In its most glaring form, this look is known as the Iguana Stink Eye.

On the top of the iguana's head, between the raised areas created by the parietal bones, lies a small, gray scale. This is the *parietal eye* (some people call it the *pineal eye* or the *third eye*). Below the scale, which is the lens of this eye, is a retina that sees light and dark. It also detects movement of light and dark and so can see shadows moving overhead, usually long before we more poorly equipped humans are aware of anything. This eye doesn't see shapes or colors, however; that's left to the regular eyes. Based on what an iguana "sees" from this eye, it moves from sun to shade. It also keeps this eye on the sky to see if that moving speck will turn into an aerial predator.

Tongue and taste . . . and smell

Iguanas, like many reptiles, have a forked tongue. Seeing the tiny forked tip is difficult, though. Most keepers become aware of it when their iguana is about a year old and the darker, deep pink tip becomes more easily visible when the iguana yawns or flicks its tongue to smell something. When an iguana flicks its tongue or places it briefly on an object being investigated, scent molecules are picked up by special receptors in the tongue. When the tongue is retracted into the mouth, it touches the ducts leading to the vomeronasal (Jacobson's) organ (refer to Figure 6-2), through which chemical signals are sent to the brain.

Thyroid problems

The iguana's *thyroid* resides in the neck, just as it does in humans. And just as in humans, the thyroid is closely involved with many aspects of iguanas' health and well being. The hormones produced by the thyroid aid in skin production and shedding; regulating metabolism, energy, and activity levels; growth; and temperament.

The thyroid needs iodine to function properly. Fortunately, feeding a properly constructed plant diet provides all the iodine an iguana needs. You never have to add iodized salt to its food. Unfortunately, some plants contain *goitrogens* — compounds that bind the iodine in food, preventing the body from using it. You can easily deal with this problem by simply not feeding your iguana a lot of these vegetables: broccoli, cabbage, cauliflower, bok choy, Brussels sprouts, kale, soy (tofu), and grains.

When the thyroid doesn't get enough iodine, it becomes *hypoactive*; its function is impaired. Hypothyroidism leads to iguanas who are sluggish, lethargic, chubby but slow growing, and generally very sweet natured without having had to work much at being tamed. Keepers of such iguanas are amazed at the difference within a couple of weeks after they eliminate the large quantities of goitrogenic foods from their iguana's diet.

Hyperthyroid is uncommon in iguanas. Symptoms may include overly rapid growth, thickened bones, and a nervous, jittery temperament.

Cold-blooded: It's just a way of life

"Cold-blooded" isn't just an epithet; it's a way of life — and a very efficient one at that. Instead of continuously expending energy to maintain body temperatures within a narrow high range, reptiles make use of the free energy available in their environment — the sun. Mammals and birds must eat frequently to maintain their high body temperatures, but reptiles use the heat from the sun or, depending on the species, the sun's heat as trapped in rocks, soil, or water to raise their body temperatures. Reptiles can also affect the rate at which they lose or gain heat — by stretching and flattening their body, changing their orientation to the sun or other overhead heat source, and changing their skin color from dark to light or back again.

Iguanas are *heliotherms*, basking in warm air rather than plastering themselves to hot surfaces. They present a flattened body or laterally compressed side of their body to the heat source when they want to get warm. When they're cool, their skin may darken to absorb more heat more quickly. When they've had enough, they may move away from the heat source, or they may compress and reorient their body so less skin surface area is presented to the heat source, or they may lighten their skin to start deflecting heat waves. Their dewlap, being a flap of skin through which blood circulates, may be flared when they're absorbing heat, and relaxed or retracted when they're cooling down.

The iguana tongue is quite large and fleshy, something that is apparent as the iguana grows older and bigger. When giving an open-mouth threat, the tongue often is arched up inside the mouth. At other times, like when the iguana yawns, you can easily see the *glottis,* the airway opening into the lungs, and the iguana's many sharp teeth (refer to Figure 6-2).

Reptile tongues don't have very highly developed taste buds. They don't taste their food as much as they smell it, and so they recognize things they like — and don't like — by smell more so than taste.

Hearing

Iguanas can discriminate different sounds. They can learn their own names, the names of other household members, and other words (and concepts) such as "bath," "food," and "outside."

Green iguanas' hearing is fairly acute, unless, of course, you yell "No!" when they're doing something they really want to do. Because of their sensitivity to noise, it's a good idea not to play loud music in their room. Some iguanas even show annoyance when subjected to loud noises from the television. And you definitely want to keep their area relatively quiet during their sleep period.

Chapter 7

The Inner Iguana:
Why Iguanas Do What They Do

The iguana is a creature of its environment. When we remove an iguana from the wild, our environment becomes his environment. Unfortunately, that's not enough for these tropical lizards. Part of keeping an iguana in captivity is safely replicating the important parts of its native environment so that the iguana can move around in and interact with its captive environment in much the same way it would in the wild.

Fortunately, you don't need to build a huge, lush greenhouse and move yourself and your iguana into it (though some iguana keepers' iguanas do live in huge, lush greenhouses!). You *do* need to sacrifice some of your living space and make the accommodations necessary so that the iguana can live safely and thrive. This chapter explores some of the special features of iguanas and why you need to make the accommodations to fit them into your life and home.

Thermoregulation: Controlling Body Temperature

Iguanas use two primary means of regulating their body temperature: behavior and physiology. *Behavioral thermoregulation* is the physical activity of moving toward and away from a heat source, as well as shifting position relative to the heat source. *Physiological thermoregulation* is the changing of skin color from light to dark or dark to light.

Size matters

The larger the iguana, the more slowly it heats up and cools down, which means that larger lizards can be away from their primary radiation and convection sources for a while and not cool down so rapidly that it causes a problem. It also means that larger lizards need to warm up thoroughly before starting their daily activities, such as feeding and pooping.

✔ **Basking:** Basking is the primary way iguanas get warmed up. Being helio-therms, they're designed, so to speak, to soak up direct *radiation* (the heat that hits the body directly from an overhead heat source, like the sun or basking light) and *convected heat* (warmth that comes from heated air moving around or near a heat source). Although they can and do lie on warm surfaces, they are harmed if the only or primary source of heat is provided by a bottom heat source, like hot rocks or heating pads.

Hot rocks are often advertised with an iguana lounging on the rock. Unfortunately, hot rocks can be dangerous to iguanas — so much so that top reptile vets, zookeepers, and iguana breeders recommend *not* using them. Researchers believe that the lizards suffer from *thermal confusion:* They try to get warm by plastering themselves to the hot rock while the rest of the enclosure is so cool that more cool blood actually circulates than warmed blood. The iguana stays on the rock, trying to get warm, while its nerve endings become desensitized to the point where it does-n't feel itself burning.

✔ **Positioning:** Iguanas also affect their bodies' heating and cooling by the way they position their body toward or away from a heat source. Flattening the body out to present the widest possible exposed surface area is a good way when the radiant source is directly overhead. When the heat source is to one side (like with the morning sun), presenting the body sideways toward the heat source, along with laterally compressing the body and flaring the dewlap, helps the iguana increase the exposed surface area.

✔ **Changing color:** Color changes are another way iguanas affect how fast or slowly they gain or lose heat. Iguanas have naturally cryptic markings that help them blend into their environment — an effective way to help avoid being preyed on. Besides those static markings, however, iguana skin cells are equipped to lighten up or darken. Lightening the *ground color* (the overall skin color) results in heat loss because the body doesn't absorb as much heat. Darkening the ground color increases the absorption, which raises the body temperature.

Photoperiods: Waking and Sleeping Patterns

In the wild, iguanas awake with the sunrise and are settled in their sleeping places before dark. This pattern of waking and sleeping is adhered to in captivity. But in captivity, daytime lengths aren't usually as evenly balanced with nighttime lengths like they are in the tropics and neotropics. To ensure that your iguana gets the right day and night length, you need to produce day and night artificially by using heat/basking and UVB fluorescent lights.

The typical day/night period is 12 hours on/12 hours off. The 12 hours that the lights are on is the day period, and the 12 hours that these incandescent basking/heat lights and fluorescent lights are off is the night period. The best way to set up this environment is to use timers to automatically turn the lights on and off in the morning and evening. That way, your sleeping in or getting home late isn't a problem because the lights go on and off on their own.

Some iguanas take their behavioral cues from what's happening outside the house when they're in a room with a window. The iguana starts stirring shortly after sunrise, even if their lights haven't come on yet. An hour or two before sunset, they may be settled into their sleeping place, sleeping (or trying to) even though the lights are still on. If you find your iguana doing this during the spring and summer months, feel free to go with the flow. Let your iguana wake up naturally with the sun, turning on the heat and fluorescent lights an hour or so after sunrise (around 7 a.m.). As the sun sets later at night, go ahead and set the lights to turn off at 5 or 6 p.m. and let your iguana have a natural sunset. As long as your UVB fluorescent is properly placed and replaced annually, your iguana will be getting enough UVB during this period of reduced use of artificial lighting.

During the winter, when it's more difficult to maintain the proper temperatures in the enclosure and your iguana isn't able to get outside to soak up some natural sunlight, you can go back to a 12/12 schedule, with the lights coming on around 6 to 7 a.m. and off again at 6 to 7 p.m. Doing so ensures that your iguana gets plenty of UVB exposure as well as sufficient heat to get his metabolism working properly so he can eat, digest, and poop.

For information on what types of lights and heat sources to use, see Chapter 8.

Do the Locomotion

Iguanas basically have three speeds: stop, walk, and blur. Even though it sometimes feels like you're spending most of your time chasing down an iguana who doesn't want to be where you want it to be, the fact is that most of the time iguanas are just lounging around. When they aren't lounging, they're moving. There. And you thought iguanas were complicated.

Lounge lizard

Iguanas are masters at relaxed lounging around. Although an iguana's torso and tail are flat against the surface it's lying on, its head and legs may be doing other things. The head may be up or laying down on the surface or resting on one forearm or the other, making the iguana look remarkably like a dog in the same position (see Figure 7-1). When in a stationary alert mode, the iguana's head is usually up, and the iguana is very aware of its surroundings, as you can see by the way it's tracking movements and noises with its eyes.

Figure 7-1:
Even when an iguana lounges, he's still alert to his surroundings, tracking movements and noises with his eyes.

Photo by Melissa Kaplan

Sleeping iguanas look a lot like iguanas at rest, except their head is down and their eyes are closed. Most iguanas appreciate having something to lay their heads on when they sleep. A small pillow, rolled-up towel, stuffed sock, small, soft, plush toy, or even a pile of your clothes is appreciated. If you have more than one or two iguanas, you may find them entwined together, each with its head resting on another's body part.

Walk the walk

Iguanas have a couple of different walks. The most common one is a slow-paced stroll with frequent halts to tongue-flick and taste things in order to check them out. The stroll is the gait of choice when the iguana is walking through a new area or one that's been visited recently by other household pets or human visitors. Iguanas use this strolling gait when they climb, too.

It's truly awesome to watch an iguana, especially a large one, gracefully climb up a surface or object — seemingly using just the tips of a couple of toes.

The other walk is the "man on a mission" walk — legs moving briskly and body up off the ground, with few stops to flick, taste, or bob (see the section "Head bobbing" for more info on the bob). When an iguana uses this particular walk, you know it has a definite destination and purpose in mind.

Faster than a speeding train

Well, maybe not a bullet train, but when an iguana wants to move, it moves. An iguana can scramble from a full stop to full speed faster than you can say "iguana." Whether dashing off their basking area, zipping up the curtains, or flying down from your shoulder to leap across to someone or something else, iguanas are *fast*. Many people assume that iguanas will slow down as they get bigger. Wrong. They may be a teensy bit easier to see and catch because there's so much more of them. But slower? In your dreams.

Generally, iguanas run with all four feet hitting the ground during the course of a stride. When some iguanas really get going, they may speed along on their hind legs, tail waving back and forth for balance, the front part of their body raised off the ground. This running posture is typically in response to a perceived predator threat or fear of confinement (like when their big dumb human comes lumbering over to pick them up and stash them back in their enclosure).

Exploring the World

We humans use several senses to explore our world: sight, sound, smell, and touch. Iguanas use the same senses to explore their world. Although iguana sight, smell, and hearing may not be as sharp as ours or other animals', those senses serve the iguana quite well in its native environment. Because iguanas didn't evolve in the suburban tract home, metropolitan high-rise apartment building, or double-wide mobile home, their senses don't always serve them as well in captivity. Nonetheless, iguanas are not unintelligent, and they do learn quite a bit about this alien nation in which they find themselves.

Sight

Iguanas spend a lot of time looking and checking things out visually. Like a bird, they may cock their head to one side to see something better. They apparently have a good eye for hiding places: Take an iguana for a tour around your house once, and by the end of it, he'll have picked out several places that are good enough to remain hidden from your view for quite some time.

It's a lot farther than it looks

Iguanas in the wild leap from branch to branch with nary a thought. They do the same thing in captivity but often get very different results. Apparently, without a tape measure, igs can't calculate distances in captivity all that well. That's the only reason iguana keepers can come up with when their iguana leaps from Point A to Point B but falls somewhat short . . . sometimes a lot short. From the look on the iguana's face, it's obvious that this wasn't the intended result. Falling short may happen in the wild, but there, iguanas have lots of nice, bouncy branches to rebound off of, vines and clumps of leaves to grab onto, and leaf litter and perhaps other iguanas to fall on as they reach *terra firma*. In captivity, carpet, linoleum, and wood just don't have the same forgiving cushiony feel that iguanas are accustomed to in the wild. Fortunately, unless they have bones weakened by metabolic bone disease, or something falls on them once they land, iguanas seem to be able to fall from heights at least six feet above the ground with little ill effect except for some temporary grumpiness.

Iguanas learn to recognize their keepers and regular family or household members. They also recognize colors and shapes. That doesn't mean that they always make intelligent use of this information, but usually they do.

Sound

Iguanas learn to recognize many sounds they're commonly exposed to in captivity. From their keeper's voice to the refrigerator opening or the shower running, many sounds form an integral part of their daily routine. Iguanas react positively to some sounds but not to others. Loud, grating, or sudden strange noises can cause a fight-or-flight response. The iguana may jerk or scramble to its feet, or it may run away to hide or to get as far as possible from the sound or source of the sound.

Iguanas learn their own names and often the names of other iguanas, pets, and family members. They also learn other words. *No*, *bad lizard*, *outside*, *dinner*, *collards*, *treat*, and *bath* are some of the words iguana keepers report their iguanas recognize. This doesn't mean that they'll always stop when you say "No!" or "Baaaad lizard!" or that they'll always come when you call them by name. But *that* doesn't mean they don't understand. Think of it as a sort of selective hearing — like when you call your partner for dinner and he/she has no problem hearing you, but when you ask for the remote control and he/she is as deaf as a post.

Smell

Iguanas don't have a great sense of smell through their nose, and their tongue can't catch as much scent as a snake's, but between their nose and vomeronasal organ, which helps the brain analyze scent picked up by the tongue, they do quite well. Iguanas learn to recognize the smells of their new home, foods, and fragrances, as well as when their female humans are ready for some vigorous courtship.

When an iguana smells something new, he tries to figure out what it is. One main category of interest to iguanas is food. One way they check to see if something is food is by trying to eat a piece of it. Carpet, T-shirt, homework, ham sandwich, used paper towels in the kitchen garbage, your award-winning bonsai tree — the nose, tongue, and teeth are sure to check it out.

Touch

On the face of it (or would that be "on the scale of it"?), iguanas don't seem to have much of a sense of touch. After all, they do dumb things like cling to a hot rock or light bulb while burning their skin off, don't they? But they also seem to have a strong hedonistic streak in them. Given a choice between pillow or no pillow, an iguana chooses a pillow. Give them both a hard place and a soft place to lounge around on, and the soft place generally wins out.

This predilection toward comfort isn't truly related to sense of touch but more toward an overall feeling of comfort. Iguanas are sensitive to touch, however, whether it's us touching them or them touching something else. They may not be able to tell the difference between suede and velvet, but they're definitely able to distinguish between pleasure and displeasure.

If your iguana is the trusting sort and is leaning over into your hand with his eyes closed while you're petting him, he may fall over if you suddenly stop and withdraw your hand. This is particularly true if he is on the edge of his shelf or enclosure. So, if you're going to stop the petting session, be sure to give your ig a little warning first. Usually, all you need to do is keep your hand on him when you stop petting and make sure he opens his eyes and regains his balance.

Social Communication

Iguana communication is physical. Their words are formed by the arrangement of their body and body parts (posture), movements (stylized walking, strutting, bobbing), and use of three-dimensional space (where they're in vertical space, seeking height or flattening out). Iguanas, then, have developed a limited (in human terms) vocabulary, one that — like some spoken languages — has some very subtle nuances in pronunciation. They're easily able to communicate with other iguanas in this language of the body. But, although iguanas are able to learn some spoken words or sounds that we make (such as their names or the sound of the refrigerator door opening), they can effectively communicate to us only in the language they know best. It's up to us to learn to read their language — interpret their postures and movements — to understand what they're saying. Once we learn their language, we can also use some of their "words" to talk to them.

Posture

The usual iguana-at-rest-but-alert posture is rather like a dog. The body is flat on a surface with knees bent, feet back, and forearms flat, but the head and neck are raised. From this position, it's easy for them to go to sleep. Sometimes they doze with their head up but eyes closed, but usually the head goes down onto the surface they're lying on — or on their arms or resting on some object. When they're in deep-sleep mode, their fore- and hindlegs may be extended back along their sides ("the swimmer" position); some may even throw one of their legs up over their tail.

From the sphinxlike starting position, it's also easy for them to raise up into an alert crouch or into a full standing position. The crouch may be in response to something that mildly startles the iguana or to some serious petting by you, as the iguana arches its back to meet your hand.

When two iguanas, generally two males, are battling one another for dominance, the one giving up adopts the "surrender" posture. It almost looks like a dog soliciting play: The forelegs and hands are on the ground, elbows slightly flexed for rapid movement if necessary, the body is low to the ground, and the hindquarters are slightly raised. The head and neck are plastered to the ground. This is the subordinate iguana's way of signaling that he is lower than a worm and of no threat or competition to the dominant iguana. For now.

The dewlap

The dewlap is more than just a solar heater; it's part of the iguana's communication system. When it's tucked up tight or flared stiffly out, you can read the iguana like a book.

When the dewlap is tucked up under the chin, an adult or juvenile iguana is signaling submission or a state of nonaggression. A baby iguana who's trying to present as nonthreatening a profile as possible keeps his dewlap tucked up tight, too.

When dewlaps are relaxed, they flop down and sway when the iguana moves. In large iguanas, especially males, the dewlap is long, wide, and luxuriously silky, hanging in folds like a curtain.

When the dewlap is rigidly extended, its leading edge actually slants forward a bit (see Figure 7-2). This flaring out is used both offensively and defensively. Offensively, it may be part of a threatening gesture, a warning that here is a big iguana not to be messed with. It typically occurs when something or someone new enters the iguana's environment. Being unsure what it is or what type of threat it may present, the iguana issues a preemptive warning first.

Figure 7-2: The dewlap is more than just a solar heater; it's part of the iguana's communication system.

Photo by Melissa Kaplan

When the flared dewlap is combined with the tall stance, laterally compressed body, and erect nuchal and dorsal crest, the iguana is seriously working at intimidating someone or something. If the iguana is at a level higher up than the object of its intentions, it may also lean over to make sure that the object gets the full effect of the posture. Funnily enough, iguanas on the floor lean over, too, trying to intimidate the person or animal standing over them. If they're presenting this posture to you, and you lean over them, some keep leaning until they flop right over.

The swagger

The swagger is a male thing, carried out by an iguana threatening, or trying to court, a human or another iguana (or dog, cat, stuffed toy animal, etc.). In this stylized walk, the body is compressed laterally to make it look taller, and the lizard stands on straightened legs. As the lizard walks, the tail is slightly arched up behind the hind legs and may be swished from side to side. The dewlap is fully extended downward. When approached, such iguanas lean over away from you or circle around you, attempting at all times to present the biggest possible broadside profile to you to maintain their threatening or "come hither" look.

Tail twitching

The tail twitch may be part of the swagger, or it may be done when the iguana is at a standstill. The last half of the tail twitches, much like the tail of a cat who's stalking a bird or ball of yarn. It seems to signify a condition of mixed motivations — like when a male iguana wants to attack its female human keeper to mate with her but knows that such an action won't be received with the same spirit in which it was intended. In such a mixed-emotions state, the iguana may be hunched up, the body in compressed and broadside presentation, but with the head down, dewlap semirelaxed, similar to the submission/subordinate position, with the tail twitching slowly back and forth.

The eyes

Eyes wide open or eyes wide shut, iguanas are quite expressive with their deep brown to light hazel eyes. The one look that every iguana keeper becomes familiar with is the infamous "iguana glare" or "stink eye." Whether delivered straight on or thrown back over the shoulder, the glare is the primary way disgruntled iguanas put their annoying keepers in their proper place.

Iguanas also communicate with their eyes closed. When the eye closest to you is closed but the other eye is open, it's actually a sort of compliment. It means that the iguana is comfortable with you but is keeping an eye out on what's going on around him.

When you first get your iguana, chances are he'll spend a great deal of time in your presence with both eyes closed. This is his way of escaping from the overall stress of the situation, with the new home, people, noises, smells, routines, and strange new foods leading to sensory overload. He closes both eyes as a way to reduce the stimuli and shut everything out. As time goes on, and your iguana becomes acclimated to you and his new home and family, you'll find that the closing of both eyes happens rarely. Eventually, you'll see that it most often happens when you're engaged in a petting session — and the closed eyes and relaxed posture reflect iggy nirvana. You'll also find that it happens when they've insinuated themselves among your fragile bric-a-brac, and you have the nerve to start yelling at them as you move everything away to extricate them.

Head bobbing

Head bobs are probably the most expressive part of the iguana language. Bobs are used in greeting and dismissal, as bragging and warning, to attract and repel. Bobs best illustrate the iguana's adaptation to communicating with humans. Bobs also take different forms.

- ✔ **Greeting bob:** This bob begins with the head swung up and held for a beat or two and then bounced up and down a few times. This bob is also used in some dismissal and annoyance situations. (You can greet your iguana by bobbing your head. In fact, if you have several iguanas, you can start a bobbing session by walking into the room and bobbing first.)

- ✔ **Territorial bob:** These resemble the greeting bob, except that they are usually accompanied by a slight raising of the body from a prone position and at least a slight dewlap flare.

- ✔ **Annoyance and dismissal bob**: These also resemble the greeting bob, but they are often done without the initial upswing, and the bouncing is repeated several times more and is faster than a greeting bob.

- ✔ **Shudder bob:** This is the big daddy of all bobs. The initial movement is a side-to-side movement of the head as it vibrates, or shakes, rapidly, followed by the upswing and bouncing of other bobs.

A lovesick iguana

I had a lovely blue-colored iguana named Freddie who persisted in trying to mate with me every year. After the first year, when he found out that I was not particularly receptive to his attentions, he stopped going for my neck but still tried to grab me by the hand . . . just in case I changed my mind, I guess. He knew that once he bit me, the result was very little contact with me for several days after the bite. When he was separated from me or reduced to minimal contact with me, he turned very dark, stopped eating, moped around, refused to bask, and became dehydrated. The tail twitching seemed to be an indication of his being torn between the two conflicting wants or needs. The want or need to mate (grabbing me with his teeth was the second step in the courtship, after stalking and presenting) was in conflict with the knowledge that if he did bite, he'd be ostracized for several days.

Be careful when you bob. If any of your iguanas aren't tame yet, for example, your greeting bob may be interpreted as a territorial or dominance bob. The untamed iguana may accept you as the dominant iguana — or may decide to contest you for the dominant position. Also, *how* you bob when you bob at your iguanas is very important. If you use the wrong bob in the wrong context, you may actually incite your iguana to an undesired reaction.

Hissing

Iguanas hiss by forcing air back up through their mouth. A low, guttural click-hiss is the most commonly heard hiss. The mouth is wide open, the tongue is arched, and the body is in full lateral compression mode — unless you happen to be holding a thrashing, untamed iguana at the time, in which case the iguana is puffed up and hissing, while at the same time trying to rapidly reduce the skin of your hands and arms into material suitable for composting.

Click-hissing is an amazingly loud sound, combining elements of a sharp clicking sound with a brief hiss, sounding something like "kikhh!" I had one female who seemed to be perpetually annoyed with all the males, including ones twice her size. She was very particular about her night sleeping spot, and I could hear her 20 feet and three rooms away when one of the males had the audacity to try to appropriate her spot for himself.

When we try to soothe or hush our children or even dogs and cats, we tend to use a "sh-h-h-h" sound. To an iguana (and many other lizards) our sh-shing sounds more like a hiss and is likely to be responded to as if we had hissed at them rather than tried to soothe them. Iguanas do, however, respond to baby talk, the soft, high-pitched nonsense chatter we make to babies.

If you're trying to tame a particularly stubborn iguana, you may want to try a little preemptive click-hissing yourself, combining it with an open-mouth threat. It often startles the iguana enough to make it stop thrashing around and focus on you as something other than a determined predator or whatever it is the iguana thinks you are. Once you have its attention, you can resume the quiet talking. Click-hissing isn't the key to instant taming, but it often breaks down a barrier or two once they hear you speak their lingo.

The open-mouth threat

Iguanas use an intimidation technique employed by many snakes and lizards — the open-mouth threat. When it's open wide and showing the deep pink interior, glistening teeth, and fleshy, arched tongue, the iguana mouth is indeed impressive. Of course, it's far more impressive on a highly motivated, 15-pound male than it is on a 90-gram finger-sized baby iguana.

When a healthy iguana opens its mouth, it's a great opportunity for you to check the mouth out. Not only can you see the nearly transparent teeth, pink tongue tip, and glottis at the back of the tongue, but the color can also help you assess the iguana's health. See Chapters 20 and 21 for common injuries and diseases and what symptoms to look for.

The slightly opened mouth

It may look like a smile, but it isn't. It's a sign of borderline aggression. (Iguanas can't smile. It's a muscle thing — or lack thereof.) The partially opened mouth and alert posture reflect an iguana who's waiting to see just how foolish you're going to be before deciding just how to react. A bite? Nip? Tail thrash? So many painful (to the human) options to choose from.

When you see your iguana with its mouth partly open, you need to assess the context to determine if the behavior is a sign of something you need to worry about. An iguana who is used to being hand-fed treats, for example, or who is having a hard time breathing due to a respiratory infection, may sit with the mouth partly open. In the former instance, the iguana is waiting for another delectable offering. In the second, the poor lizard is trying to get more air into its lungs. There is a third instance in which this partial gape may be used: to pant. Because iguanas don't sweat, they have adopted other ways to help cool off. Opening the mouth for some evaporative cooling is one of the things they do.

"If I Only Had a Brain . . ."

Many new iguana keepers initially make the mistake of thinking that their iguana is just a creature of pure instinct — that it's incapable of any sort of learning or thinking . . . or plotting. Once they give their iguana an opportunity to develop, though, the keepers realize just how much of a brain they have.

But if he's so smart, why is he so dumb?

Iguanas do amazingly well for wild animals dropped into a completely alien environment, surrounded by creatures who don't speak their language. They're assaulted on all sides by things strange and new. They're also equipped with a sometimes unhealthy curiosity. That's why they do what to us appears to be really dumb things.

- ✔ Eating nonfood items is at the top of many iguana keepers' lists. An incredible array of household items have been surgically removed from the intestines of iguanas: pennies, pushpins, balloons, masses of human hair, tacks, condoms, bark chips, small stones, and even a pair of silk panties. This begs the question of whether it's the iguana being dumb or the human needing to be a bit tidier.

✔ When iguanas are stressed or entering a shed period, or they just decide that they don't like their usual basking areas, they usually seek out someplace cold, dark, and usually tight-fitting in which to spend the day. Although this doesn't seem like very smart behavior, it's their way of escaping from their reality for a bit. An otherwise healthy iguana can be allowed to remain in such a place for a day or two, but eventually, the reason for the behavior must be determined and dealt with.

Thinking like an iguana

Iguanas always have a reason for doing what they do. Your problem is that those reasons may not be obvious. Instead of dismissing the behavior or incident, especially if it's one that can lead to physical harm to the iguana, you need to evaluate the overall situation — not only the behavior or incident but also the events surrounding it. Iguanas are very sensitive to their humans and react with abnormal behaviors when their humans are out of sorts or dealing with unusual stresses. Try to look at things through your iguana's eyes, through the eyes of a wild animal living in a strange place.

Part III
Setting Up the Environment

The 5th Wave   By Rich Tennant

"I built the iguana cage myself. He seems to like the chandelier over his food bowl, but we're replacing the sconces over the fireplace with recessed mood lights."

In this part . . .

Before you bring your iguana home, you first need to get his (or her) enclosure ready and checked out for temperatures and day/night cycles. Doing this first means less stress for you and your iguana because he will have everything he needs to get started out right, right from the start. And a happy iguana is a healthy iguana (well, not necessarily . . . see Part VI for iguana health issues).

Chapter 8

Basic Supplies

● ●

● ●

*K*nowing how to set up an enclosure and how to get it ready before bringing your iguana home isn't all you need to learn about making a home for an iguana. You also need to know what to look for in an enclosure, the difference between lighting and heating, about the problems with maintaining humidity, and more.

Every year, pet store shelves and reptile magazines have more new products marketed directly to iguana and other reptile keepers. Many of the products look great at first glance but often turn out to be inappropriate, or even dangerous, for iguanas. In this chapter, you'll find out about enclosure design and size, lighting, heating, humidity, and ventilation.

Enclosures

Whether you call them enclosures, tanks, or cages, they all share one thing in common: They provide an enclosed space in which to house something. The problem with so many of the enclosures on the market today is that most of them were designed to house something other than green iguanas. The rectangular glass tanks most often seen in pet stores are just fish tanks with some sort of top fit on or built in. Wire mesh cages are modeled on cat, dog, rabbit, and ferret cages. Enclosures made of plastic, wood, melamine, or powder-coated wire are usually designed so generically that they create more problems than they're worth.

The following sections look at the importance of the enclosure dimensions, as well as shapes and the types of features you need to be able to best care for your iguana.

Size

Hatchling iguanas are tiny, ranging from 2.5–3 inches snout-vent length (SVL) and 7–9 inches snout-tail length (STL). When you're holding an iguana that's barely bigger than your thumb, it's difficult to visualize how big it will get. If you've never raised a hatchling to adulthood, realizing just how fast iguanas grow is impossible. Because of these things, the majority of new iguana keepers start out with an enclosure that's too small. A lot of things have to fit into that enclosure — water bowl, food plate, heating and lighting equipment, basking branch, hide box, perhaps some decorations — along with that little munchkin who will grow one or more feet a year for the next several years.

Some iguana folks who are poorly educated in basic biology will tell you that iguanas (and other reptiles) won't outgrow their enclosure and that, if you keep an iguana in a small enclosure, it won't outgrow it. Wrong. What you get is a weak iguana who isn't able to exercise the way he needs to, who gets increasingly territorial over his increasingly smaller home range, and who is highly stressed and ultimately takes his frustrations out on you.

So what size tank do you need? You can use a simple calculation to determine the enclosure size needed for your iguana:

- ✔ To figure out how wide (from left to right) the enclosure should be, multiply the snout-tail length by 1.5–2.

- ✔ To figure how deep (from front to back), multiply the STL by 0.5–1.5. (***Note:*** Hatchlings need a minimum depth of 1 foot; juveniles and adults need a minimum depth of 3 feet.)

- ✔ To figure how high (from top to bottom), multiply the STL by 1–1.5. (***Note:*** The minimum height for juveniles and adults should be 5–6 feet tall.)

For example, if you have a hatchling that's 8 inches long, her enclosure needs to have the following dimensions:

Width: 12–16 inches (8 x 1.5–2) (30.5–40.6 cm)

Depth: minimum12 inches (8 x 0.5–1) (minimum 30.5 cm)

Height: 8–12 inches (8 x 1–1.5) (20.3–30.5 cm)

But — and this is a big *but* — by the end of her first year, she'll have grown a foot or more in overall length. By the time she's full grown, she'll be even bigger yet and need a much larger enclosure.

Table 8-1 lists the average size (in snout-vent length and snout-tail length) for the first seven years and the minimum enclosure dimensions needed for each. Keep in mind that these dimensions don't take into account the additional width, depth, and height needed to accommodate your iguana's future growth — just what the iguana needs at that point in time. Bottom line? Unless your iguana is full grown, when its snout-tail length is more than two-thirds the enclosure width, it's time for a new enclosure.

Table 8-1	Recommended Minimum Enclosure Dimensions	
SVL (in inches)	*STL (in inches)*	*Minimum Dimensions (in feet)*
2.5–7	9–18	3 x 1 x 1.5
8–10	20–28	3.5 x 1 x 2.3
11–12	28–36	4.5 x 1.5 x 3
12–14	30–42	5.25 x 1.75 x 3.5
14–16	35–54	6.75 x 2.25 x 4.5
18–20	45–60	7.5 x 2.5 x 5
20–22	50–66	8.25 x 2.75 x 5.5
20–24	50–72	9 x 3 x 6

How do these sizes compare with the enclosures you might be tempted to buy when getting a hatchling iguana? Well, a 20 gallon tank is 2' x 0.9' x 1.08', quite a bit smaller than the 3' x 1' x 1.5' your hatchling needs to get him through his first year.

Most new iguana keepers try to economize — or listen to recommendations they shouldn't have — and start out with a 10-, 20-, or 30-gallon enclosure, believing that it'll last them for at least a year or two. Two problems occur with these small tanks: Iguanas quickly outgrow them, and it's nearly impossible to set up the required thermal gradient in the 20- to 30-gallon tank (it's impossible in the 10-gallon tank). If you start out with a smaller tank, you have to buy a larger enclosure before the year is out, or you'll end up with a miserable, stressed, malnourished, and aggressive iguana.

If your iguana is already an adult but small for his age due to an inadequate diet, don't think you can get away with building an enclosure for the size he is right now. Once you put him on a proper diet, you'll see a growth spurt and continued growth over the next several years.

Shape

When you look around at enclosures in pet stores and pet catalogs, you see three basic shapes: cubes, coffins, and telephone booths (see Figure 8-1). None of these is appropriate for a juvenile and adult iguana.

Make it big enough to bask!

When an iguana is basking or cooling off, all the body — including the tail — needs to be in that basking area or the cooler area. Health problems, including thermal burns, occur when part of the iguana is in the basking area while the rest of him is in the cooler area. If he's trying to get warmed up, his sensors will keep telling him he's still too cool because of that part of his body and tail that are outside of the warmest area. Conversely, when he's trying to cool off, his body temperature will not drop as it should if part of him is still exposed to the basking heat.

If your enclosure isn't wide enough for your iguana to lie stretched out with most of his body and tail in the basking area, or most of the body and tail in the cooler area, then he can't thermoregulate properly. This will ultimately cause stress and other health problems. Iguanas prefer to lie flat when basking and sleeping. Being forced to live diagonally in a too-narrow enclosure also prevents them from being able to thermoregulate properly and causes stress, which can lead to illness and injury.

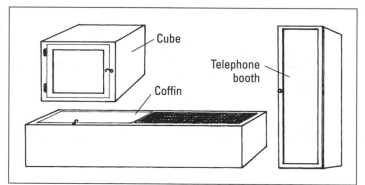

Figure 8-1:
None of these iguana enclosure shapes is appropriate for your iguana.

Cube

Telephone booth

Coffin

So what does an iguana need? Well, if you picture a wide bedroom closet that's deep enough for a couple rows of shoes, with lots of height to stack things on top of the hanging clothes, you've got a good picture of the proper shape for an iguana enclosure. In fact, many iguana keepers turn over such a closet in a bedroom or family room to their iguana, setting it up with climbers, additional shelves, heat and fluorescent lights, and so on.

A baby iguana does well its first year in a 55- to 125-gallon coffin-shaped enclosure. Juveniles need increasing amounts of both vertical and horizontal space. And adults need the most of all. If you hunt around, you may be able to find an individual or a small company that makes or will custom-make an enclosure of the right size and shape for your growing lizard. If you have the luxury of getting a custom-made enclosure — or the skill to make one yourself — the following sections can give you ideas on the type of enclosure you should try to create.

The perfect enclosure

The ideal enclosure has ventilation panels on both ends and in the roof. It has front-opening doors that make getting the iguana in and out of the enclosure and cleaning and servicing the enclosure easier. The roof, sides, and back are all or partially made of wood, enabling you to securely install shelves and climbers. The hinged wooden roof also makes installing the light fixtures easier. The floor is covered with linoleum, which curves up the walls a few inches so that no crevices exist for feces and urates to become trapped when you're cleaning the enclosure.

A double-duty enclosure

If you live in a climate that gets hot during the spring, summer, and fall, think about making a convertible enclosure (see Figure 8-2). Make the sides and front of the enclosure out of a plastic-coated heavy wire or rigid plastic mesh. Put casters on the bottom to make rolling it outside easier. In order to make the enclosure usable during cooler evenings and colder seasons, make wood and/or clear, rigid plastic panels to cover the mesh. You can use slide bolts or even Velcro strips to attach the panels to the enclosure's frame. Make sure to use a clear plastic or Plexiglas panel in the front so that your iguana can see out!

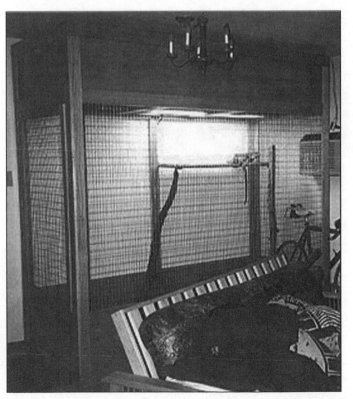

Figure 8-2:
A collapsible wood-frame and wire enclosure.

Design and photo by Jennifer Swofford

Many people buy wire mesh cages to house their iguanas, including wire cages made specifically for iguanas. Unfortunately, heating them properly is very difficult because there is nothing to hold the heat in. If you can't keep the iguana's room 80+ degrees Fahrenheit all day, every day, you need to use an enclosure with solid walls or have solid panels that can be attached to cover the mesh during the winter months and cooler evenings throughout the year. You may be able to wear warm clothes and put on a sweater when it's cool in the house, but your tropical lizard needs tropical temperatures all year round.

Outdoor enclosures

Appropriate outdoor enclosures have many of the same features as indoor enclosures (see the earlier sections for details). In addition, the enclosure needs to be secured against busy little fingers, which is essential if you you're planning to leave your iguana outside when you're at work or overnight. Neighborhood kids and curious, hungry raccoons are equally adept at getting through latches and slide bolts. Figure 8-3 shows an outdoor enclosure made of PVC pipes and wire mesh.

Figure 8-3:
A PVC-mesh outdoor enclosure is a comfortable and safe option when you want your iguana outside.

Design and photo by Catherine E. Rigby

If you are going to make (or have custom-made) an outdoor enclosure, keep these things in mind:

 ✔ Outdoor enclosures are made from wire or rigid plastic mesh. The mesh comes in a range of gauges (the size of the squares in the material), enabling you to select a size that's too small for your iguana to slip through but large enough for comfortable climbing and lots of sun and air movement.

✔ Never use poultry (chicken) wire for your iguana's enclosure. As the iguana grows, his weight alone can exert enough pressure to sever his toes when he has climbed and is hanging on the wire. This wire is also excellent for slicing off bits of the iguana's rostrum when he rubs his nose against it.

✔ The frames for large outdoor enclosures must be sturdy; wood, as shown in Figure 8-4) and PVC pipe are excellent for framing. Frames do more than hold up the sides, keep the roof on, and provide something on which to hang the door. They provide a secure support for the roosts. Climbers can be made from sections of mesh, branches, or other materials. As with climbers in indoor enclosures, they need to be securely anchored.

If the enclosure is going to sit on the ground, the floor can be made of mesh and then covered with soil and planted with safely edible foliage and plants. This kind of floor prevents an iguana from being able to dig his way out and other animals from digging their way in. If the floor is raised off the ground, the mesh allows feces and spilled food to fall through to the ground, keeping the enclosure (and iguana) cleaner and enabling you to easily wash that stuff away with a hose and water. If you're planning to put a water tub for swimming, soaking, and pooping in the enclosure, be sure to support the raised flooring so that the heavy tub doesn't pull the mesh floor away from the frame. Your iguana may well spot the gap before you do and decide to take a neighborhood tour without you. A similar subfloor support is required if you're making the raised iguana enclosure large enough for you to walk into.

Figure 8-4:
A wood-framed enclosure made with starplate connectors.

Photo by Jennifer Swofford

If you have a small enclosure, make sure that it sits on something to keep it off the ground. Doing so not only protects the iguana from small, multilegged, ground-dwelling organisms but also helps satisfy the iguana's need for height to feel safe, especially when he's outside where he lacks the security of solid walls and glass around him.

Lighting Sources

Iguanas need light. That seems pretty obvious. But they need different types of light for different reasons and at different times of the day:

- Iguanas need to have bright, white light during the day. The bright light not only tells them that it's daytime, but when you use the right light, it also provides the increased heat they need during the day — especially in the basking area.

- Iguanas need special fluorescent lights to get the ultraviolet rays they need to ensure that they produce enough vitamin D, which helps them metabolize the calcium they need to maintain their health.

- Iguanas need heat at night, which can easily be provided by certain types of colored light bulbs.

Something to remember about lights is that some are also heat sources. For information on products that simply provide heat, see the section "Heat Sources."

Daytime light and heat

You can easily provide both the bright light and basking heat iguanas need either by using the reptile basking lights or by using household incandescent lights. Several product manufacturers make reptile basking lights. Some look like regular incandescent bulbs, and others are pear- or spotlight-shaped with silver on their top surface that's supposed to focus the light and heat downward. Some of these lights are made with lightly tinted glass that's supposed to make your reptile look better — to you. That doesn't necessarily mean your iguana *is* better. The reptile heat and basking lights tend to be expensive and are available at most pet stores or from mail-order pet suppliers.

Fluorescent lights generally don't generate enough heat to keep the enclosure at the required thermal gradient, even when you have two or more fixtures installed. So when designing your iguana's enclosure or free-roaming basking area, you need to install both fluorescent *and* incandescent fixtures to ensure both the proper light and heat.

To save some money, you can use a regular household incandescent bulb to provide your daytime light and heat. When used in a metal reflector hood, their light and heat are focused toward the point where you've aimed the fixture. Make sure that you use a fixture rated the wattage of the bulb you're using and that you secure the fixture so it can't be toppled or clawed down.

Nighttime light and heat

Some lights are made for nighttime use for reptiles. These nocturnal reptile lights emit a dim purplish light and come in assorted watts. You may also be able to find dim blue, green, or red incandescent bulbs made for household light fixtures. Stay away from the clear party bulbs because they produce a very bright light through their clear glass. The bulbs that provide the heat you need with reduced visible light are opaque or frosted.

Iguanas, never being creatures to make their keepers' lives easy, have preferences for the color of their nocturnal light. Some are fine with the blue or purple light, but others do better with the red or green. Be flexible. And if your iguana is agitated at night under a different colored bulb and doesn't settle down within an hour or so — and nothing else in the environment inside and outside his area has changed — try another color.

If your iguana is in a room with a window, keep the curtains open or shades open to let in any light from the outside at night — moonlight, starlight, and distant streetlights all can provide gentle, indirect illumination that doesn't disturb the iguana's sleep or the biochemical processes that take place during sleep periods.

Emergency night lights

Most iguana keepers find that they want to check up on their iguana at night to make sure that he's still there or still breathing, or just to see what cute position he's fallen asleep in this time. Turning on a light or using a flashlight is disruptive, to say the least.

An iguana who is startled awake may do nothing more than open one eye and glare at you. At other times, though, or with an iguana of less sanguine temperament, the iguana becomes so startled that he'll launch himself across the sleeping area or enclosure in a blind panic. Having a dim night light in the room or enclosure helps you see your iguana as well as helps calm the iguana by allowing him to see his surroundings when he awakes suddenly. The light from a power strip or heating pad control is usually just enough light for this purpose.

Let there be light . . . and heat

One thing iguana keepers learn is that all light is not heat, and all heat is not light. Sound confusing? Well, it is, until you get your products sorted out and decide which of them works best in the environment you set up for your iguana.

Light-emitting heat sources include the reptile basking lights, nocturnal reptile lights, incandescent light bulbs made for human household use, and infrared lamps used in food services to keep food warm. Non-light-emitting heat sources include ceramic heating elements (CHEs), reptile heating pads, human heating pads, and infrared heat panels (see the section "Heat Sources" for more info on these). Fluorescent lights and fixtures were designed to put out as little heat as possible; even though some fixtures may get warm, they are not considered heat sources.

Ultraviolet light

Many iguana keepers find the whole heating and lighting issue — with the different types of equipment, temperatures, photoperiods, and do's and don'ts — hard enough to deal with. When you throw in having to learn about ultraviolet light, well, you can hear the screaming from a long way off. But ultraviolet lighting is one of the most crucial aspects of your iguana's care, right up there with diet and the rest of the environment.

Seems like it'd be easy enough to go out and get an ultraviolet (UV) light. But it isn't. About the only easy thing is this: Lights that produce UVB also produce UVA, so you need only one type of UV light. From that point on, however, a lot of misleading information is out there. The result is that many iguana (and other reptile) keepers often get the wrong type of light.

What you can use

For the purposes of keeping reptiles, the safest artificial source of UVB and UVA is fluorescent lights that are specially made for reptiles. They are special in that they don't produce harmful amounts of UVA, UVB, or UVC (C as in "causes skin cancer"). You can find these special fluorescents at pet stores, through herp supply catalogs, and through online herp supply sellers, and sometimes you can buy them direct from the manufacturers or their distributors. Many just-for-reptiles fluorescents are out there, some producing more UVB than others. The oldest tube on the market is Durotest's Vita-Lite. Another good product is the Zoo Med Reptisun and Iguana Light. These Zoo Med lights are identical to the Durotest light except for the packaging.

Make sure the reptile fluorescent you get puts out at least 1.1 percent UVB. Reptile fluorescents that put out less than 1.1 percent UVB emit too little UVB to enable sufficient quantities of vitamin D to be produced, which results in metabolic bone disease. The same is true for the compact (also called *plug-in*) UVB-producing fluorescents. Several UVB-producing fluorescents are on the market that produce 3-, 5-, and 7-percent UVB, but no studies have been done to show whether they are in fact better than lights producing amounts between 1.1 percent and 2.9 percent.

✔ Some iguanas seem to act differently under different brands of UVB fluorescents, becoming edgy or aggressive under one but not another. If your iguana is calmer when his UVB light is turned off, or if he's calmer when he's outside his enclosure than he is when he's inside when the UVB light is turned on, try another brand.

✔ Because UVB fluorescents over time produce less UVB, you need to replace the UVB fluorescent every 9–12 months.

✔ Because all of the iguana's skin is involved in the production of previtamin D, the UVB-producing fluorescent needs to span as much of his body as possible. Although a 15-inch tube may look fine for your hatchling, he's going to need a 24-inch tube by the end of his second year. And, ultimately, he's going to need a 48-inch tube or two 24-inch tubes.

✔ Some fluorescent fixtures are sold with plastic diffusers that are meant to be placed on the fixture to completely enclose the fluorescent tube. Don't use the diffuser when installing a fluorescent light for your reptile. These diffusers block the transmission of the ultraviolet wavelengths, resulting in metabolic bone disease.

What you can't use

Here are ultraviolet light sources you *can't* use:

✔ **Fluorescents made for use in offices, factories, and homes:** These lights are made to eliminate or greatly suppress UV emissions to prevent the prolonged exposures that can cause health problems and fade fabrics.

✔ **Tanning fluorescents:** They emit dangerously high levels of UVA and UVB.

✔ **Fluorescents made for plants and aquariums:** Plants, fish, and coral have very different UV requirements.

✔ **High-powered lights:** There is a new product that combines high-output UVB and heat. These lights produce significantly more UV than standard fluorescent tubes to the point where there is concern about their safety — for both the reptiles and their keepers — when used in the home environment.

✔ **Window glass:** Because window glass is made to keep out as much as 96 percent of the sun's UV, you can't provide UVB to your iguana by planting him near a closed window or his glass-fronted tank near an open one.

Heat Sources

Infrared lamps (like those in restaurants and cafeterias) are used by some iguana keepers. These large bulbs produce a red light as well as infrared heat (see the section "Lighting Sources" for details). But fixtures don't need to produce light to produce heat. Appropriate heat sources that don't produce light include the following:

- **Human heating pads:** Human heating pads are large, relatively inexpensive, last for years, and are a useful addition to the iguana enclosure or free-roaming basking or sleeping area. They are less likely to malfunction than made-for-reptile products. They are also easily cleaned and disinfected, can be easily moved to new locations, and can be used inside and under tanks.

- **Pig or farrowing pads (also called *pig blankets*):** These are rigid fiberglass panels covering heat elements. They are sturdy, easy to clean and disinfect, and come in a variety of sizes with a flexible metal-wrapped cord. They radiate heat and are useful in providing bottom heat that rises. You can order them through farm supply catalogs as well as through herp supply catalogs. You may also be able to order them through your local farm and ranch supplier.

- **Infrared ceramic heating elements (CHEs):** The infrared heat produced by a CHE is focused downward, resulting in a relatively small cone-shaped zone of heat. Useful for heating up a small enclosure, infrared CHEs may not do more than provide a limited basking area for a large iguana in a large enclosure.

    If you decide to use a CHE, you *must* install it in a fixture with a porcelain, not plastic, socket. The heat thrown upward from the CHE is hot enough to melt plastic and start a fire.

- **Infrared panels:** These are large panels made to install against a wall, and they heat up a larger area than a CHE.

How many overhead radiant heat sources you need depends on how well insulated your iguana's enclosure is and the ambient room air temperature. You know you have enough when your thermometers show that the heat sources are producing enough heat to maintain the necessary temperatures.

Substrates

Substrate is what you put on the floor of the enclosure so that the enclosure itself is spared as much direct contact as possible with what comes out of both ends of the iguana: spilled food and water from the front end and feces and urates from the back end.

Many substrates are packaged and marketed to reptile keepers. Unfortunately, most of these products are downright dangerous to use for iguanas.

Safe substrates

Safe substrates are nontoxic to the iguana, can't be easily ingested — intentionally or accidentally — and are easily cleaned and disinfected or removed and disposed of. The easiest substrate of all is linoleum — just line the floor and the first couple inches of the bottom of the walls with it. By curving the linoleum up onto the walls, you ensure that no sharp right angles exist for feces, urates, or other biological material to flow into or get trapped in, where they form a breeding ground for bacteria. Linoleum can stand up to repeated cleanings and disinfectants.

Disposable substrates include paper towels, newspapers, or plain newsprint. Newsprint and newspapers outgas noxious chemicals, which, in the enclosed environment of a reptile enclosure, may lead to unsuspected health problems. Some claim that newspapers have a bactericidal effect on wastes. Maybe so, but wastes shouldn't be allowed to sit in an enclosure long enough for bacteria to start colonizing the enclosure. Plain paper towels, while more expensive than newsprint or newspapers, don't outgas chemicals and are easily scooped up and disposed of.

A third alternative is the artificial grass carpeting designed for indoor and outdoor use. This floor covering comes in different grades that range in price from relatively inexpensive to expensive. The inexpensive, flexible grade is fine for reptile enclosures. (Always get enough to make a couple of extra pieces to fit the enclosure so that when you take the soiled one out for cleaning and disinfecting, you can put a dry, clean piece in the enclosure right away.) One risk is associated with the artificial grass: the loose ends. The cut edges can unravel over time. One way to avoid this problem is to cut the piece 2–3 inches bigger all around than you actually need, fold over the edges, and use a running stitch to baste them down.

Unsafe substrates

Unsafe substrates can be described in one word: *particulates* — bits and pieces of substances made to put in the bottom of enclosures, such as sand; sand-like particles made from calcium; wood chips, bark pieces, shavings, or mulch; shredded, compressed, or pelleted paper; cat litter of any type; gravel of any size or type; crushed walnut shell; corncob pieces; soil; litters; and other particulate substrates sold specifically for lizards.

Some of these products have been marketed for other pets through the years and have documented problems, such as dust and molds causing respiratory and eye irritations. Others cause problems specifically for iguanas and other reptiles who actively explore their environment with their tongue. In the case of iguanas, the particles can cause lacerations of the mouth, throat, and intestinal tissues if the pieces have any rough edges or protrusions. They can also cause impaction. In this case, if the keeper is lucky, the vet can operate to successfully remove the impaction. If both the iguana and keeper are unlucky, the impaction kills the iguana.

Some iguana keepers use alfalfa pellets, which are safely edible, if a few are eaten now and then, because they break down in the moisture in the gut and are utilized as food. However, when they get wet, by spilled food or water or by feces and urates, the pellets begin to decompose in the enclosure, growing bacteria and mold colonies. These growths are not something you want your iguana walking through, eating, or breathing. So, in a pinch, they're okay, but it's best to seek a permanent, less potentially harmful, substrate.

Humidifiers

Humidifiers sold for human use can help raise the ambient room humidity in the iguana's room. If your iguana's enclosure is large enough and you can secure a humidifier so that the iguana can't knock it over, you can put one right in the enclosure. Some iguana keepers prefer the units that produce a warm mist; others prefer the cool mist. The bottom line is that both put water droplets into the air, boosting the humidity level and moisturizing the air that the iguana breathes. When setting up a humidifier, be sure to follow the manufacturer's instructions for care and maintenance. You can run the humidifier all day and night or just during the daytime hours. But be sure to check it one or more times a day to make sure that the water level is within safe limits.

If you use a warm-mist humidifier in your iguana's enclosure, make sure he can't get right next to the mist as it comes out of the unit — some are hot enough to cause burns and eye injuries.

Chapter 9

Furnishing the Iguana Home

. . . .

In This Chapter

▶ Creating your iguana's roost *and* giving him a way to get to it

▶ Adding safe plants to your iguana's enclosure

▶ Giving your iguana something to look at

▶ Setting up your house for a free-roamer

. . . .

The iguana enclosure, lights, and heat form a basic structure, something like an empty house or apartment. But before an empty house or apartment can become a home, you have to move in your furniture, put pictures on the walls, decide where you're going to put your car keys and mail when you come home, and so on. Making your iguana's enclosure an iguana home is really no different.

Some of the things that go into making an iguana home are necessary for the health — physical and mental — of your iguana. As much as possible within the confines of captivity, you are working to satisfy some of the key needs and instincts of your iguana. The happier your iguana is with his home within your home, the healthier he will be overall.

Making a Roost

Roosts, also called perches, are high places for your iguana to hang out while doing the things he likes best: sleeping, basking, and observing (see Figure 9-1). Iguanas are arboreal lizards; they prefer being up high where they can look over and down on things. It gives them a sense of security, especially in new situations.

Figure 9-1:
The climbers and roosts in this indoor enclosure offer a sense of security and comfort for animals that like sleeping, basking, and observing from on high.

Photo by Jennifer Swofford

Location, location, location

The iguana's roost should be up high. One of the mistakes many new iguana keepers make is that they put their iguana's enclosure down on the floor where the iguana has to look up at everything — and where he has to watch big, scary, stomping human feet come perilously close to kicking or smashing him. This stuff may seem a little absurd to you, but look at it from the iguana's point of view, especially a hatchling iguana. Your new iguana doesn't know you aren't out to get him, and he doesn't yet understand the concept of glass — that it functions as a barrier.

An enclosure on the floor is also perfectly placed for dogs, cats, and very young children to come and stare and stare and stare some more at the iguana. The only things in the wild that stare so determinedly at an iguana (besides an iguana researcher) are other iguanas or predators of iguanas. A baby iguana can tell that your furry pets and children are not other iguanas, so he will probably go crazy trying to escape, go numb with fear, or suffer from episodes of acute stress. Not good things for iguanas of any age.

If you can't make an enclosure at least 6 feet tall for an adult iguana, you can get away with making it 3–4 feet tall *if* you raise the enclosure up off the ground. As an added bonus with a raised enclosure, the space under the table or inside the cabinet makes a convenient place to store some of your iguana's belongings — lights, cleaning supplies, carrier, spare bowls, towels, and so on.

Keep things on an even keel

Iguana keepers often make the roosts on the diagonal, thinking that it's normal for arboreal lizards. Although it is normal for many arboreal lizards — and iguanas can and will hang out on vertical or diagonal planes once in a while — iguanas are committed to comfort, preferring to spend most of their time lying on a horizontal surface.

Depending on how tall your enclosure is, you can put in two or more shelves. Iguanas frequently develop favorite spots for different activities: High perches are favored for basking and keeping an eye on things; a slightly lower roost may make the perfect sleeping place. Placing shelves 12–14 inches apart also puts iguanas in different places within the vertical thermal gradient, increasing your iguana's choices in thermoregulating.

Materials

Roosts can be made out of almost anything that's safe, comfortable for the iguana, and easily cleaned and disinfected. The easiest ones are those that don't take a lot of work on your part to fashion or install:

- ✔ **Wood shelves.** Wood shelving or planks, 10–12 inches wide and as long as you need to fit inside the enclosure from side to side, are easy to fabricate and install. The lumberyard or builder supply store can cut the length you need, leaving you to do the sanding and finishing. A clear coat of environmentally friendly varathane or washable paint safe for children's rooms helps make the shelves water (and feces and urates) resistant, which makes cleaning and disinfecting them easier.

- ✔ **Melamine shelves.** You can find these shelves at the builder supply store where they stock the materials for building closets and household shelving. Melamine is pressboard laminated with a plastic resin that can withstand cleaning and disinfecting, although it doesn't do well if you scrub too vigorously with an abrasive pot scrubber.

- ✔ **Plastic-covered modular metal shelving designed to build closets and shelves.** The shelving comes in several lengths and can be cut to the length you need. The narrow round bars that form the shelves are spaced 1 inch apart. The shelving comes in two widths — 12 and 16 inches — which is nice if you end up with a very large male in a deeper-than-average enclosure.

When you buy any of these modular shelves, be sure to buy the hardware — including all the structural supports — that comes with it. That hardware provides a sturdier support for your growing iguana than standard shelving hardware. If you want to have a more flexible arrangement for wood and melamine shelves, you can get the metal tracks and hardware that enable you to raise or lower the shelves — useful if you start out with an adult-sized enclosure for your baby iguana. Because iguanas need to be within 18 inches of the UVB fluorescent, the shelf for a 2-inch tall hatchling needs to be closer to the fluorescent than the shelf of a 6-inch tall adult. Installing the shelving on adjustable tracks means you can easily lower the shelf as the iguana grows larger and taller.

Serious injuries can happen when the shelving or other heavy furnishings are not properly secured in the enclosure. Iguanas are inquisitive lizards, and some spend hours trying to figure out a way to get out of their enclosure, including climbing things you never intended them to climb and jumping on things not meant to be jumped on. Be sure that all shelves are securely anchored to the side and back walls of the enclosure. If you're installing a free-standing platform, use L-brackets to anchor the uprights to the base and top, and rope, bungees, or other strapping to secure the entire structure to something solid, like the wall behind it.

Natural resources can lend some interesting natural and functional beauty to your enclosure. But before collecting branches and decorative rocks from a site, make sure that doing so is legal. Before using rocks, you must clean them, boil them for 30 minutes, and then cool them. Wood should be cleaned, soaked in a bleach-water solution for 24 hours, rinsed thoroughly, and then soaked in fresh water for another 24 hours. Then let it dry thoroughly in the sun. Smaller pieces of wood can be cleaned and baked in an oven set at 200–250 degrees Fahrenheit (93–120 degrees Celsius) for 30 minutes.

Creating Climbers

Climbers are sort of the highways and byways in your iguana's enclosure. Iguanas use climbers to access the different levels within the enclosure as well as for entertainment and exercise. Climbers can be made out of a wide range of materials. The key things to remember are that they must be safe for an iguana to use and firmly anchored to prevent them from coming loose and falling when an iguana is on — or under — them.

Healthy iguanas are easily able to climb vertical surfaces, given enough texture to sink their claws into. Assuming that the enclosure is large enough, you can construct a combination of vertical and horizontal climbers throughout the enclosure.

Putting shelves in glass houses

Installing shelves in glass or Plexiglas enclosures is a bit difficult — nothing is available to screw the hardware into. You can use blocks of wood, brick, or architectural glass bricks to form a base across which a piece of wood is anchored, which forms a sort of free-standing platform. For the wood, you can use a suitable piece of 1-inch thick board that's 4, 6, 10, or 12 inches wide or a piece of branch or driftwood.

Whatever looks like it's climbable probably is. Rope-wrapped boards, branches, carpet-covered PVC pipe, bird ladders, ladders made of interlaced rope, rope and wood ladders, ladders made of modular closet shelving turned sideways, layered fishnet, rigid plastic mesh, carpet, hardware cloth (plain or plastic coated), and fabric designed for making gym bags or beach cover-ups are all things people have used to create climbers for their iguanas.

Sisal (hemp) rope is inexpensive and found at hardware and builder supply stores. When you use it to create a climber by wrapping it around a board, use a heavy-duty electric stapler to lock the rope strands to the board. Otherwise, as your iguana grows and gets heavier, the rope starts slipping.

You can affix carpet to wood or PVC pipe by using an appropriate glue. You can also glue carpet to the inside wall of the enclosure to make a vertical climbing surface. The only problem with this type of climber is that if your iguana has an accident or decides to poop-paint, you have a tougher job of getting the climbers clean and disinfected.

Although you can potty-train iguanas by working with their natural daily cycles (see Chapter 17), accidents sometimes happen, or your iguana simply gets mad at — and gets even with — you. The result is heavy-duty cleaning and disinfecting of the enclosure and its furnishings, including climbers. When you choose your material and install the climbers, keep in mind that at some point you may have to remove them to thoroughly clean and disinfect them, or you may have to do it while they're still in the enclosure.

Adding Plants

Plants can liven up an enclosure, help keep the humidity up, and provide some visual screening so the iguana can hide behind them when he wants a little privacy.

Tiptoeing through the carpet

Carpet has gotten a bad rap from herp keepers and vets because fibers from some carpets may get caught on lizard toes, sometimes wrapping around the toe. As the iguana grows, the carpet strands get tighter and eventually cut off the circulation, leading to tissue death. Conscientious lizard keepers, however, regularly check all the toes (and tail) to make sure that nothing is caught on them, that no unshed skin remains, and that no injuries have occurred to them. When done regularly, such inspections catch any fibers caught on the toes so they can be removed before they become a problem.

Live plants

Live plants pose a couple of problems that fake plants don't. Because the plants are alive, your iguana assumes that you have nicely provided fresh salad for him to forage through whenever he likes. The plants you select must be safely edible — as well as free of pesticides and other harmful chemicals (see Appendix A). You also need to accept the fact that the plants are going to get eaten, clawed, walked on, and smashed when the iguana decides he wants a cool belly tickle from the leaves.

If possible, buy your plants from nurseries that propagate their own stock because they can tell you for sure whether any chemicals (pesticides, herbicides, fungicides, or fertilizers) have been used in growing the plants. If you can't find such a nursery, keep the plant out of the enclosure for a week or so while you water it several times to allow any chemicals to leach out through the bottom of the pot. You should also clean the leaves. If cleaning them individually is out of the question, spray the tops and undersides of all the leaves with a mild, soapy water solution, using an environmentally friendly soap. Water the plant several more times after washing or heavily spraying the leaves with plain water to ensure that all the diluted soap is washed through as well.

Plants need to be securely installed in the enclosure. If hung, they need to be hung far enough away from the iguana so that the iguana can't play Tarzan and leap from his shelf to the potted plant. Although a hatchling iguana won't cause a problem, a 5-pound iguana doing a belly flop right on a potted plant suspended from a simple hook will. You're likely to have both iguana and partially unpotted plant going splat on the floor of the enclosure, something that's far less amusing if the pot shatters under the iguana's belly.

On the plus side, watering the plants helps keep the humidity level up, both from the water evaporating from the soil as well as the moisture respired from the leaves. You can also spray the leaves themselves with water, which also keeps more moisture in the air as the droplets evaporate.

Many people believe that animals instinctively know what is good or safe for them and what is not. Although that's true for an animal in its native environment, once you change the environment or move the animal to a new environment, that line of thinking can be deadly for an animal left to its own devices. Given that some iguanas have been known to eat just about any object that wasn't nailed down, you can't assume that your iguana will know whether or not a live plant put into his environment is poisonous. You have to do the research and ensure that only safely edible live plants are used. See Appendix A for a list of toxic plants.

Fake plants

Fake plants may sound icky, but some great-looking silk and polyester plants are available now in craft stores and specialty silk flower shops (where a simple bouquet can run into hundreds of dollars).

On the downside, some of the more inexpensive plants have very thinly covered wire that pops through once the plants have been bent around a couple of times as they're arranged and rearranged again. The exposed wire can be dangerous because the iguana can get poked in the finger — or eye — by a piece of metal. Another downside is that the leaves and flowers of some fake plants come off with little pressure, making it a bit too easy for a curious iguana to pull one off. If you have chosen a fake plant with very small parts, your iguana may swallow them, leading to injury or impaction. You can easily reduce this risk by selecting plants with large leaves and flower petals made with sturdy, thickly covered wire.

On the positive side, some fake plants are sturdy. Even a large iguana can climb some big, well-supported fake plants and lie on smaller ones without destroying them . . . at least not right away. Fake plants can also be scrubbed clean and disinfected if the iguana poops on them, something you can't always easily do with a live plant. Spraying a fake plant with water also helps keep the humidity up.

Iguanas try to eat fake plants initially, giving the leaves tentative bites, perhaps shaking a leaf a bit, trying to figure it all out. Once they realize that a plant is not edible, they leave it alone. They may give it another try off and on through the years, just in case a fake plant has been magically transformed into the real thing.

A Room with a View

There's no doubt about it: Iguanas prefer to look at an interesting view rather than a boring one. Maybe that's an obvious statement, but given the number of iguanas kept in dank garages and basements, with nothing of interest to look at, day after day, year after year, well, it apparently isn't as obvious as it seems.

Position the enclosure so that your iguana can look out a window or at a room where humans spend a lot of time. The window can look out at a street, a back yard, or even a patio or tiny apartment balcony that has a few potted plants (visited by butterflies) and a bird feeder or two.

The iguana's enclosure needs to be far enough away from the window so that the heat of the sun coming through the window, and the glass or plastic front of the enclosure, doesn't build up to fatal levels. Like heat building up inside a closed car on a mildly warm day, heat from the sun combined with the heating equipment in the enclosure can result in an iguana that's quickly dead from hyperthermia.

Putting Up the Fluorescent Lights

Iguanas need ultraviolet light to help them get the UVB exposure they need to keep their metabolism working properly. To provide the necessary ultraviolet light, you use fluorescent lights made especially for reptiles (see Chapter 8 for details).

The thing about ultraviolet wavelengths, however, is that they disperse rapidly. Only one-quarter the amount of UVB hits the surface 2 feet away from the fluorescent than hits it at 1 foot away. To ensure that your iguana gets the most out of the fluorescent light, install it so that the fluorescent tube itself is no more than 18 inches above the iguana's body; ideally, you want the fluorescent tube no more than 10–15 inches away from your iguana.

Born Free: The Free-Roamer

There's an alternative to keeping an iguana enclosed most or all of the time. Many iguana keepers set their iguanas up as free-roamers. Free-roaming doesn't mean that you just let your iguana go wherever he wants and do whatever he wants. You still need to set up basking areas, including UVB-producing fluorescents if you can't ensure that he'll get exposure to direct sun often enough through the year to make them unnecessary. You also need to set up a feeding place so that he knows where to find food and water whenever he wants it. And getting your iguana on a regular potty schedule reduces, if not eliminates, the chance of accidents around the house.

Setting up a free-roamer's environment

Free-roamers can be kept restricted to a single room or given the run of most or all of the house. If some part of the house is to be kept off limits and a family member has trouble remembering to close doors, you can install automatic door closures on those doors. If the iguana is confined to one room, you can replace the solid door to the room with a screen door that has sturdy mesh strong enough to withstand an iguana who wants out. If keeping the room warm enough is a problem, you can cover the screen with a panel of plastic or Plexiglas.

Setting up the basking area

Keeping in mind the need for heights and a view, you need to set up a basking and sleeping area where the iguana can be 4–7 feet above the ground (see Figure 9-2). A shelf securely mounted to the wall or the top of a large piece of furniture, such as an armoire, a bookcase, or a cabinet, works well. A curtain rod may look like a good place, but the iguana will keep using the place long after he's large and heavy enough to bring the curtain and its rod crashing to the ground.

Figure 9-2: Even free-roamers need basking areas.

Photo by Ann Marsden

Providing light

In a large wood enclosure, you can easily mount the light fixtures on the ceiling of the enclosure. Installing light fixtures, both incandescents for heat and at least one fluorescent for UVB, takes a little more creativity for free-roamers.

Incandescent fixtures can be mounted on the wall a foot or two above the basking/sleeping shelf. A fluorescent fixture can be mounted sideways on the wall or suspended from the ceiling. (If you choose to suspend it from the ceiling, be sure to buy the special anchor screws made to support heavy objects hung from drywall and acoustic ceilings. You can find the anchors, along with the rope or chain used to hang the fixture, at hardware stores.) You also need a small drill to drill holes through the fluorescent fixture's plastic casing, unless you buy a fixture designed to be installed flush against the ceiling or the underside of a cabinet. Just how much weight should the chain or rope and anchors support? Fifteen to 20 pounds — the weight of a full-grown iguana — plus the weight of the fixture and fluorescent tube.

You can find fluorescent fixtures at pet stores, lighting stores, and builder supply stores. The ones sold in pet stores tend to be big and bulky, in shades of black and brown. Utility fixtures found in hardware and builder supply stores are generally white and, well, utilitarian looking. A third, generally more attractive option, is a fixture designed to be installed under cabinets in kitchens and workshops. These fixtures are usually white, have a very low profile, and have a sleek design. They come equipped with a plastic diffuser that should not be used when the fixture is for your reptile. You will need access to enough electrical outlets for the heat lights, pads, and UV fixtures, as well as space for any timers you want to use. Because iguanas try to climb just about anything, it's a good idea to secure the electrical cords to the wall so they don't hang around providing too much temptation.

Heating a free-roamer

Because the heating equipment doesn't work as efficiently in a cool room, a space heater is useful most of the year to raise the ambient room air temperature without having to heat the entire house. Be sure to get one that is sturdy enough not to tip over and that has an automatic turn-off mechanism if it does tip over. And be sure to follow the safety tips provided by the manufacturer.

Keeping humidity levels right

Maintaining adequate humidity is a bit more difficult for free-roamers. Daily baths, supplemented by frequent sprays of water several times a day, helps a great deal. Running a humidifier or fogger during the day can also help keep the room humidity up.

Iguana-proofing your home

Anyone who has had children knows what it means to child-proof a room: You make it safe for infants and toddlers who are starting to explore their world with their fingers, toes, and mouths. Iguana-proofing a room is done for similar reasons: to make it safe for an inquisitive iguana who thinks that everything exists for his climbing, digging, hiding, and toppling pleasure.

Start going around the room, looking at it from the iguana's point of view. See any hidey-holes under cabinets or any upholstered furniture he can wriggle into? Plug 'em up! See those delicate porcelain and crystal knickknacks you've collected over the years sitting there so beautifully on the sideboard? Hide 'em! And what about those books, CDs, or tapes piled haphazardly in the bookcase? Straighten 'em up or put 'em behind closed doors!

Most iguanas won't open cabinets (though some have been known to do so) and probably won't stick their toes or tongues into electrical outlets (assuming that you have any left over after plugging in all their equipment), but if you're concerned about them doing so, you can find plug covers and child-proof door latches at any hardware store. See Chapter 3 for more tips on what to look for when you iguana-proof your home.

Natural selection: Letting your iguana decide

Okay. So you've spent days thinking about your iguana's room — planning, trying arrangements out, changing them again, rearranging furniture, and generally making yourself crazy — and you've finally come up with the perfect basking area. The only problem? Your iguana won't go near it. You put him on it, and he just up and walks away. You put him on it again, and he gives you the stink eye and walks away again.

What's going on? Just that your iguana doesn't like the spot you've picked out for him, no matter how much logic, effort, and good intentions went into it. Although it's generally unwise to allow your iguana to train you, in the case of setting up basking and sleeping areas, it's best to let the iguana help decide where they're located. You obviously don't want him someplace that's truly unsafe, but you do need to accommodate his internal sensors that tell him whether a place is safe and secure and comfortable for him.

I mean *really* iguana-proofing your home

I can't stress hard enough or often enough the importance of iguana-proofing a room — or house — before you let your iguana start having time out of his enclosure. Like all reptiles, iguanas are very squishy, and the smaller they are, the squishier they are. This means that they can and most definitely will squeeze through that narrow, dark, dusty slot between your dishwasher and kitchen cabinet. This means that they will find that one opening tucked up under the bathroom or kitchen cabinet that you yourself couldn't find without contorting yourself into bizarre and entertaining postures while juggling a hand mirror and flashlight. This means that they will rip that little tear in the bottom of your bed or sofa bed into a slightly larger tear, squeeze through, and somehow make themselves comfy within the mattress springs.

Tools of the iguana-proofing trade include long sticks (walking sticks, long snake hooks, even golf clubs, all work well); rolls of duct tape; bright flashlights and spare batteries; hand mirrors; a stick to tape a mirror onto for easily checking under and behind large pieces of furniture; screwdrivers, pliers, and wrenches for dismantling large pieces of furniture; drills and jigsaws for dismantling built-in cabinets when your iguana finds that iguana-sized hole you missed; and a dictionary of colorful alternatives to the cuss words sure to stream from your mouth when you find yourself having to use more than the first couple of items in this list.

Chapter 10

Keeping Your Iguana Comfortable

*R*egardless of an iguana's age and size, he needs a lot of equipment and paraphernalia: daytime heat lights, nighttime heat sources, fluorescent fixtures, climbers, basking shelves or branches, a hide box, a water bowl, and a food bowl. Many iguana keepers also put in a tub large enough for the iguana to bathe (and, hopefully, to poop) in. Plants, real or fake, are often added to soften the look and help humidify the enclosure. And additional shelves and climbers to add variety and interest for the iguana are common features in the well-cared-for iguana home. Combine all this stuff with an active, arboreal, tropical lizard averaging 5–6 feet long and 12–18 pounds, and you're needing an enclosure nearly the size of a small bedroom. All that's missing is cable TV and maid service. (Oh, wait — they *do* have maid service.)

You have gone to all this trouble to make him feel welcome and to keep him safe and healthy. Now you need to keep him happy. Read on to find out what you can do to make him more comfortable and secure.

Give Him a Place to Hide

Enclosure size. It's one of the biggest factors in keeping your iguana happy. As preceding chapters explain, iguanas need space: space to explore, space to bask, space to climb, and space to feel safe and in control — generally from on high.

Can you make an iguana enclosure *too* big? No. But, if you put a very small iguana inside a very large enclosure, it can cause stress unless you also install some small iguana-sized hide boxes for him. As he grows, change out the hide boxes for larger ones or discard them altogether when he no longer uses them. Starting a hatchling out in an adult-sized enclosure means you have to build or buy fewer interim enclosures — leaving you a lot more cash to spoil your new baby with.

Watch the Thermometer

You'll find that your heating equipment needs will change throughout the year as the weather shifts from warm to cold to warm again. Placing thermometers throughout the enclosure is critical so that you always know at a glance what the temperatures are and whether you need to make alterations in the heat output.

To increase the heat in the enclosure, you can

- Change to a higher wattage bulb (as long as your light fixture supports the higher wattage).

    Make sure that you have light fixtures that can safely house the highest wattage you need.

- Install a second light fixture. By installing two or more sockets, you can add more lights to provide more heat when needed.

- Install an infrared heat panel, pig blanket (large, rigid panels with embedded heat cables), or second heating pad.

- If the lights are installed outside the enclosure, move them closer to the enclosure (watch for fire hazards!).

- Install a space heater to heat the room instead of the entire house. By increasing the ambient room air temperature, the heating equipment in the enclosure will work more efficiently.

Once you start adding up all these fixtures needed for heat and light, you begin to see why you need access to several electrical outlets and power strips.

To decrease the heat in the enclosure, you can

- Plug the light or ceramic heating element (CHE) into a dimmer switch and ramp it down.

- Plug the infrared panel or pig blanket into a thermostat made to regulate its output.

- If the lights are installed outside the enclosure, move them farther away from the enclosure.

- Switch to lower wattage bulbs.

The reptile basking lights and household incandescent bulbs are all suitable for daytime use but can't be used at night to provide heat. Iguanas, like all animals, need a dark period at night. Although they may sleep with lights on, they're not sleeping well, and ultimately they'll suffer from behavior- and stress-related symptoms. At night, if you're using a heat source that emits light, the light needs to be dim — best provided by bulbs that emit purple, blue, green, or red light. Need a reminder as to the proper day and night temperatures? See Chapter 3.

Keep the Air Moist

Most iguanas are native to the tropics where the general humidity and frequent rains are interspersed by an annual dry season. Some iguanas come from areas that are somewhat drier than we'd think based on our idea of tropical wet forests. Because you can't be sure where your iguana came from, you need to err on the side of caution and provide as much humidity as possible.

Sounds simple, but the reality of producing the 80 percent or so humidity recommended for iguanas is nearly impossible. Most iguana keepers find that keeping the humidity up around 50 percent is difficult, especially when the central heating or air-conditioning may be running during the winters or summers. The final kicker is that when the high humidity levels are attained, lovely colonies of mildew may end up growing on the walls. When you have to choose between having fungal growths destroying the drywall or protecting your house by reducing the humidity level, protecting the house usually, and understandably, wins. So what do you do? Read the following sections.

Humidifying the room

To humidify the air in your iguana's room, you can run a humidifier all day and night or just during the daytime hours. (Be sure to check it one or more times a day to make sure that the water level is within safe limits.)

Another way to increase the humidity is to put a large pan or plastic tub of water in the warm side of the enclosure. The bigger the tub's surface area, the higher the rate of evaporation. Some iguanas soak in this water, which also helps humidify them. Because so many iguanas decide that the water tubs are a nice place to poop, make sure that you can easily get the tub in and out of the enclosure to clean and disinfect it as needed. Even though the tub or pan is filled with plain water, the container itself can get scummy after awhile, so periodically clean and disinfect it even if your iguana isn't using it for his toilette.

Plumbing for iguanas

Some iguana keepers take the "How do I deal with the waste water?" situation into consideration when designing their enclosures. A raised floor allows the tub to be recessed into the floor. You can put a drain in the bottom of the tub leading to a receptacle underneath that can more easily be removed to empty the waste water and any feces or food in the water. A few iguana keepers even plumb their iguana enclosures — install water pipes and fixtures to give them running water, which makes cleaning and refilling the tub easier. Similarly, misting systems can be installed in the ceiling of the enclosure, with the system set to turn on and off automatically throughout the day.

If you start seeing mildew growing on your walls, cut back the hours the humidifier is in operation. If your walls are white, you can apply a bleach-water mixture to kill the fungus. If your walls are painted or covered, you can test various household mildew products in an inconspicuous place to find one that won't discolor the walls. Use these products when the iguana is out of the room and give the room time to air out before returning him.

Spraying water

Using a spray bottle filled with water is one of the easiest ways to help keep your iguana humidified. Just set the nozzle to a broad, gentle spray or mist, and spray. There's no need to add any vitamins or emollients to the water. The water itself does the job of helping increase the humidity right around the iguana. Spraying is especially nice when the iguana is shedding because it keeps the loosening flaps of skin from drying out, making them shed off more easily. As the water droplets evaporate, they humidify the air the iguana breathes. You should spray several times a day during the daytime period, giving your iguana enough time to dry off before he goes to sleep.

If you have a big iguana or several iguanas, or your hand gets tired squeezing the sprayer's trigger, try this: At your local home builder supply store, you can find a heavy-duty pressurized spray bottle. After pressurizing the bottle using the plunger handle at the top, you simply press and lock down a button and then just hold the bottle while it emits a fine spray for a couple of minutes.

If you keep plants in the enclosure, spray them when you're spraying the iguana. The overall humidity in the enclosure increases as the water droplets evaporate. You can place saucers under the plants to catch water that drains out of the bottom of the pot when you water it, which also contributes to the overall humidity.

If you put your iguana outside in a sunning cage during the day, you can buy various types of attachments for your garden hose. Screwed onto the end of the hose, the attachments can either stand on their own or be placed on top of the enclosure. When the water is turned on, they emit a fine, continuous spray of water as long as the water flows through the hose.

Keep any eye on the cage furnishings to make sure that they aren't affected by the constant mist. Check the wire mesh for nicks in the plastic coating that may allow rust to start. And check the wood to make sure that it isn't starting to rot. Most importantly, make sure that the iguana has a dry area to lie in so he can thermoregulate his body temperature. Hide boxes should remain dry all the time. Follow the manufacturer's directions for cleaning the misters.

Let Him Cool Down When Necessary

When is hot too hot? Although iguanas are from the tropics and neotropics, temperatures above 98–100 degrees Fahrenheit (36–37 degrees Celsius) can be dangerous, even fatal, if an iguana is unable to move into a cooler area.

When the weather is very hot, you can stock up on iguana ice. No, that doesn't mean icing your iguana. It means making ice that he can use to cool himself or that you can use to ensure he has fresh, cool water to drink and to provide some humidity in his outdoor (and indoor) enclosure. For example, regular ice cubes placed in a bowl melt on a warm day, providing cool water. Or you can make ice in the water bowl itself: Fill the bowl ¾ full of water and freeze it. Pop the bowl-shaped cube out and make some more. You can freeze and store several such blocks, wrapped in foil or plastic wrap or bags, to be used as needed. Cubes of iguana salad can also be frozen and placed in the food bowl with fresh salad — the frozen salad helps keep the fresh salad cool longer. Setting the food bowl in a larger container that has been lined with ice is another way to keep food cool on a sweltering day.

Making your own drip systems

Some iguana keepers make their own drip systems by using plastic water, milk, or juice bottles. You can fill a soft-plastic gallon milk or juice bottle with water and set it on top of a sturdy cage on a stack of paper (such as newsprint) or over a plant. Puncture a portion of it with a thin, sharp object, like the tip of a paring knife. Then arrange it so the water can drip inside the enclosure. A plastic liter soda bottle needs to be punctured first. Then you fill it, put the cap back on, and turn it upside down until placing it on top of the enclosure. If you place a wad of paper under the punctured bottle, the water saturates the paper. Once the paper is soaked through, it starts dripping water from several places.

Can't set up a cool misting system for your iguana on a hot day? Fill plastic soda bottles up to ⅔ full of water, put the caps back on, and then freeze them. When you need to "turn the air conditioner on," just pull one of the bottles out of the freezer, wrap it in a terry cloth towel, and place it in the iguana's enclosure. The iguana can lie on it or next to it.

Keep the Air Flowing

Iguanas need a flow of fresh air through their enclosures. It not only keeps their environment from becoming stale but also helps reduce the bacterial and fungal growths associated with high humidity.

When you're using a commercial glass or plastic tank, the floor, walls, and all or part of the top are solid glass or plastic. There may be only one or two pieces of screen (depending on the size and design of the tank) on the top. This setup doesn't allow for any air flow other than the warm air that rises through the open areas in the top. Because there's no way to increase air flow in this type of tank, get that outdoor enclosure set up as soon as possible so that your iguana can spend some time in the fresh air.

Some enclosures made of wood or melamine have ventilation panels, but they're installed opposite of one another — both at the bottom on opposing walls or near the top on opposing walls. This setup allows air to pass through between them but does little to create an air flow through the enclosure as a whole. You can increase the ventilation by drilling clusters of ⅛–¼ inch holes into the side of the tank where you need them.

When building or designing an enclosure, put a ventilation panel at the bottom of one wall and near the top of the opposite wall. In addition, you can install a panel at the top of the back wall or in the top of the enclosure. To reduce the risk of injury from snout rubbing by an iguana who's trying to force his way out of the enclosure, make the panels out of masonite pegboard or similar material rather than wire mesh. An alternative to buying ventilation panels is to create your own. You can drill several rows of holes, each measuring ⅛–¼ inch in diameter and spaced ½ inch apart, in a rectangular pattern in the areas you want the ventilation panels.

If you find that your ventilation panels are a little too effective during the winter, resulting in the enclosure losing too much heat, you can cover part of the panels to reduce the air flow. If you put a ventilation panel at the top, cover that one first. A folded towel works well because it still allows some air through but helps to retain the heat in the enclosure. Solid wood or plastic panels can be custom-made to fit over the ventilation panels, attaching to the enclosure with Velcro strips, latches, or slide bolts.

Chapter 11

The Great Outdoors

Iguanas are children of the sun and fresh air. Taking them outside on a regular basis is an important part of maintaining their physical and mental health. Where you live and what your daily schedule's like are going to determine how often you can get your iguana outside and how long he can stay out there. In temperate climates, iguanas can spend most of the day outside during the spring, summer, and early fall. If you live where the weather is a little less clement, you may have to limit your iguana to a couple of the warmest hours on your days off. If you can provide artificial heat for your iguana when he's outside, he can stay outside on cooler days. Where winters are warm and mild, iguanas can be housed outside all year when they're provided with heat and shelter from the wind and rain.

If you're starting to think that taking him outside isn't going to be as simple as just dropping him in your backyard while you go off to do some errands, you're catching on to iguanas! In this chapter, I explain how to introduce iguanas to the outdoors, how to ensure their safety, and how to enjoy places other than your own backyard.

Spending Time Outside

Taking an iguana outside, whether for just a few minutes or for several hours, requires advance preparation. Needless to say, the longer the period of time you plan on having him outside, the more planning and preparation are required on your part. You need to remember a few key things about your iguana:

> ✔ No matter how old or how tame, he still has the instincts and responses of a wild animal: He won't always think and react like you do to sights and sounds.

✔ He can probably read you better than you can read him.

✔ No matter how big or old, he can still move faster than you can.

The two safest ways for your iguana to spend time outside are either in your hands and arms or in a sunning cage. If he isn't in a cage, then you should be holding him. Or, if you have placed him on you while you're sitting or lying down, place your hand on him to be ready to grab him. A small iguana can be held in your cupped hand. Larger iguanas can lay along your forearm, with their shoulders, neck, and head cradled in your hand and fingers (see Figure 11-1). You can also hold them up against your chest as you'd hold a baby, with your hand on their back at all times.

Pick a calm area

When you first take your iguana outside, do it in a relatively quiet area and on a relatively calm day. The more movement (breeze-tossed bushes and trees, kids playing ball or racing their bikes, cars whizzing by) and noise (kids, traffic, loud music, wild frat house party next door) your iguana is exposed to, the more confusing and scary everything will be to him. Sensory overload leads to an iguana who either wants to dive down your shirt, cling to the top of your head, or head for the nearest tall tree. And based on the number of iguana keepers who — after being turned away by the fire department — frantically call all the tree trimmers in their city phone book, trying to find one who'll make an after-hours service call, the tall-tree scenario is an all-too-common one.

Avoid distractions

During your first forays outside, eliminate your own distractions. You need to be *focused* on your iguana, not merely aware of him while you're watching to make sure that the kids are safe in the pool and that the dog doesn't dig up your prized geraniums while you're simultaneously picking earwigs out of your roses. Leave the cell phone and pager inside, too.

Pay attention!

You need to be very aware of what's going on around you and the iguana, not only in your yard and the sky overhead but also in the yards around you or out in the street. If the kids next door are playing ball, is there a chance it'll come sailing over into your yard? Do large, noisy trucks come rumbling down the street a few feet away or emergency vehicles race by with sirens screaming? Is your door-slamming teenager or spouse due home soon? You need to extend your awareness out in all directions to listen and watch for sounds and sights that may startle your iguana into flight.

Figure 11-1:
Holding a
juvenile or
an adult
iguana.

Photo by Melissa Kaplan

A word on leashes and harnesses

One of the first things many overeager but naive iguana keepers buy, along with that hot rock and bark substrate, is a leash or harness. The packaging implies that your iguana will happily be walked like a dog or sit quietly lounging about, with not a care in the world. Yeah, right. Assuming that you don't break any spikes, limbs, or his tail while getting the harness on, something may break as the iguana struggles to get out of the harness or tries to make a run for it. Alligator-rolling, thrashing, and panic all pretty much describe a harnessed iguana who doesn't want to be in a harness. So do broken bones, eye and ear injuries, and strangled, limp lizards.

The problem with leashes and harnesses is that they're not designed with the iguana body and behavior in mind. They're primarily designed for rabbits, cats, and ferrets — furry mammals who've been highly domesticated. They're not designed for lizards with floppy dewlaps, spiky crests, razor-sharp teeth, and lashing tails. And if you put the harness on tight enough so that the iguana can't wriggle and squirm out of it, then the harness is on tight enough to break spikes. It isn't a big problem with a baby iguana, whose spikes are barely visible along his back, but on a juvenile or an adult iguana, serious injury and infection can result.

It's a bird! It's a plane! It's going to eat me!

Although you know that Superman isn't about to eat your iguana, your iguana isn't so sure. To him, anything flying overhead — whether it's a hummingbird or helicopter, jet plane or paper kite — is probably out looking for lunch. When you first begin acclimating your iguana to the outdoors (be it outside in your yard, walking down the street, or driving down the highway), his parietal eye (see Chapter 6) is on duty, alert to overhead predators. The more you take your iguana out and expose him to things flying overhead (birds, planes, hot air balloons, freeway overpasses, whatever), the more he'll become used to filtering out these moving shadows and the less nervous and flighty he'll be.

Explore slowly

Walk around with your iguana, talking softly to him, petting him. Let him look around at everything. Give him a verbal as well as physical tour of the yard. You may feel like an idiot as you babble on about this bed of roses, that tree stump, the mound of herbs over there, and point out all the nice veggies you planted for him. But the sound of your voice will help soothe him.

Iguanas learn some things by exploration and some things by watching others. If you have a pet that uses a dog or cat door, expect that your iguana will figure out that the pet door is an easy way to let himself out when you're too busy. If you have such a door, be sure to block it when your iguana is free-roaming in the house, lock him out of the room with the pet door, or get one of those pet doors that are coded to open only in response to a signal from a special collar worn by the pet.

Run, Run, Runaway! Finding an Iguana That Gets Away

The first thing to remember is that, no matter how many years you've been together, no matter how tame and affectionate your iguana is with you, he's still a wild animal — one endowed with a marvelous sense of smell and adventure and, apparently, a mischievous sense of timing. Iguana keepers who for years have let their iguanas roam through the yard or sun themselves on the deck, or who've just plunked them down on a lush and tasty bush, sooner or later find out that past behavior is no guarantee for the future. Some iguanas may only run a short distance before stopping, just enough to give you a heart attack. Others have taken off, never to be found again or, sadly, found dead. Still others take off and, if lucky, survive the elements, cats, and malicious stone-throwing kids to end up in someone else's possession, never to be returned.

If your iguana does get away, here's how you can make the search more effective:

✔ Don't look for the iguana. If you deliberately look for the iguana, your eyes will miss him. After all, the markings and colors of an iguana, as vivid as they may be when he is in your arms or sitting in his enclosure, are there to help your iguana disappear when sitting in a tree. And disappear they do. So, instead of looking for your iguana, divide the area to be searched into smaller sections, unfocus your eyes, and just stare at an area. Be quiet, relax your breathing, don't move, and don't think. Just let your eyes wander from ground up into the bushes and trees and along walls and outbuildings. If your iguana is there, his shape will suddenly jump out at you as your brain registers a shape or outline line that shouldn't be there. If the iguana isn't in the section, move to the next one and continue.

✔ The best time to look is when your iguana is likely to be out sunning after the overnight cool-down. Look on exposed branches, walls, the ground against walls, and rooftops during the mid to late morning or midafternoon. As the morning and afternoon progress, the iguana is more likely to lounge where there is quick access to leafy cover.

✔ You can also search at night, armed with a strong flashlight. If you're lucky, your light will annoy the iguana as he tries to sleep, and you'll see the eyeshine as he glares at you. Some iguanas may go to ground at night, crawling under houses through the ventilation holes or behind pool heaters or other warm equipment in outbuildings and on the grounds.

✔ Leaving favorite food out, keeping the sunning enclosure open, and putting out his favorite toy may lure your runaway back home. Don't give up looking and do let the local animal shelters, herp societies, and reptile rescues know that your iguana is missing.

Sunning Cages

As you have probably already figured out, providing the perfect captive environment for your iguana isn't necessarily a guarantee that he'll appreciate it the way you do. No matter how wonderful you are, how bonded you become with your iguana, and how much you have created a miniature iguana Garden of Eden in your yard, the leaves and flowers will always be tastier over in the next yard, street, or field.

The best way to make sure that you won't be out frantically beating the bushes looking for an iguana who has decided to hit the road is to put your iguana in an outdoor enclosure. There, he can get all the sun and fresh air he wants, in a secure environment. If you can't build a large enclosure (see Chapter 8), you can probably buy or build a wire enclosure to use as a sunning cage. Wire enclosures made for mammals and birds can be used. To make the sunning cage more comfortable, cover the floor with some soft towels. You may need to use bungee cords or bolt snaps (from the hardware store) to better secure the door to the cage.

Setting your sunning cage on a stand has several benefits (see Chapter 9). An added benefit *outside* is that if ants become a problem, the legs of the sunning cage's stand can be set in containers half-filled with soapy water. Wide-mouth containers also keep other potentially dangerous insects, such as scorpions, out of the cage. Because venomous spider bites can severely harm an iguana, keep an eye out for spider webs and get rid of them as soon as you spot them.

Iguanas need to have access to shade in their sunning cage. Shade enables them to retreat from the direct sun and lower their body temperature when they start getting too hot. Shade should be provided over one-third to one-half of the top of the cage. You can find orchid shade cloth in several densities at plant nurseries, builder supply stores, and nursery or garden supply mail-order companies. An alternative to using this type of shade cloth is to plant edible climbing plants next to the enclosure and train them to grow up and over it. The leaves from Nasturtium, grapes, vining geraniums, and Hibiscus are all colorful, attractive, and yummy. You'll have to provide shade some other way until these plants are well established and providing the shade you need.

Going on Outings

At times, you *have* to take your iguana out (like when going to the veterinarian), but don't think that those necessary times are the only times your iguana *should* go out. Iguanas are intelligent enough to take an interest in their surroundings and apparently enjoy going new places and seeing new faces — faces preferably attached to humans who'll lavish attention on them. One of the ways to increase and maintain the level of socialization is to reinforce the behaviors by regular contact with people and locales outside your own home.

As with anything else, going out requires some preparation and the right mindset. In the beginning, it's especially important that you select your destinations carefully so that you interest your iguana, not completely stress him out to the point where he fights every time you try to take him on an outing.

You may want to start out by going to friends' homes — friends who like your iguana and accept your craziness in having one. (Going to public beaches and parks may or may not be a good idea, depending on the general community attitude toward exotics in public.)

Humans and their iguanas have also been welcomed in a number of different places. Pet stores (watch out for mites), feed and grain stores, hardware stores, bookstores, art stores, office supply stores, and banks have all been popular destinations.

A wonderful destination is any place where the public has come to learn and where you can engage in educating the public about iguanas. Teachers are often thrilled to have a parent come into the classroom and share an iguana with the students. It gives the students an opportunity to learn without realizing it. Herp societies and reptile rescue groups often appear at community events where teaching takes place under the guise of having fun. Call the organizations near you to see if they're interested in having you and your iguana volunteer for their events.

Grocery stores, health food stores, ice cream or other snack shops, and restaurants are inappropriate places to take your iguana. Another clue to an inappropriate destination is a sign on the door says "No Pets Allowed." Although these signs may have been posted with dogs and cats in mind, some establishments have decided that all animals (except service animals) are to be excluded.

The time will come when you're out somewhere and you come across a customer who's clearly afraid of iguanas and not interested in hearing about how wonderful they are. Even if you're in a store you've been in before, the one who should leave is you (with your iguana, of course), regardless of how unreasonable or ungrounded the customer's reaction is. Responsible iguana keeping includes knowing where you're welcome and where you're not, learning to read people's discomfort or fear, learning how to respond to their feelings, and knowing when to bow out gracefully. In a public human versus iguana dispute, the human will prevail. Even if your iguana is better behaved than that particular human.

Road Trip!

Okay, your iguana is comfortable with you, and you're comfortable that you've honed your peripheral vision and sixth sense, and now you're ready to roll. The next problem to address is getting from home to your destination.

Riding along in my automobile

The usual mode of transportation is a car, small truck, or van — in other words, a passenger vehicle. There are two schools of thought on the best way to transport an iguana in a passenger vehicle: Keep the iguana enclosed in a box or carrier, or don't. Without a doubt, keeping him enclosed in a carrier is safer. For the iguana, it means less bouncing around if you are in an accident. For you, it means you're not distracted by an iguana who decides to go where he shouldn't or by an iguana who decides for some reason that the back of your neck looks awfully tempting to climb on or bite.

✔ **Pet carrier:** Confining a small iguana to a cardboard box or pet carrier (adapted to prevent his squeezing through the holes in the sides and wire door) is not a problem, because small iguanas easily fit inside them. Although you can find carriers and collapsible cages made for large dogs and birds, they may be too large to fit in your car. The downside to confining an iguana to a carrier with mostly solid walls or a cardboard box means that he's not able to see the sights.

✔ **Back seat:** An alternative to total confinement is to block off the area behind the front or back seat so that the iguana can't come up front and try to climb your chest or creep under the brake pedal while you're driving. Collapsible gates made to keep dogs confined in the back seat of a car or the rear cargo area of a van or sports utility vehicle can be used for iguanas, too. If your iguana is still small enough to slip through the mesh, you can use wire or plastic ties to fasten hardware cloth or smaller gauge plastic mesh to it until your iguana gets too big to slip through.

If you have a rear cargo area behind the back seat or in an extended cab pickup truck, you can actually set up a roost for your iguana. A crate topped with a folded blanket or pillow; a log mounted on a toolbox, or a hammock affixed to the interior provides a comfortable perch with a view. Some dedicated iguana keepers even choose the model of their new car or minivan because it has an electrical outlet in back that they can plug a heating pad into — to keep their iguana warm even on cool days and nights.

✔ **Up front:** Even with all the potential dangers, some iguanas do get to ride in front. Some iguanas happily spend time on their hind legs, front toes and claws on the window sill, watching the world go by (see Figure 11-2). (A towel attached to the front dashboard with Velcro helps provide a secure footing.) Or they perch themselves on the top of the front seat. Iguanas can be trained not to intrude into the driver's space, but iguanas, like toddlers, often figure that rules are made to be broken. There are never any guarantees that they won't decide to break the driver's space rule at an inopportune time.

If you're going to let your iguana ride up front, it's best to do it when you have another human along who is comfortable holding and working with iguanas. The passenger can sit in the passenger seat, holding the iguana and gently restraining or redirecting him if the iguana decides that riding on top of your head will be much more fun.

Figure 11-2:
When you take your iguana on a car ride, make sure that he's safely confined or caged. If you want to let him roam and enjoy the view, do it when the car's stopped.

Photo by Adam Britton

Public transportation

If you rely on buses or taxi cabs to get around, then a secure carrier is a must. To make less of a disturbance, be sure to cover any gates or wire mesh on the carrier with cloth. People will assume that you have a dog or cat in there and won't freak out seeing a scaly green nose poking out at them.

Generally speaking, airplanes don't allow reptiles in the passenger cabin. A decreasing number of airlines are accepting reptiles for shipping in the pressurized cargo area.

Don't be a sneak. If you're going to be traveling and spending the nights at motels or hotels, call around first and determine which ones accept pets. If you're flying, don't sneak your iguana onboard. Too many people lose their herps during the flight, or they're spotted by freaked-out passengers. Although the airline can't exactly kick you off midflight, the personnel can be less than pleasant about things. Show you're a responsible iguana keeper by *being* a responsible iguana keeper.

But, officer, I can explain . . .

As one dedicated iguana keeper found, being distracted by an iguana doing her pre-poopy dance on the car upholstery can be quite expensive. When the police officer asked what happened, the woman mumbled something about a dropped water bottle, too embarrassed to admit that she was trying to get paper towels under her iguana's tush before the iguana slimed the seat with a load of feces and urates. The driver's insurance company ended up shelling out $5,000 to fix the car. Imagine how much less amused they would have been had they known what she was really doing.

Overnight express — no kidding

If you have to get your iguana somewhere and driving him there by car won't work, consider overnight express mail service from the post office. Call the post office to confirm that overnight service is available from the starting-point zip code (the zip code of the post office station you're shipping from, which may be different from your home address) to the destination zip code. If no overnight express mail service is available, then start calling the airlines to see who'll accept your iguana and what their requirements are.

To ship your iguana, you need to pack him properly:

1. **Obtain or make a sturdy, Styrofoam/polystyrene foam-lined cardboard box large enough to hold the iguana and his tail comfortably.**

   You can sometimes scrounge them up from pet stores.

2. **Pour in foam or cornstarch peanuts to a depth of 3–4 inches.**

   This step provides some cushioning for the inevitable knockabouts the box is going to receive.

3. **Put your iguana in a pillowcase (or a larger cloth sack if he's too big for a pillowcase) and close the open end with a rubber band. Then fold the rubber-banded top over on itself and wrap it with several windings of duct or masking tape.**

   Doing so prevents escapes if the box is damaged during shipping. For a small iguana, some crumpled paper or terry cloth towel can be put in the pillowcase to give him something to grip. You can even put in a shirt that smells like you so that your iguana doesn't feel like he's in a totally alien environment.

4. **Clearly label the outside top of the box with the recipient's name and address and the name and address of the sender.**

   Cover the addresses with clear mailing tape to prevent the ink from bleeding if the box gets wet.

5. **In large letters, write** LIVE HARMLESS LIZARD **on the top of the box.**

6. **Label all sides of the box with** LIVE HARMLESS LIZARD **and** Keep at room temperature (75°F/23°C) **and** This Side Up.

7. **Before placing the iguana inside, poke air holes in the sides and top of the box, making sure that they go through the inner foam core.**

8. **Just before you're ready to leave for the post office or other shipper, put the bagged iguana in the box.**

   If the weather is going to be cold, you can activate and tape a couple of small heat packs (hand warmers available at camping and sporting goods stores) to the inside top of the box. Because your iguana is safer being a little too cool than too hot, it's best to forgo heat packs unless you know that the weather's going to be cold and that keeping the iguana at room temperature for most of the trip is going to be difficult.

9. **Seal up the box, taking care not to cover the air holes. Stow the box safely in your car and go.**

Packing up and shipping off your iguana this way can be a scary thing. Fortunately, being comfortably situated in a dark space will reduce the stress on the iguana. You can ease your own stress by making sure to keep the tracking number and the recipient's phone number, and call to make sure he arrives safely.

You can help ensure your iguana's safe arrival by not shipping him during the coldest months of winter or hottest months of summer, or when a cold snap or heat wave has been predicted. No matter how many warnings and instructions are on the box, someone may drop the ball at the most inopportune time. By timing your iguana's shipping right, you can prevent temperature-related fatalities.

In case there is a problem along the way, make sure the post office has both your phone number and the recipient's. An additional benefit to doing so is that, in many cases, the receiving post office will call the recipient first thing in the morning to tell the recipient that the package has arrived.

One Final Warning

Taking your iguana out can be risky. The iguana can run off, leaving you to try to chase him down. He may bite, whip, or scratch someone — or jump on someone who really doesn't want an iguana attached to his or her body. You need to learn how to read your iguana's behavior — his intentions and response to situations as well as his actions — to provide the safest possible experience for you, your iguana, and the general public. Be courteous and take paper towels, a surface disinfectant, and hand disinfectant with you. Accidents do happen, and you want to be sure that people touch your iguana with clean hands and that they go away with clean hands. You can't tell just by looking at someone if he or she is immunocompromised and may become ill from contact with surface bacteria.

Public outings can be a great way for the public to see that iguanas are not all scary, dangerous, uncontrollable beasts. Ultimately, though, *you* have to decide if you're ready for outings and car trips, how you'll do them, how you'll transport your iguana, and whether the benefits are worth the risks. Being smart and playing it safe can reduce the all-too-frequent bad press both iguanas and careless herp keepers get.

Part IV
Basic Iguana Care

The 5th Wave   By Rich Tennant

"His diet consists of a lot of greens and vegetables, which he eats sporadically all day long in short feeding bursts. Fortunately, the iguana does too, so we can time their meals together."

In this part . . .

You have an iguana. Now you need to care for him. Feeding your herbivorous iguana means more than just throwing together a bunch of plant stuff from the market or school cafeteria salad bar. In this part, you discover the ins and outs of leafy greens, vegetables and fruits, and why some should be avoided most of the time. You will also find out the best ways and times to feed your iguana to ensure that he eats as much as he needs and is able to digest it under optimal conditions. As no meal is complete without something to drink, you'll also find out how to get that all-important moisture into your iguana.

This part also addresses the problems that arise when you need to be away from your iguana for a period of time. How you prepare your iguana for your departure and how you deal with him once you return home can go a long way towards understanding what he's going to do and reduce your stress levels when you find yourself having to deal with what he actually does.

Chapter 12

Cleaning and Caring for Your Iguana

In This Chapter

▶ Keeping your iguana — and his environment — clean

▶ Disinfecting

▶ Staying safe when you clean

An important part of your iguana's daily and long-term care and health is keeping him and his environment clean. Not coincidentally, this is also an important part of keeping you and your family healthy, too.

Cleaning and disinfecting are addressed separately in this chapter because they're two separate processes, each accomplishing something different. One reason iguana maintenance costs are so high is that you need to keep the things you use for your iguana separate from your household cleaning supplies. Doing so prevents inadvertently poisoning your iguana or his environment with toxic substances and also prevents any cross-contamination between the iguana's wastes and your family.

This chapter also gives you a couple other pointers on caring for your iguana: how to get them detached from clothing and skin (yours) without hurting them and how to keep their claws trimmed.

Rub-a-Dub-Dub — Cleaning the Enclosure

Cleaning removes the organic debris that accumulates in the normal course of day-to-day living: spilled food, feces, urates, saliva, various body secretions (blood and seminal fluids), and shed skin. You need to clean enclosures and surfaces before they can be effectively disinfected. Daily removal of the organic matter helps to reduce the growth of bacteria and fungi between the regular weekly full cleaning and disinfecting. Removing wastes as soon as they're spotted also helps reduce the probability that the iguana will contaminate himself by coming into contact with the feces and urates.

To clean the enclosure, follow these steps:

1. **Remove the furnishings that are not affixed to the enclosure itself: heat pads, bowls, branches, and so on.**

2. **Start the dishes soaking in one container or sink and start the branches, if soiled, in another.**

3. **Wash out the enclosure, using hot, soapy water.**

   The hot water and soap help loosen the stuck-on debris and flush the surface.

4. **If any resistant spots remain after your initial cleaning, use a blunt knife, like a butter knife or putty knife dedicated for this purpose, to scrape them off.**

   Baking soda is good for when you need a little extra ooomph. Sprinkle some on your sponge or directly on the surface area to be scrubbed. You can wet resistant pieces with soapy water and let them sit for a few minutes. Then sprinkle some baking soda on a damp sponge and rub the areas. Rinse thoroughly to remove the debris, soap, and baking soda.

5. **Rinse everything off, using clean water.**

   Ridding the enclosure of all soap residue is important because the residue can interfere with the disinfectant's effectiveness.

If you can't easily rinse your enclosure (in a sink, a bathtub, or outside with a hose), then use a fresh sponge or cleaning cloth dipped in fresh water, wringing it out in a waste container so that you don't contaminate the fresh water with soap or debris.

Any soap safe for animals and children is safe for iguanas. Many environmentally friendly household and dishwashing soaps are available at the supermarket and health food store. Follow the directions on the package for making a dilute solution. *Don't* use soaps or cleansers that are abrasive or that contain pine scents or phenols. And don't use cleaners that contain bleach or ammonia.

Regular household sponges, including those made for nonstick cookware, are great to use for your iguana's enclosure and for his food and water bowls. Just be sure to keep his cage-cleaning sponges separate from his food and water bowl sponges — and keep them all separate from your own household sponges.

What the daily cleaning involves

A simple daily cleaning may involve taking out wastes and changing the substrate. If the walls, climbers, or roosts have been pooped on, you should clean and disinfect them. Clean and disinfect water and food bowls daily.

Keep a spare set of bowls around. That way, you don't have to wait until you've washed and dried the dirty ones to put fresh food and water in the enclosure. Also keep extra pieces of substrate (like indoor/outdoor carpeting) on hand so you always have a clean, dry piece to put in the enclosure, which gives you plenty of time to wash, disinfect, and thoroughly dry the soiled piece.

What the weekly cleaning involves

You should do a thorough cleaning and disinfecting weekly. Empty the inside of the enclosure of all removable objects and then clean and disinfect (see the section "Disinfecting") the floors and walls. If you have ceiling-mounted lights, periodically turn them off, unplug them, and wipe down the fixtures (not the bulbs) with a damp cloth to remove dust. Human heating pads should be turned off, unplugged, wiped down with a damp, soapy cloth, wiped clean, and then wiped down with a disinfectant.

Bathing Your Iguana

Unlike mammals and birds, iguanas don't clean or groom themselves. Iguanas in the wild seem to rely on brushing against rough bark and plunging into bodies of water to remove the grime and parasites that they pick up over the course of living their lives. Given that a captive iguana probably doesn't have much rough bark to rub against or pools to dive into at will, the task of keeping him clean falls to you. To bathe your iguana, follow these steps (remember, though, that "bathing" an iguana *doesn't* mean using soap on him *or* in the water):

1. **Run the water until it's chest deep (the iguana's, not yours!) at the deep end where the drain is.**

   This depth makes the water about iguana-hip deep at the shallow end. If your iguana isn't used to bathing, put less water in the tub and see the following section for tips on getting him comfortable.

2. **Let him soak to his heart's content.**

   If you leave your iguana in the tub long enough for the water to start cooling off (a good bath temperature for iguanas is 85–90 degrees Fahrenheit [29–32 degrees Celsius]), run more warm water into the tub, draining off a little of the cool water.

   The noise of running water can be quite loud in a tub/shower enclosure. If your iguana gets stressed by this noise, fill a pitcher with warm water at the sink and pour it gently into the tub.

3. **When he's done soaking, blot him off to remove the drips and send him on his way.**

4. **Thoroughly clean and disinfect the tub.**

Are sponges dangerous to iguanas?

A hoax warning has been recirculating through the Internet for years. The warning says that pot scrubber sponges are manufactured with a chemical that kills pets. Fact is, they aren't and they don't. The sponge wrapper does indicate that you shouldn't use the sponge to clean aquariums. That's because, according to the manufacturer, little bits of the sponge or scrubber material can be scraped off and clog the filters or be taken in by the fish when they breathe with their gill structures. These sponges pose no threat to iguanas, though the scrubber side may be dangerous to plastic and Plexiglas by scratching the surface.

If any individuals in your household are at high risk for contracting bacterial infections, have your iguana use a different bathroom than the at-risk family members use. Even if you take precautions to thoroughly clean and disinfect the tub, walls, and floor, accidents and distractions can and do happen.

Daily baths are a good idea for several reasons. Iguanas get to soak, which is good for their skin. They get to loll about in an environment that has higher humidity, so they're inhaling air that has more moisture in it. Another benefit is that many iguanas drink deeply when their bodies are in water. But perhaps the most popular reason why iguana keepers bathe their iguanas daily is that most iguanas poop when they're in water. Keeping the enclosure clean is very easy because it's a lot easier to drain the bathtub, thoroughly rinse off the iguana, wash the bathtub out, and then disinfect it before the next use by human or iguana.

Iguanas who are new to baths frequently freak out. Acting like you're trying to kill them, they thrash wildly, scrambling about trying to launch themselves out of the tub, over your head, and out of the room. This scene is enough to make many iguana keepers shrug, dry themselves off, and never try it again. Which is a shame because, if you keep it up, starting off with very shallow water and over time gradually deepening the bath water, iguanas come to tolerate a bath quite well, if not actually look forward to a luxurious soak.

Bath tips

Iguanas are excellent swimmers. They're able to hold their breath for extended periods of time, easily staying fully submerged for 20–30 minutes at a time. This ability tends to freak out iguana keepers who haven't previously seen their iguana looking dead, lying on the bottom of the bath tub. This is not to say that iguanas can't drown. They can. One of the dangers of leaving them unattended in the bath for long periods of time is that the water cools and they get too cold to move. Or something may panic them, causing them to thrash about and inhale water into their lungs.

Some iguana keepers make it easier for their iguana to climb in and out of the tub by placing a rubber bathmat or a rubber-backed bathroom rug over the rim of the tub. Terry cloth towels can be attached to the inside and outside of the tub with Velcro strips. The towels can be easily removed and tossed into the washing machine if they get soiled. If your iguana is bothered by the slick surface of the wet porcelain, put some decals on the bottom of the bathtub (those used to provide a nonslip surface for young children). Another trick is to put a terry cloth towel or rubber bathmat in the tub so the iguana has something to stand on that won't slide out from under him.

If you have two or more iguanas, poop them in the tub, clean and disinfect the tub, and then put them all into the refilled bathtub for a long soak. Obviously, you can only do a joint bath if the iguanas are compatible with each other. If you have iguanas who don't get along with one another, you have to give them each their own soaking session.

Although a long soak in a warm bubble bath may sound like a little bit of heaven on Earth to you, it's not such a good idea for your iguana. In fact, because soaps and disinfectants can irritate their skin, eyes, and mouth, it's best to use just plain water when bathing and rinsing them.

Getting rid of stubborn dirt

Once in a while, especially when taking in an iguana who was ill-cared for, you'll see some feces or undetermined soiling stuck on and between the scales that won't come off with just a good, long soak. Here are a couple of suggestions:

- After you let the iguana soak for a while, use a washcloth or soft children's toothbrush to gently rub at the soiling to remove it.

- If it's still stuck on, you can put a drop or two of a child-safe soap or shampoo on the cloth or brush and work it in; then let the iguana soak some more in fresh, warm water. In 15 minutes or so, work on it some more. You may need to do this several times to get the soiling all off. Whatever remains ground-in will come off when the skin next sheds.

When you're done, toss the washcloth in the washing machine and wash it with hot, soapy water and bleach. The toothbrush can be washed and left to soak for ten minutes in the same disinfectant you use in the iguana's enclosure. Then rinse and dry the toothbrush when it's done soaking. Be sure to store it with the iguana's cleaning supplies and not someplace where a family member may confuse it with his or her own toothbrush.

Regular crankiness

When iguanas are in their pre-shed period (every 4–6 weeks except during the winter months), they tend to get very cranky. During these times, they may darken, stay out of their basking area, and go off food. This behavior is natural and nothing to be concerned about. But daily baths are good for them, even if they haven't eaten enough recently to have anything to poop out. Pick them up gently and bathe them. Or move them when you need to. As the months go on, they will come to know that you will be putting them down soon and not trying to engage them in a petting or play session. They will relax once they see you're heading for the bath and not the front door.

Disinfecting

Disinfecting is a process that kills or neutralizes most microorganisms — neutral as well as harmful organisms. Some disinfectants are made to kill bacteria, some to kill viruses, and others to kill fungi. *Sterilization*, on the other hand, kills *all* organisms. Sometimes, the same product can be used to disinfect and to sterilize, the difference being a matter of the concentration of the chemical in the dilute solution and the amount of time it's left in contact with the item to be sterilized. Unless extenuating circumstances exist (an iguana who is diagnosed with a highly virulent organism or zoonoses and/or an at-risk family member), disinfection, when done properly after a thorough cleaning, produces satisfactory results.

Once the surface has been cleaned and rinsed free of soapy residues, you're ready to disinfect:

1. **Generously apply the disinfectant solution to the surface.**

   Depending on what you're disinfecting, you can spray it on from a spray bottle or dip a clean sponge or cloth in the solution and apply it to the surface. Refer to the section "Types of disinfectants" for info on the types of disinfectants you can use. Whatever disinfectant you decide to use, follow the manufacturer's safety instructions.

2. **Let the solution remain on the surface for at least ten minutes.**

   To be effective, the disinfectant has to remain in contact with the surface for at least ten minutes. If you just spray it on and wipe it off, it acts only as a cleaner, doing what soap and water does for less money and with fewer toxic chemicals.

3. **If the surface is dry once the ten minutes are up, use a clean, damp cloth or sponge to wipe the surface down to remove the residue.**

   If you used bleach, ammonia, or a quaternary ammonia compound, you need to rinse or flush the surface to rid it of the chemicals. If the surface you disinfected is a heavily textured object like a basking or climbing branch, or wire or plastic mesh, you need to saturate the surface of the object to make sure the chemicals are wet enough to flow away.

4. **While you're working on the enclosure, disinfect the clean bowls by submerging them in a sink or plastic tub that's partially filled with the disinfectant solution.**

5. **When you're done cleaning and disinfecting, soak the cleaned sponges and cloths in the disinfectant solution; then rinse and dry them before using them again.**

If your iguana is a free-roamer, potty-training him or getting him to poop in the tub becomes more important because it's hard to disinfect the carpet or a couch.

General disinfecting tips

The tragic incidents of fatal salmonella infections in infants that were traced to the family's iguana or other reptile happened in families where they didn't know that reptiles can carry potentially harmful organisms. Having to regularly and conscientiously clean and disinfect so often may seem like a drag, but it can literally be a life-saving task. Following are some general disinfecting tips:

✔ Stock up on spray bottles and, if using bleach, extra sprayers (even when diluted, bleach can cause rapid deterioration of the sprayer mechanism).

✔ Have on hand several household sponges and cloths so you can use one set to clean, one to rinse, and one to wipe down after disinfecting. Disinfect them all when you are done.

✔ Store all your reptile cleaning and disinfecting equipment together, away from your household cleaning supplies. (Stashing your reptile stuff in a large bucket with a handle, or in a covered tote box, makes it easy to store and grab everything when cleaning time comes.)

✔ Label all bottles of solutions clearly. Write the recipe for the solution on the bottle to make it easier on you when making a new batch. (Even if you do this, you still need to keep them separate from your household supplies.)

Types of disinfectants

What kind of disinfectant you choose depends on the general health of your iguana and whether anyone who regularly comes in contact with your iguana is considered at-risk for medical complications. If your iguana has health problems or you have at-risk family members, you should use the stronger disinfectants; see the section "Heavy hitters: Chlorine and ammonia." If your iguana is generally healthy and you have no at-risk family members, you can use the disinfectants listed in the section "Friendlier disinfectants."

Heavy hitters: Chlorine and ammonia

The two most toxic disinfectants — to humans, animals, and the environment — are chlorine and ammonia. Both are highly toxic when inhaled and ingested, even when diluted to a strength suitable for disinfecting. Because the fumes linger, putting your iguana back into an enclosure that's still damp or contains fumes can be hazardous to his health.

To make a disinfecting solution of bleach, use 4 ounces of bleach per gallon of water. To make a disinfecting solution of ammonia, use 3.5 ounces of ammonia per gallon of water.

Never, ever, *ever* mix bleach and ammonia together in the same container or on the same surface — or even pour them down the drain one after the other. Dangerous, potentially lethal gases are formed when these two chemicals are combined. Read the back labels for household cleaners and dishwashing soaps carefully because a number of them contain ammonia even when the word is not present on the front label.

Some disinfectants made for institutions and veterinary uses, such as Roccal, contain quaternary ammonia. This ammonia compound is also hazardous if ingested (remember that iguana tongue-flicking), although it doesn't smell nearly as much as chlorine, plain ammonia, or cleaners advertising ammonia as an active ingredient. These institutional and veterinary quaternary ammonia products can certainly be used, and you may want to use them if you have an at-risk family member. They're highly toxic to you and your iguana, so care must be taken when using these products and disposing of waste water and other cleaning supplies that have been used with them.

Friendlier disinfectants

If your iguana is generally healthy and you have no at-risk family members, effective but less toxic chemical disinfectants are available, although you may have to go digging for them and pay a bit more for them.

Nolvasan is a veterinary disinfectant. This blue fluid is diluted at the rate of 4–6 tablespoons per gallon of water, so a gallon of Nolvasan lasts a long time. You can buy Nolvasan from your local feed and grain stores or through animal-supply mail-order houses. You can make up the dilute solution and keep it in spray bottles.

In contrast to bleach and ammonia, Nolvasan doesn't have much of an odor and, if used in the dilute solution, doesn't cause harm if the iguana happens to lap at it. Many iguana keepers finish their cleaning and then spray everything down with Nolvasan and let it dry. If you end up having to force-feed an

Sleeping in water

Many iguana keepers find their iguanas spending most of the day, or sleeping at night, in the tub of water in their enclosure. The iguana may be completely submerged or have his body and most of his tail in the water, or he may be draped over the edges in such a way that only part of his body is in the water.

Prolonged soaking can be caused by the temperatures in the enclosure getting too high during the day or night, the onset of shedding, or mites. If any of these is the cause, remedy the problem by checking and correcting the tempertures, getting rid of the mites (see Chapter 21), or doing what you can to ease the shedding discomfort (see Chapter 19).

If the enclosure temperatures are just where they should be, he isn't getting ready to shed, and he doesn't have mites, he may be soaking just because he wants to. Or maybe he is bored with his usual routine or just got sleepy and decided not to move to his usual sleep spot. As long as the soak doesn't go on for days and days, and he once again follows his usual eating, pooping, and thermoregulating routines, don't worry about your iguana spending a weekend at or in the spa.

iguana, you can use Nolvasan solution to soak the syringes and feeding tubes between feedings. You can also soak food and water bowls, sponges, and other cleaning equipment in Nolvasan to disinfect them.

Another option is Hibiclens, the human version of Nolvasan. However, because the veterinary version was developed for use against bacteria and viruses commonly associated with animals rather than humans, you may want to make the extra effort to locate a Nolvasan source.

What about antibacterial soaps and gels?

Several brands of antibacterial soaps are available, but they're soaps, *not* disinfectants. They're not a shortcut to the two-step process of cleaning and disinfecting. The most important part of cleaning hands and surfaces is the agitation of soap — any kind of soap — and water against the skin or surface being cleaned and then rinsing them free of the soapy water. Waterless antibacterial products are okay for use when no water is available, but they are not a replacement for proper cleaning and disinfecting of enclosures or vigorous handwashing.

Protecting Yourself When You Clean

The primary health concern when cleaning and disinfecting your iguana's enclosure (besides waking up a now crabby iguana to move him to a safe location while you mess around in his enclosure or area) is spreading around organisms that can be harmful to humans and other pets.

Disinfecting a wooden enclosure

If your enclosure is made primarily of wood, you may want to think twice about using bleach or ammonia products. Residues left in the enclosure can cause health problems for your animals, with both the liquid and fumes causing internal and external irritation and inflammation. If you do use these chemicals, be sure to flush thoroughly and allow the enclosure and furnishings to dry and air out completely before replacing your iguana inside.

Fecal-oral transmission means that the microorganism is passed either directly through mouth-to-feces contact (with the feces carrying the microorganism) or indirectly through the mouth coming into contact with something that's been contaminated by the feces.

Diseases passed from animal to human are usually transmitted by the fecal-oral route. Fortunately, we can all assume that, although an iguana may eat his own or another iguana's feces, iguana keepers and their children will not intentionally be engaging in that activity. Humans can pick up these microorganisms in other ways, however. For example, if the feces-contaminated water from a water bowl or your pan of soapy water used to clean the tank splashes onto the floor, kitchen counter, or sink, or is poured down the bathtub drain, any organisms in the feces are deposited on the surface. They may be flushed down the drain if they're in a well-rinsed and cleaned sink or tub. But if the sink or tub is not thoroughly flushed with clean water — and even if they are — organisms may remain on the surface.

Contaminated droplets on a kitchen counter or sink rim may go unseen. When the droplet, whether wet or dried, comes into contact with hands preparing food, or with food directly, the organisms are passed from the droplet to the hands or to the food, and then into the mouth.

Types of diseases

Salmonella has been the most publicized of diseases passed from reptile to human. But reptiles carry other diseases, like *E. coli* and *streptococcus*, that can be passed to humans as well.

Most of these organisms cause diarrhea, vomiting, cramps, and other salmonella-like symptoms in humans. In a healthy adult, some of these diseases may go unnoticed or be very mild (similar to a mild flu); they may be quite noticeable, like food poisoning or a bad flu; or they may be serious enough to require hospitalization. Young children with still-developing immune systems and people of all ages who have weakened immune systems are more susceptible to infection by these organisms and may suffer far worse symptoms than a healthy adult.

Who's at risk?

At risk is a term used to refer to certain individuals who are at high risk for getting sick from infectious organisms, such as salmonella. Typically, the people considered to be at risk are children under the age of 5; the elderly; and anyone with a compromised immune system, including cancer patients, organ recipients, and those testing positive for HIV or AIDS. Pregnant women are also considered potentially at risk because some disease organisms can be passed to the developing fetus. Finally, anyone who has an abnormally functioning immune system resulting in frequent illnesses can also be considered at risk. For information on iguanas and human health concerns and how to protect yourself, head to Chapter 23.

The tricky thing is that the reptiles themselves may not look sick or exhibit any signs of illness, such as diarrhea. And, to make things more confusing, the organisms may not be expelled in feces every time the iguana defecates, so having the feces tested for salmonella, for example, may well yield a false negative: The sample tested is negative for salmonella, but the iguana is passing the organism through during other defecation events.

Treating reptiles who have no signs of any salmonella infection is not recommended, even if they do test positive for it. Resistance to antibiotics is growing in reptiles and other animals. Treating reptiles who are not ill may result in humans getting infected with organisms that are resistant to the antibiotics the humans need if they become seriously ill from the infection.

Various protection tips

You can do certain things to protect yourself when you clean your iguana and his enclosure:

- ✔ When cleaning, wear gloves to prevent your hands from coming into direct contact with feces or feces-contaminated objects and wash the gloves (while still on your hands) with hot, soapy water before you start handling the bottles of disinfectant. You can wear reusable household rubber or latex gloves that can be disinfected between uses or get boxes of disposable latex or vinyl gloves from drug or grocery stores, medical supply stores, or mail-order suppliers.

- ✔ If you can, use a sink or utility area washbasin that you don't use for human food preparation, clothes washing, or human baby bathing.

- ✔ Kitchen and bathroom sinks (and bathtubs) can safely be used if you're careful to clean *and disinfect* the entire area (sink or bathtub, counters around the sink or tub, and floor around it) after every iguana cage-cleaning session.

✔ Wear your grubbies instead of good clothing when doing a cleaning job. As soon as you're done, toss them in the washing machine.

Be smart, take these simple precautions, and enjoy your lizard. Just knowing that your iguana may carry diseases and taking care of him and his environment properly drastically reduce the chances of infection.

Detaching Your Iguana from Your Body and Clothing

If this topic sounds amusing to you, you've never had an iguana apparently Velcro-ed to your clothing or flesh. Those sharp, hooked claws are made for sinking into soft things, penetrating enough to prevent the iguana from falling. The claws that enable him to scale a tree in a blinding flash are the very same ones that will shred the top layers of your epidermis.

When an iguana is on cloth, you can't just pull him straight out from the surface he is on, nor can you pull him backward. First try pushing him gently forward. If he walks with a nudge in that direction, you can gently lift him up as he walks, allowing each foot in turn to disengage from the cloth. The other way is to lift each foot individually (with a small iguana, you can use one of your fingers to lift both of his front feet or both of his hind feet at the same time), making sure each claw is free from the cloth.

If your iguana is on your bare skin, the claws disengage a little easier than they do from cloth. If an iguana is in your hair, you need to take care in disentangling your hair from his toes. If you pull too soon, you may injure your iguana's toes. The best thing, of course, is not to let your iguana go on your head to begin with, especially if you're alone with no one else around to help you get him off.

If you pull an iguana away without getting all of his claws out of the cloth, you may find yourself with one less claw to clip during the next pedicure session — as the claw is left dangling from your shirt or from the bloody tip of your iguana's toe. If this situation happens, follow the instructions in Chapter 20 for treating an injured claw.

Claw Trimming

Regularly trimming iguana claws means that handling your iguana will be more pleasant because your arms won't be slashed and shredded by the razor-tipped claws. Trimming the claws is important when you're in the process of taming your iguana, as well as later when your iguana is over 12 pounds and decides to climb your bare leg or arm.

Many iguana keepers think that if they trim the claws, their iguanas won't be able to climb. Fortunately for both the iguana and the iguana keeper's arms, this is not true. The entire claw isn't clipped off, just the thin, razor-sharp extension on the tip of the main claw. Plenty of claw is left for the iguana to climb the things he has to climb on in captivity.

The biggest risk in claw trimming is trimming the claw too short (see Figure 12-1). Blood vessels and nerves are in the main claw, but they only extend about halfway between the end of the toe itself and where the main claw ends. Since you're not trimming into the main claw, there's little risk of cutting the claw so short that you cut into the blood vessels and nerve area. If you do, it's easily dealt with.

When you get ready to trim claws, have close at hand an open container of a blood-stop product (sold in pet stores and through mail order) just in case you accidentally cut through the blood vessel and nerve area of the main claw. If you see a droplet of blood at the tip of a clipped claw, just dip it into the container of blood-stop product. You can use cornstarch to do the same thing. Chapter 20 has more info on how to treat injured claws.

Figure 12-1:
Make sure that you don't trim the claw too short; otherwise, you may cut into a blood vessel.

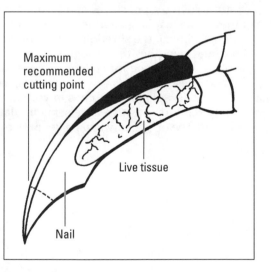

Maximum recommended cutting point

Live tissue

Nail

When you set the clipper on the claw and apply gentle pressure and then hold it, rather than cutting through, give your iguana an opportunity to tell you that you're too high up the claw. He tells you by jerking his hand, trying to get it away from you. If you wait and watch for that signal, then reposition the clipper (moving it farther down the claw or reangling it), and *then* cut, you avoid hitting the blood and nerve supply.

When to trim

You can start trimming hatchling iguanas within their first couple of months. They don't actually need to be trimmed because their claws aren't long enough to scratch you, but starting early gets them used to the sight and feel of the clippers — and of you touching and manipulating their toes.

During the main growing seasons of spring, summer, and fall, you may need to trim the claws at least once every two weeks. Because individual claws sometimes grow at different rates, you may need to trim once a week, trimming different toes each session. During the winter, when the growth rate is slowed, you may be able to go longer between trims.

Regular claw trimming sessions are a great time to check your iguana's toes and feet for any signs of injury or retained shed.

What to use

Several different clippers are sold in the pet stores and through mail order for all clawed pets. Some of them, such as the guillotine style of clipper, tend to shred the end of the cut claw. Although the shredding may not be so bad on a dog or cat who goes outside and smoothes their roughened claw tips by walking on concrete or asphalt, it isn't good for an iguana. Feces and food can get caught in the rough edges. These materials can then be tracked around wherever your iguana walks or inserted into scratches in your arms. Clippers that look like children's safety scissors — with a little semicircular cutting edge cut out of the blades — are the ones many iguana keepers prefer.

Chapter 13

The Good, the Bad, and the Processed: Nutritional Requirements

. . . .

In This Chapter

▶ The general nutritional needs of iguanas

▶ How to provide a proper, nutritious diet

▶ Where to find the foods you need and how to prepare them

▶ Whether to use commercial foods, multivitamins, or calcium supplements

. . . .

Some iguanas are more adventurous than others about testing new foods, which can work in their favor if, for some reason, their regular food sources disappear (like after a fire, long drought, or flood) or if they're displaced to a new location with plants not familiar to them (your home, for example). However, the choices they make can be risky. Although some choices may help them to survive in the short term (if the choices don't kill them first), some of those foods may not be the best for long-term survival.

What this means to you, the iguana keeper, is that you can't let your iguana dictate what he will or will not eat. You may need to work very hard and be very patient to get him feeding on a proper diet. Once you're assured that he is getting what he needs, you can play around with other suitable foods. If he doesn't like something, well, that's okay as long as he's getting the nutrition he needs from what he does eat.

What They Need: An Overview

Research into green iguana nutrition shows that, like humans and other animals, they need more carbohydrates than protein, a lot of fiber, and not too much fat. They also need vitamins, minerals, and trace elements. They can obtain almost all of what they need through a proper selection of fresh leafy greens, vegetables, and fruits.

Although ways exist to ensure that you're feeding a healthy diet and to determine whether your iguana may need additional nutritional support when he's sick or she's gravid, you have to rely on assessing your iguana physically according to growth norms and blood work every year or two to make sure everything is working smoothly. Reptile nutrition research indicates that the following ranges are appropriate for green iguanas:

15–35 percent kilocalories (kcal)	Protein
55–75 percent kcal	Carbohydrates
Less than 10 percent kcal	Fat

A healthy adult, then, would be fed a diet composed of 75 percent kcal from carbohydrates and 15 percent kcal from protein, while a hatchling, juvenile, sick, or gravid iguana will get more protein and, relatively speaking, less carbohydrate. Does this mean you have to become a nutritionist to figure out how to feed your iguana? Fortunately, no, not if you follow some sound iguana dietary recommendations and then do some experimenting on your own, in conjunction with your observations of your iguana's color and behavior and information provided by regular lab work and discussions with your reptile vet.

A Proper Diet

All iguanas are herbivores, which means their diet consists solely of plants, vegetables, and fruit. The challenge is trying to get your iguana to eat all the protein, fiber, and carbohydrates he needs based on the plant foods available to you in your local markets. Iguanas can only take in a certain amount of food, so you need to find a way to provide the quantity of nutrients needed without forcing them to eat more than they can pack in their gut.

Feeding an iguana is more than just throwing together a bunch of vegetables, greens, and fruit. Some foods are good; others are not so good. Some are fine on an occasional basis; others should be avoided altogether. If you're not using commercial iguana food (and I recommend that you do not, at least not as the sole source of your iguana's diet), you need to understand how much of an iguana's diet should come from each group (veggies, greens, and fruit) and what particular food items in each of those groups are best.

Protein

All plants contain some protein; certain plants contain more than others. Some of the higher protein plants have other things in them that make feeding those plants to your iguana on a regular basis a problem. A proper diet contains a mix of foods to provide the necessary protein while reducing the amount of undesirable things in the diet.

When we think of protein, most of us think in terms of animal protein — the protein that comes in things like hamburgers, chicken, and other meats. Your iguana, however, being an herbivore, needs *plant* proteins. So will one bite of your hamburger or turkey sandwich kill your iguana? No. But no one knows how much animal protein is too much or how much may be safe. Too much animal protein can lead to irreversible kidney failure.

Alfalfa: Not just for horses anymore

Mature alfalfa is packed with protein, calcium, and fiber. You won't be setting a bale of hay in your iguana's enclosure, however. Instead, alfalfa can be obtained in several forms that make mixing it into the iguana's vegetable and fruit salad easy:

- You can find powdered alfalfa, alfalfa tablets or capsules, and alfalfa tea at the health food store (or from vitamin mail-order suppliers). All these products are made from the mature leaf. Because they are pure leaf, you add less to the salad than alfalfa in other forms.

- You can find alfalfa pellets made for small mammal feed at the pet store. The pellets are made from both the mature leaf and stems, mixed with vitamins and minerals, and compressed. Be sure to read the labels to ensure that alfalfa is the first listed ingredient and that no animal matter is mixed in.

- Also available at the pet store are small packages of dried alfalfa hay, sold for small mammal bedding. This is the least desirable form because you have to pick out the stems, strip off the leaves, and grind it all down.

- Alfalfa pellets and minibales of dried hay can also be found at feed and grain stores. (If you're going to use the alfalfa pellets, you can presoften them in water or fruit juice if they don't break down in the iguana salad within 24 hours.)

- You can grow your own alfalfa, either from seed or by planting alfalfa sprouts, harvesting the grass once it matures.

Use mature alfalfa instead of alfalfa sprouts. Mature alfalfa is higher in nutrients, including protein and calcium, than alfalfa sprouts. You'd have to feed an awful lot of alfalfa sprouts to your iguana to equal the nutrition of a small amount of mature alfalfa, so much so that your iguana wouldn't have room to eat any of the other foods he needs.

If your iguana doesn't like the taste of alfalfa (and some don't, initially), the alfalfa powder, pulverized tablets, and tea seem to be the least objectionable of the forms. You may want to use them instead of the pellets, adding the alfalfa in small amounts, gradually increasing the amount over a two-week period as your iguana adjusts to the flavor. Although some iguanas will eat their salad with the alfalfa powder or dried leaves sprinkled on top, many won't. If your iguana is in the latter group, you can mix the alfalfa into the salad, dispersing it throughout the vegetables and fruit.

"Beans, beans, the magical fruit . . ."

When people think of plant proteins, beans (kidney, garbanzo, navy, lima, white, black-eyed peas, pinto, black, and so on) are usually the first plants that come to mind. Although beans are high in protein, they're also high in phosphorous and very low in calcium. Some, like garbanzo and soy, are also high in fat. Plain, cooked beans can be used on occasion to provide some variety. If you buy packages of dried beans rather than the already cooked and canned beans, you have to cook the dry beans first, following the directions on the package.

When including cooked beans in your iguana's food, mash or cut the beans, especially if you have a small iguana. Some small iguanas have swallowed whole beans and raw peas that caused an obstruction or that passed through the entire digestive tract and were excreted still in one piece.

Although all the beans mentioned in this section grow in pods, you don't usually find them that way in the store. You can find other members of the legume family still packed in their edible pods: green beans, snow peas, snap peas, pole beans, and so on. You can serve these fresh beans to your iguana raw.

Tofu

Tofu, made from soybeans, is a well-known plant protein source widely used in some Asian and vegetarian cooking. Soy has some problems, however, which make it inappropriate for use as the primary protein source for iguanas. The soft and hard types of tofu are high in fat. Excessive amounts of fat can impede calcium metabolism, so low- or nonfat versions should be used if you're going to offer tofu.

The other problem with tofu is that it's *goitrogenic*, meaning that it binds the iodine in foods, preventing the body from being able to use it. Because the thyroid gland depends on iodine to function properly, feeding too much tofu can result in *hypothyroidism*, a disorder of the thyroid gland that slows the metabolism and causes muscle and joint aches. Besides soy beans and tofu, other goitrogenic plants include broccoli, cabbage, kale, Brussels sprouts, bok choy, soy, and corn. The best way to avoid hypothyroidism in your iguana is to feed these goitrogenic foods sparingly.

Vegetables

Forty to 45 percent of your iguana's food should come from vegetables. Vegetables include hard things like raw green beans, snap peas, snow peas, squash, parsnip, turnips, carrots, and sweet potatoes. Well, squash is technically a fruit, but because of its nutritional value, I include it in with the vegetables. In other words, vegetables are pretty much anything that isn't a leafy green.

Good vegetables

Good vegetables for your iguana include green beans, pole beans, or snap peas; yellow/orange vegetables such as squash, sweet potatoes, yams, or carrots; and some alfalfa. Some other foods that can be used in addition to these foods include cassava (*Manihot esculenta*, sometimes sold as *yucca*), nopales, and other *Opuntia* cactus pads and fruit, as well as more mundane things like turnips. Vegetables such as sweet peppers and mushrooms, and any herb your iguana likes, can be added now and then to vary the flavor and textures you offer.

Use vegetables with lots of calcium oxalates, such as carrots, only occasionally. Calcium oxalates bind calcium, preventing the body from being able to use it. A diet high in calcium oxalates can cause *metabolic bone disease (MBD)* (see Chapter 21 for details). Calcium oxalates can also cause the mineralization of soft tissue — small crystals form in the muscles and organs, causing pain and organ dysfunction.

Bad vegetables (Yes, there are such things)

Some vegetables are marginal in terms of nutrition: iceberg and romaine lettuce, cucumbers, onions, olives, tomatoes, zucchini, radishes, and such. They're great for humans who want to lose a few pounds, but they are exactly the kinds of vegetables that you *don't* want to feed your iguana. Including these foods in your iguana's diet in place of more nutritious foods means you reduce the overall nutrient content of the diet, which, over time, can lead to malnutrition and health problems. If your iguana likes these "junk" foods, offer them as occasional treats, not as a diet staple.

Leafy greens

Leafy greens should comprise at least 40–45 percent of your iguana's diet. Make your primary leafy green selections from collards, dandelions (those grown for humans as well as the pesticide-free ones in your garden), mustards, and escarole. Occasional add-ins include kale, bok choy, chard, broccoli leaves, and endive. Some things to keep in mind:

- Not all leafy greens are good for iguanas, nutritionally speaking. Greens that have too little nutrition include iceberg, butter, Boston, and head lettuces. Romaine is widely available and can be used in combination with more nutritious greens, but it isn't good enough to use by itself for more than a few days (such as when you run out of all the other greens and need to get to the store to buy more).

- Some greens contain high levels of goitrogens, while others contain high levels of calcium oxalates. Because you can't completely avoid feeding your iguana foods containing calcium oxalates or goitrogens, the trick is to be careful in selecting the greens and vegetables you do feed and to ensure that your iguana is getting enough calcium and iodine.

Finding the foods

You can find the fresh vegetables and leafy greens you need in supermarkets in metropolitan areas. In smaller towns or smaller markets in a sprawling metropolis, the store will usually order the greens or vegetables you need if you ask it to. Some produce managers may not be familiar with the food item you're looking for. Give them as much information as you can, including other common names, alternate spellings, and botanical names. A photograph or drawing of the plant may even be useful. If you live in an area where good quality and selection of produce is hard to find all the time or during parts of the year, consider growing your own. If you can't find the seeds locally, you can order them through mail-order seed and garden companies.

Because leafy greens are an important part of their diet, you may want to make the trade-off by feeding vegetables lower in goitrogens and calcium oxalates while still providing sufficient protein and moisture. For example, feeding winter squashes more often than carrots reduces the amount of calcium oxalates but still provides the other nutritional benefits of orange vegetables.

Fruit

Fruits don't add a lot in the way of nutrition. In captive diets, they comprise the smallest portion of the iguana's diet, just as fruits do in the wild. Added to the vegetable-alfalfa salad, fruit adds necessary moisture as well as a little color.

As you have probably guessed, there are good fruits and not-so-good fruits. Deciding what fruits you can feed your iguana becomes a matter of trading off nutrient contribution and the overall level of goitrogens or oxalates.

- All fruits are low in calcium (except figs) and high in phosphorous. Some are goitrogenic.

- Some fruits (the apple, mango, papaya, plum, and strawberry) are low in calcium oxalates, especially in the small quantities added to the iguana diet.

- Other fruits (the rhubarb and star fruit [carambola]) are very high in calcium. Don't feed these to your iguana.

Bananas, grapes, peaches, nectarines, berries, melons, and citrus fruits make tasty treats and can be used occasionally in the salad. Many iguanas seem to relish banana peels as much as or more than the banana itself. Because commercially grown bananas are all sprayed with fungicides, buy organically grown bananas if you want to let your iguana eat the skin.

Grains

Through the years, grains — often in the form of bread and noodles — have been recommended for green iguanas. As with a number of other plants, grains have some nutritional problems associated with their use, including poor calcium:phosphorous ratio. They also don't contribute that much to the fiber or protein content of an iguana diet, and some are also goitrogenic. On the whole, it's best not to include grains as a dietary staple. Instead, offer them on occasion as treats or tasty additions to the main diet.

✔ Cook noodles, pasta, and rice before feeding them to your iguana. Noodles and pasta should be cut into small pieces. (If the noodles and pasta are leftovers from one of your meals, make sure that sauces have been washed off, especially if they are rich, spicy, or fatty, or if they contain cheese and other dairy products.)

✔ You can crumble bread and mix it in the salad or offer a small piece by hand.

Some iguana keepers find that, when they need to get their iguana to take oral medication, the iguana takes it more willingly if it's spread on or rolled up in a piece of bread. Water-soaked bread can also be a way for you to get a dehydrated iguana to get some more fluids in when he isn't drinking enough.

A few iguana keepers have reported that their iguanas exhibited signs of allergic reactions after eating wheat. If your iguana wheezes, salivates, gasps for air, regurgitates, or has diarrhea after eating bread, pasta, or a commercial iguana food or other product containing wheat or oats, get him to a reptile vet and discontinue feeding foods containing wheat or oats.

Preparing Fresh Food

If you don't already have a food processor or chopper, treat yourself to an early birthday present: You're going to need it. Although baby iguanas don't eat very much and it may not take much time each and every morning to manually mince, chop, or shred your baby's vegetables and fruit, a larger iguana can consume astounding quantities of salad as well as a bunch or two of greens each day.

- ✔ Finely chop or shred hard veggies such as green beans and squash. (You can microwave squash for a short time. Doing so makes removing the skin and cutting them into pieces — and then shredding them — easier.)

- ✔ Finely chop or mash fruit.

Some iguanas show a preference for slightly larger-than-rice pieces of food. If your iguana is like this, that's fine. The reason for processing the food into small pieces is so that iguanas can fit more inside of them. A little bigger or smaller is fine, depending on the iguana's preference. Most, however, don't like vegetable mush, and big chunks can be dangerous!

Frozen Dinner, Anyone?

If you need to rely on frozen foods for a period of time, do so. Either buy commercially frozen foods or freeze your own:

- ✔ Buy produce when it's plentiful, put the shredded or chopped foods in labeled and dated food storage containers, and stash them in your freezer. You can even make large batches of salad and freeze them in containers that contain a couple of days' worth of food in each.

- ✔ When freezing your own, be sure to start with fresh, high-quality produce. Freeze leafy greens separately because many become mushy and can slime a salad if premixed into the vegetable-alfalfa-fruit mix.

- ✔ For baby iguanas, you can freeze the food in ice cube trays, placing the frozen cubes in a food storage container. The vegetable-alfalfa-fruit salad freezes and defrosts much nicer than chopped greens, and both do better when frozen separately. You may want to experiment with small amounts first to see how your iguana responds.

- ✔ If you're using frozen foods, be sure to replace the thiamine (vitamin B1) lost from the green vegetables and leafy greens by mixing some thiamine into the defrosted salad.

Some iguana keepers report that their iguanas refuse to eat defrosted vegetable-alfalfa-fruit salad. Although the defrosted salad looks a bit different in color than fresh salad, there's little difference otherwise. If your iguana turns his rostrum up at a bowl of defrosted salad, don't give in. He may well just be trying to train you to give him what he's used to. Frozen food comes in handy during the winter as well as when you have to travel and can't find a caretaker to "cook" for your iguana, so getting him used to eating it is better for both of you.

Finding thiamine

Thiamine (vitamin B1) occurs naturally in plants and animals. When fish and green plants are frozen, the enzyme thiaminase destroys the thiamine when the food is defrosted. Over a period of time, iguanas fed primarily on defrosted green plants develop a thiamine deficiency. Because many of the signs of thiamine deficiency are identical to those of metabolic bone disease (calcium deficiency), someone not familiar with the problem of thiamine deficiencies in plants may mistreat the condition, giving extra calcium instead of thiamine.

Finding thiamine (vitamin B1) is now very easy. Check out your local health food stores and the vitamin supplements aisle at your supermarket or drug store. Thiamine can also be ordered from mail-order vitamin suppliers. Another source is brewer's yeast. This yeast, which is not the same yeast used to make breads rise, is often sold as a nutritional supplement for humans and pets. Look for it in health food stores, health food aisles of supermarkets, and pet stores. Until thiamine became so widely available as a stand-alone supplement, iguana keepers had no choice but to use brewer's yeast to replace the thiamine. Brewer's yeast, however, is high in phosphorous, so try to obtain a B1 supplement instead of using the brewer's yeast, especially when you need to be concerned about metabolic bone disease, such as when feeding a gravid iguana or one recovering from MBD.

What about Commercial Foods?

Pet food products are made to satisfy the pet owner's desire for a quick and easy way to provide nourishment to pets. However, these foods tend to be very high in protein, often using animal protein sources rather than quality plant protein sources. They're often high in fat, which impedes calcium metabolism. The plants most often used are corn, grains, and soy — all foods with minor to serious health impacts when fed consistently and in quantity to iguanas.

If you're going to use a commercial food product, look for a product whose main ingredient is alfalfa and that has little to no corn, grains, or soy. Food products to avoid include those whose first listed ingredients are corn, wheat, wheat middlings, oats, soy, or soy protein; those that have any animal protein (vertebrate and invertebrate); and those whose primary ingredients (besides the extensive listing of vitamins and minerals) are highly goitrogenic plants, problem fruits, and flowers.

If you're feeding your iguana any of the pelleted, chunked, or powdered dry food products, keep these points in mind:

✔ If you use an alfalfa-based food product, make sure that the pellets or powder are thoroughly moistened by presoaking them in water, if the salad itself doesn't have enough moisture to break the pellets down or moisten the powder. Or you can add a bit of water or fruit juice to the salad to enable it to break down the pellets or moisten the powder.

Although many commercial foods instruct the iguana keeper to feed the food dry, feeding a dry food without thoroughly moistening it leads to increased dehydration in iguanas. There's also some risk that the sharp edges of the pieces may cause injury to the gums and tissues farther down the digestive tract.

✔ Frozen products have a higher moisture content but generally have even less nutrition than their dry counterparts. The other concern with frozen foods is the loss of thiamine when the food is defrosted. See the sidebar "Finding thiamine" for details.

Do not use commercial iguana food as the primary or sole component of your iguana's diet. Instead, use it as a *supplemental* protein source. Or you can feed it on an occasional basis as a sort of treat food (if your iguana likes the taste), adding it in or replacing some or all of that day's alfalfa with the commercial food product.

To Supplement or Not

Top reptile veterinarians recommend that iguanas be given both a multivitamin supplement and a calcium supplement. The multivitamin is to ensure that they're getting what they need because it may be missing from their diet. (Many vegetable crops are grown in mineral-depleted soil and may not have what we think they have, nutritionally speaking.) The calcium supplement is recommended because a strictly vegetarian diet is high in phosphorous and low in calcium, and metabolic bone disease (calcium deficiency) is one of the most common health problems with captive green iguanas.

How much vitamin and calcium supplementing you need to do is based on the iguana's age and health status (see Table 13-1). Give just a little pinch when needed.

Table 13-1:	Supplement Schedule	
Age/Health Status	*Multivitamin/Week*	*Calcium/Week*
Under 1 year old	4–5	7
1–2 years old	3–4	5–6
Over 2 years	2–3	4–5
Prebreeding/gravid	2–3	5–6
Sick/emaciated, over 1 year	3–4	5–6

TIP

Top dressing versus mixing it up

No doubt about it, having a tasteless or unpleasant-tasting dry powder on the top of your food is a turnoff. Many books recommend sprinkling the vitamins on top, probably because that's the only way to be sure an iguana who isn't warm enough to begin with, or has a reduced appetite due to illness, is getting all the vitamins. With a healthy, properly heated iguana who virtually vacuums his food bowl clean, this is a nonissue. So be a thoughtful iguana parent and mix the vitamin and calcium supplement into the salad. As the small amounts of powder are spread throughout the salad, they become tasteless and invisible. If you can see the powder after you mix it in, you added too much.

Multivitamin

Several multivitamin supplements are on the market for reptiles, and you can find them at many pet stores and through mail-order herp supplier companies. Or you can use a human supplement, such as a crushed Centrum tablet, which has all the vitamins and minerals and trace elements. Just use a small pinch per serving or the equivalent if adding it to whole batches of salad.

Several spray-on-food vitamins are available. You can compare their list of ingredients with the powdered reptile multivitamins, such as Reptivite and Vitalife, and with Centrum. Keep in mind, though, that several reptile vitamin products don't contain the full spectrum of vitamins, minerals, and trace elements.

Some vitamin products have a taste that your iguana may not like. He may cheerfully gobble down your salad on the days the vitamins are not added but turn up his nose and walk away on vitamin days. If that's the case, you'll have to try another brand. You can always donate that unused bottle to a reptile rescue so that it doesn't go to waste and haunt you every time you open the cupboard.

Calcium

Multivitamins have some calcium but not enough for iguanas, so you need to add some more. In order to provide a balanced diet and boost the calcium needed based on age and health status, you can just add a small pinch of calcium to your iguana's salad.

Vitamins to skip

Spray-on-body vitamin products are available. Although iguanas can absorb some water through their skin, whether or not they can pass vitamins through is questionable because the skin is also made to keep a lot of things outside the body. There's also a dosing problem: These products are formulated generically; yet the vitamin and mineral requirements for a carnivore are probably different from those of an omnivore or an herbivore, like the green iguana. It's probably best to stick with a vitamin that gets into the body by the traditional route — through the mouth. You can also skip vitamins that are to be added to water: They are only good if your iguana drinks the whole thing, but the water will get all slimy from the vitamins long before then.

Most of the calcium supplements sold for reptiles have vitamins A, D3, and E added to them, as well as phosphorous. The reason is that these vitamins and minerals are required for the body to properly metabolize the calcium. But, because these are things your iguana already gets enough of in his diet and multivitamin product, the last thing he needs is more of them. So, when looking for a calcium supplement, look for a plain calcium carbonate supplement — one with no other vitamins or phosphorous added in.

You can buy calcium carbonate tablets or capsules at health food stores, grocery stores, drug stores, or through mail order. You can ask your pharmacist to order food-grade calcium carbonate powder for you. Tablets need to be ground to a powder; capsules already contain powder and just need to be pulled apart to release the contents.

Chapter 14

Brunch Is Served

. . . .

In This Chapter

▶ The right time of day to feed your iguana

▶ What to serve the food in and the best ways to serve it

▶ The facts about overfeeding

▶ How to store foods to keep them fresher longer

▶ Food-safety issues and tips

▶ Ensuring fiber year-round for proper digestion and gut function

. . . .

*O*kay, so you've created the perfect environment, slaved over a kitchen counter putting the finishing touches on a gourmet salad (many iguana keepers find that their iguanas eat better than they do), composed the salad and greens just so on your baby's plate, and . . . nothing. Either your iguana doesn't budge or he walks over, takes a sniff, cocks a suspicious eye at you, and walks away. You stand there, bereft and more insulted than a master chef after being told his four-star soufflé tastes like sludge.

What happened? That depends on your iguana and the overall situation. If you have a hatchling, he doesn't understand what you've put in front of him. And if he's hungry, he still isn't going to sample it with you lurking around; iguanas, like many prey animals, are vulnerable when they're feeding. If your iguana is older but new to you, he may be experiencing diet shock — not recognizing that the multicolored stuff is food. Newly acquired adults and established iguanas, who may have been fed a very different diet, may need some time to get used to it.

How and when food is served may also have a lot to do with your iguana's receptivity to it. Food service also has a lot to do with how your iguana is able to digest the food and make use of the nutrients.

When to Serve

When it comes to feeding your iguana, you need to pay attention to his natural daily rhythms. Not the rhythms you try to overlay on him to fit your schedule, but the ones that have evolved over millions of iguana years.

After your iguana warms up in the morning, his thoughts will turn to food. In the wild, iguanas generally eat once a day. In captivity, most iguanas also do all their eating at one time and then spend the rest of the day lounging and basking, sometimes interrupting that by another visit to the potty place. Some get up and eat again in the early to middle afternoon and then return to their basking place for a few more hours of heat and digestion.

Iguanas do best when you feed them in the morning. If you have to leave for work before 9 a.m., just place the food out right before you leave. If you're home in the mornings, get the food out by 10 a.m. or so. Leave the food in place, replenishing it as needed, throughout the day. Throw away (or compost) the old food at the end of the day.

Some iguanas prefer to eat their greens instead of the vegetable-alfalfa-fruit salad. If this describes your iguana, try placing the salad out in the morning and the greens in the afternoon after the salad has been eaten.

If you work at night, you need to figure out a way to ensure that your iguana is getting fresh food (and a clean enclosure) reasonably early every morning. Some iguana keepers tend to their iguana's needs before they go to bed. Others set their alarm and get up to feed, clean, and spend a little time with their iguana before going back to bed for another several hours.

Having salad and greens already processed and stored in the refrigerator makes serving up food in the mornings quick and easy. Some iguana keepers go one step further and put single servings of food in individual bowls or plates; then they wrap them and store them in the refrigerator, leaving the person who actually serves the food with nothing more to do than whip off the cover and put the bowl in the feeding area.

How to Serve

You'll be happy to know that serving, at least, is a relatively simple affair. The main thing you need to do is pick out a plate, bowl, or dish that your iguana can easily see into and reach his head and neck into. As the iguana grows, you'll need to use bigger serving pieces because not only will his head (and floppy dewlap) get much bigger, but so will the quantity he eats.

For baby iguanas, the bowls and crocks sold in pet stores for reptiles are too big. They may have a small capacity inside, but they're too tall for a hatchling iguana. By the time a young iguana can easily see and reach into the bowl, the inside of it will be too small for his head and his appetite. Some pet stores carry some square, low-rimmed dishes that work well for both food and water for small iguanas. So do plastic and metal jar lids from various food containers and the plates from some microwavable frozen meals. They have very low rims, enabling an iguana to get right up into his food if he needs to.

Use your imagination — and common sense — when looking for serving pieces for your iguana. Sturdy paper plates are fine, but stay away from flimsy paper or foam: Your iguana may decide that they're just as tasty to eat as the rest of his food. Double-welled dog and cat bowls, if they're the right size for your iguana, work well for his food and water. Metal pie plates are great for large iguanas. Jelly roll pans, with their shallow rim and wide, flat surface, are perfectly sized for large iguanas or when you have more than one iguana eating at the same time.

To mix or not to mix

Here's one area where there's no wrong way to do it . . . well, depending on your iguana's eating habits. Some iguanas plow through whatever you put in their bowl, no matter how it's arranged or mixed together. Others want to eat the leaves first and then the salad, although others eat the salad first and then the leaves. With these iguanas, you can put the salad and greens in a serving dish large enough to hold both types of food and let them go at it however they want.

Other iguanas, especially ones new to the foods in the recommended salad, may be picky at first. They may stick to eating only the leafy greens because they recognize only them as being food. They may ignore the salad completely, perhaps pooping on the salad as a commentary on your taste in food, as they go on to gorge on the greens.

Picky eaters

Iguanas can be picky eaters — really picky. Fortunately, it's a condition that's reversible. All you have to do is retrain yourself.

To get reluctant iguanas to eat the proper foods, you need to stick to giving them the right food daily, even if they won't eat it initially. Assuming that your iguana is in good general health, going several days without food won't kill him. Remember that iguanas are ectotherms: Slowing down the metabolism (by staying a bit cooler) slows down the rate that calories (energy) are burned, meaning that an otherwise well-fleshed, healthy iguana will take a long time to starve to death. Nonetheless, it takes a considerable amount of willpower not to give in to that little green glare.

Most iguanas, once they realize that you are not giving in, do give up and start eating. But what happens if yours doesn't? If you can't stand it any longer, or the iguana wasn't particularly healthy or well fleshed to begin with, you can do this: Start by giving him the food he wants but mix it with a little of the food he should be eating. Every day, gradually decrease the amount of bad food and increase the amount of good food until he is, within a week or so, eating only the proper food.

Once he is eating the basic salad and leafy greens, you can try adding a new food item in small amounts. Some new foods he'll like right away; others may take awhile for him to get used to. Some iguanas like a particular food for a long time, and then suddenly one day they treat it like poison. Assuming that nothing is wrong with the food itself, don't worry about it. Chances are that sometime down the line, he'll like it once again. The same thing happens with a new food that he absolutely won't touch right now. Try again in six months or a year, and you may find that he digs into it with relish.

Dangers of Overfeeding — Not!

Can you overfeed an iguana? Nope. Not when you're feeding the right foods. You do need to limit the intake of certain foods — the ones high in goitrogens and calcium oxalates, as well as junk foods. Other than those foods, however, you can let iguanas pig out to their hearts' — and hind guts' — content (see Figure 14-1).

Food consumption changes with the seasons, as well as when the iguana sheds every four to six weeks. In the spring and summer, iguanas tend to pack away a lot of food (the warm season is the time of year in the wild where the food is most plentiful). During the winter, iguanas taper off their food intake. Although they don't stop eating completely, they may only feed lightly or feed once every other day or so. Even though you're providing the same temperatures and photoperiod, their senses — including the parietal eye — trigger normal winter responses in them. In the wild, the winter is the dry season where little food is available, so iguanas reduce their activity levels to match the reduced quantities of plants available to eat and the lower nutritional content of those plants.

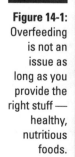

Figure 14-1: Overfeeding is not an issue as long as you provide the right stuff — healthy, nutritious foods.

Photo by Melissa Kaplan

Who's the boss?

Iguanas can be *very* effective trainers of humans. One iguana I took in had — for over two years with her prior humans — refused to eat the recommended foods. Her humans swore that they had tried everything I suggested to get her off monkey biscuits and other unhealthy foods. But nothing worked.

She refused to eat for me, too. She refused for over two weeks, every day watching the other iguanas dive into the platters of salad and greens. Finally, hunger got the best of her, and she sampled the salad. Suddenly, there was no stopping her. She made it very clear to all the other iguanas, many of whom were bigger than she was, that she was going to eat first every day. The alpha male let her do it, too. He'd bob his head when he decided that she'd had enough time for herself, signaling to the others that they could move in and start eating. When her former owner came over one day to watch the feeding, he was astounded to see his girl eat everything she had refused to eat for years.

Storing Foods

Storing iguana salad and greens is a simple matter. The best tip is to use proper food storage containers for the salad. They keep the salad fresher longer than those recycled food containers (like a margarine or whipped cream tub).

Shelf life varies. Determine how long your refrigerator and storage containers will keep the salad fresh-looking and -smelling (some iguanas won't eat it once it starts to oxidize) and then store the salad in containers holding the quantity that will be used up during its shelf life. Containers of salad in excess of that quantity can be stored in the freezer. (Remember to add some thiamine to the defrosted salad before feeding it to your iguana if you end up feeding a lot of defrosted salad.)

Leafy greens will keep for 3–5 days in a zipped storage bag as long as they're dry and the air is squeezed out when you close the bag each time. Leafy greens tend to turn mushy when frozen, so you may want to buy them fresh during the week.

When leafy greens are mixed in with the salad and then stored in the refrigerator and freezer, the combined salad tends to go slimy and smelly sooner than when the salad is stored without the leafy greens. If you're serving them mixed together, you may want to store them separately, mixing them just before serving.

Food Safety

Much of the produce we find in our markets is contaminated with salmonella, just as poultry and eggs are. Although some supermarket chains certify their produce as being pesticide free, not all do. Plants are often purchased with soil still clinging to them and insects crushed or drowned deep in between leafy greens. (And you thought being a vegetarian was healthy!) Fortunately, these are all food-safety issues that can be easily dealt with.

Washing and cleaning

You can wash produce under running water, removing any dirt, roots, and stems at the time. If you are concerned about infections, you can spray vegetables and greens to kill salmonella, and other infectious organisms that are increasingly prevalent in our food chain. Keep two spray bottles — one of vinegar and one of hydrogen peroxide — by your sink or use one of those commercial sprays available at markets and health food stores. Clean, spray, rinse, and then blot the vegetables dry. Once you have processed them (greens torn and spun dry, and vegetables and fruits chopped or minced by hand or machine), pack the mixed vegetable salad into clean food storage containers. Store them in the refrigerator, or some in the refrigerator and the rest in the freezer. Pack the greens into zipper plastic bags, squeezing the air out as you close the bag.

Laboratory research has found that spraying plant and animal food with 3 percent hydrogen peroxide and 100 percent vinegar is effective in killing salmonella, shigella, and E. coli bacteria. One interesting finding is that it's more effective to spray them on one after the other, in any order, rather than to combine them together in a single spray bottle. Rinse foods and surfaces with fresh water after spraying.

Serving

Always serve food and water in clean bowls. If you're in a hurry on work or school days, keep a supply of clean bowls ready to go, dropping the used ones in the sink to soak until later. Leftover food should be disposed of every day.

Clean and disinfect food and water bowls every day. If the bowls are clean other than food residues, you may want to disinfect them by spraying them with vinegar and hydrogen peroxide (see the preceding section). If your iguana has a habit of walking in his poop, however, use a disinfectant such as properly diluted bleach or chlorhexidine diacetate (Nolvasan), soaking the cleaned bowls in the solution for at least ten minutes.

Because iguana enclosures are kept warm, place the food on the cool side of the enclosure. The coolest place is at the far end of the cooler side, down on the floor.

A fun way to vary the way you offer greens or provide treats is to hang some leafy greens (a tasty source of fiber) in their enclosure, using a binder clip (from an office supply store), chip bag clip (from a grocery store), or greens hanger (from a bird supply store) to hold a leafy green or stack of leafy greens onto the side of your iguana's enclosure.

If the weather has turned warm and even the cool side is warmer than usual, set the food bowl in a pie plate that contains bags of ice. The ice surrounding the bowl of food helps keep it cooler longer.

Fortunately, once your iguana is eating heartily and you figure out how much to serve him, you won't have much in the way of leftovers. If leftovers are in the iguana's feeding area, don't save them for the next day or leave them in there for the next day's meal. Toss them out or, better yet, toss them into your compost pile.

Iguanas got guts

The design of the reptilian gut aids in the digestion of food because the folds in the stomach and intestine slow the food's passage. The result is that food is kept in the stomach and intestine longer, giving the enzymes and gut organisms more time to work on it.

Part of your job as iguana keeper is to provide what your iguana's digestive tract needs to function most efficiently. You have to ensure that the diet is healthy and that your food preparation maximizes the food's capacity to be broken down so that as many of the nutrients as possible are made available for use by the iguana's body. This is actually very easy to do: Just provide the proper temperatures and basking area in your iguana's environment and shred or finely chop the food into very small pieces so the gut organisms can more easily break it down.

You also need to make sure that they're getting enough fiber year-round to ensure proper gut function. The leafy greens, hard vegetables, and alfalfa will provide the fiber he needs.

Besides fiber content, activity and temperatures also affect the rate of digestion:

- A more active lizard is going to digest his food faster than an inactive one.

- Higher temperatures speed the activity rate of the gut, moving food through the gut more quickly. When temperatures are higher than they should be, during the day or night, it can cause food to be passed too rapidly through the gut, which will negatively affect overall growth and development.

Chapter 15

But Iguana Go with You! (What to Do When You're Going Away)

Many people get reptiles as pets because they think they'll be able to leave the reptiles home alone when they go away for several days or a week. Silly people. If you have read several chapters in this book already, you've probably guessed that when it comes to green iguanas, the only answer to the "Can I leave my iguana home alone over the weekend?" question is "Babysitter!"

Getting a babysitter doesn't sound too difficult, but wait until you try to actually find one who knows about and is willing to handle green iguanas. And what about your iguana? Should he have a say in who you select? Will he even notice that you're gone? Read on to find out.

When Your Iguana Can't Go with You

If you're going to be away for 24–36 hours, you can probably get away with leaving your iguana alone. Two or more days, however, increases the risk that something may happen. If you're lucky, that "something" may only be your iguana pooping in his water and/or food bowl your first day away. Although a healthy iguana can go a couple of days without food, he does need drinking water available for when he's thirsty. Unfortunately, your thirsty iguana may drink the only water available, even if it happens to be foul. Or he may tip his water bowl over, soaking his enclosure but leaving nothing to drink. And if you aren't so lucky? Well, among other things, make sure that your home insurance policy covers fires.

Iguanas in schools

Iguanas who live in schools pose serious problems because they're generally left at school on weekends, school holidays, and summer vacations. Every year, several schools pay hundreds of thousands of dollars due to fire damage. Worse still is the number of iguanas who are severely stressed, malnourished, and generally unhealthy because of inadequate diet and feeding and because most schools turn off the power during extended breaks. Even if they keep the power supplied to the classrooms and labs, the air-conditioning and heating are turned off, resulting in iguanas who end up severely ill or dead from hypothermia or hyperthermia, depending on the time of year. Classroom reptiles should be checked daily by someone knowledgeable about their care and able to physically handle them, or they should be taken home by the teacher — not students — on weekends, vacations, and summer breaks.

If you're away at work or school for regular periods of time, five days a week, week after week, your iguana gets used to your schedule and to your being gone. This regular cycle of your being home and gone, home and gone, becomes part of his daily routine. Your iguana may even be used to your having a social life outside of your house, adapting to these relatively short periods of time you spend away from home during the week and on weekends. But longer absences, ones not punctuated by your presence at home, are noticed. And they cause him stress — often severe stress.

Stress can lead to various behaviors, including trashing the food and water you left for him and redecorating the enclosure. Redecorating may just mean ripping up the substrate and pulling down his climbers. It can also mean pulling down light fixtures. Because light bulbs are made of glass, the result is often shards of glass all over the enclosure. Other times, the heat fixture may be twisted or may fall just the right way, resulting in the heat source being close enough to a flammable material to start a fire. Not a few homes and school buildings have been destroyed by fire from iguana heat lamps when the humans were absent.

A bored iguana may also try to dig his way out of his enclosure, spending hours scrabbling and clawing at the floor or walls, hitting or rubbing them with his snout. Eventually, claws get ripped out, and the snout gets severely contused or breaks open. So, along with cleaning up the rest of the mess you find in his enclosure, you need to clean dried blood off the enclosure, furnishings, and your very unhappy iguana.

Recruiting a Babysitter

Although there will be times when you can take your iguana with you on vacations and other trips, there will be other times when you can't. To ensure that your iguana is as safe as possible while you're gone, you need to find someone who is able to care for him. Ideally, you want

- ✔ Someone who is responsible and will show up when and as often as agreed on

- ✔ Someone who isn't afraid of iguanas and will actually touch and hold them

- ✔ Someone who will visit at least once a day during daytime hours

- ✔ Someone who will follow your instructions about feeding and cleaning

- ✔ Someone who can easily take your iguana to the reptile vet if something happens or your iguana gets sick

- ✔ Someone who can go out and buy additional food or replacement equipment and supplies if something breaks or runs out while you're on an extended trip

This ideal person tends to preclude the 13-year-old down the street and your son's party-hardy college roommate. It may also rule out your mother if she's terrified of the iguana and your own children if they're uncomfortable with or dislike the iguana.

Finding a babysitter

Finding a babysitter isn't something you should do when you realize that your long-planned-for vacation starts next week. If you regularly take trips out of town on business or just for fun, you should start looking for a qualified iguana sitter at the same time you start looking for an experienced reptile vet: when you first get your iguana. In many instances, finding a reptile vet you like and can work with is considerably easier than finding someone to take care of your iguana for three or four days.

If no one in your family or close circle of friends is experienced enough or comfortable enough to do a good job, you need to look further to find a qualified iguana sitter. If you have friends who are just as picky about the care of their iguana as you are, perhaps you can trade services, with you caring for their iguana the next time they go out of town. If you don't know any other iguana keepers, contact the local herp society to see if any members do iguana sitting.

You can let your fingers do some work, too. Use the Internet to look for local iguana keepers who may be able to iguana sit. Iguana e-mail discussion groups are a good way to meet other iguana keepers, and there are Web sites with lists of iguana keepers who iguana sit. You can also check the Yellow Pages and pet stores, and check with your vet to find out about reputable pet sitters. Because many pet sitters don't have experience with iguanas or may not be knowledgeable about proper iguana care, expect to do some careful screening and make as many calls as necessary to find one or more who is experienced with iguanas.

Reptile vets may be a good resource for another reason: They may have veterinary technicians or other staff who are experienced in handling iguanas and who may be willing to sit for you. The nice thing is that they should be able to tell if something is wrong with your iguana and know of a good vet to take him to. If your iguana requires special daily care, such as injections, vet techs are experienced in giving them.

Don't assume that all reptile vet techs and staff know proper iguana care, such as diet, interpreting behavior, and so on. As with other people, you may still have to teach them how and why you want things done the way you do. You should also watch them handling your iguana to make sure that they know how to do it properly and safely.

The minimum care you should accept

Okay, you have tried and tried, but the Iguana Babysitting Goddess hasn't blessed you with the prefect sitter. Is it time to cancel your vacation? Maybe not. But it is time to decide how much you're willing to compromise in the care you want for your iguana. Here's the minimum care you should accept:

- Although you ideally want someone who can stop in twice a day, once a day can do if necessary.

- You need someone who can handle dishing out the salad and greens, even if that person can't handle adding the vitamins and calcium supplement.

  Unless your iguana is gravid or recovering from metabolic bone disease, he will do fine missing his supplements for a week or so. Otherwise, you can mix small amounts of the vitamin and/or calcium supplement into the food you prepare and stash it in the refrigerator or freezer for use by the iguana sitter while you're gone.

- You need someone who won't hesitate to get into the enclosure to do the necessary cleaning and feeding and to check out the equipment.

- Mostly, you need someone who isn't afraid of iguanas because if that person is, your iguana will know and may well exploit the sitter's fear mercilessly — whipping, lunging, or possibly even snapping at or biting him or her.

- There's another reason that you want someone who isn't afraid of iguanas, especially if your iguana is tame: You need the sitter to *handle* your iguana while you're gone.

Ideally, you want a sitter who will spend some quality time with the iguana during every visit — perhaps letting him free-roam for a while, getting him into the bath, and just sitting and petting him for ten minutes or so. These are activities your iguana enjoys when you're home. Having someone do them while you're gone helps reduce his stress levels a little. You also want the sitter to be able to catch, pick up, and handle your iguana in case something happens and the iguana needs to be removed from the enclosure or taken somewhere.

Some iguanas may take advantage of being let out of their enclosures and go hide somewhere or squeeze themselves in someplace from where it's difficult to extract them. Having a sitter who knows how to find them and extract them helps ease your mind and the sitter's mind.

What about Boarding My Iguana?

A couple options are available for boarding your iguana: a veterinarian's office or another iguana keeper.

Although reptile vets are able to handle iguanas appropriately during office visits and when you have to leave them for a few hours or overnight, longer stays may pose a problem. Few vets have boarding facilities for anything other than dogs and cats. Your iguana will be sitting in a steel cubicle surrounded by species he may not like or may be frightened of. And it's difficult to heat a cage or open-fronted steel box.

Boarded dogs and cats also don't require as much daily care as an iguana. With dogs and cats, the general care is food (from a box, bag, or can), water, and some time in the dog or cat run while the cages are being cleaned. Your iguana, on the other hand, requires very special food as well as food preps, needs very specific day and night temperatures, has daily bathing needs, and must be taken out for a stretch under the close supervision of someone who's comfortable handling him. Often, there's simply not enough time or staffing for a vet's office to handle all the daily clinic needs, basic boarding duties, and quality cuddle time with a lonely iguana who has stress-induced diarrhea. Based on the number of stories I've heard about iguanas who have returned home with injured tails, limbs, and snouts, vet office boarding should be a last choice.

The best option for boarding your iguana, if it comes to that, is finding another iguana keeper whom you know and trust to care for your iguana. If you don't know of anyone yourself, try the online Iguana Sitters listing, at http://www.icomm.ca/dragon/sitter.htm.

The bottom line is that boarding an iguana anywhere is very stressful for the iguana. While boarding in an iguana-friendly environment with humans who understand iguanas and who will spend some time every day in social contact (rather than just doing feeding and maintenance) will *not* eliminate the stress, it will reduce it. The benefit is that, instead of coming home to an injured and ticked-off iguana, you come home to one who is merely ticked off. If your iguana already knows and likes the person who will be boarding or babysitting, it can help reduce the stress even more, so try to arrange some "get acquainted" time for your iguana and the human who will be caring for him during the weeks prior to your departure.

Preparing for Departure

Obviously, your iguana will do best if you simply don't leave or if you take him with you. Because that may not be possible, you can do something to help reduce the overall stress and increase the likelihood of his continuing to eat and poop while you're gone: You can transition him into your absence by having the iguana sitter start working with the iguana several days before you leave.

The initial meeting

If the iguana doesn't know the sitter, this meeting and interaction before you leave is important for several reasons. First, it gives you a chance to see whether the sitter really does know what he or she is doing when it comes to handling iguanas. Second, you get a chance to see whether your iguana likes the person. If he is comfortable with the person, he'll wear his usual colors; if he likes the person, he'll wear his happy colors. If your iguana rapidly turns dark or brown and doesn't lighten back up until you hold him for a while or until after the person leaves, it's a clear sign that your iguana doesn't like the person. If this person sits for you, chances are your iguana won't eat much, may vigorously redecorate his enclosure with organic substances, or may just sulk in the darkest, coolest part of his enclosure while you're gone.

You think I don't know you're leaving?

As you have probably figured out by now, iguanas recognize objects and their humans' behavior patterns. If you travel regularly on business, don't be surprised when your iguana recognizes the signs of your impending trip. Iguanas have been known to start acting out before their keepers leave when they see evidence of an upcoming trip: suitcases and travel bags. If you see that your iguana's behavior changes when he sees your bags, keep them out of his sight until you're ready to leave. Doing so reduces the overall length of time he is under increased stress.

Eventually, though, your iguana will get used to these routine absences. In this type of situation, you may be able to prepare your iguana for your absence by letting him see the bags the day before you leave.

Trial run

When an iguana sitter is suddenly sprung on an iguana — one day the keeper is there and the next day not — the iguana will not be happy. The result will be an iguana who eats little to nothing while his keeper is gone or who acts out at the sitter, biting, whipping, poop painting, food fighting, or sulking in a corner the whole time. A free-roamer may just crawl under a piece of heavy furniture and hide, refusing to come out until you come home and drag him out. On the other hand, your iguana may be a perfect angel for the sitter and act out when *you* come home. And all of this is why, before you leave, you want the sitter to do a trial run.

A trial run involves having the iguana sitter come over several times during the week or so before you leave. During the visits, the sitter should hold and talk to the iguana, take him out of his enclosure, give him baths, and move him from his free-roaming basking area to another spot or put him back in his enclosure. The sitter should also clean the enclosure just as he or she would if you weren't there and take out the old food and water bowls and put in fresh food and water.

During the first visit, you should be there, talking with the iguana and the sitter while the sitter works with the iguana. On subsequent visits, start making yourself scarce. By the last trial visit, don't be in the room at all.

Finding a sitter who will do three or four previsits like this may be hard. It may be harder to explain to prospective sitters why you want the trial run done. The reasons, though, are simple: You want your iguana to have as normal a routine as possible when you're gone. Having him cared for by someone he knows and who has fed, cleaned, and handled him before — with you there — means he is more likely to accept this person doing all these things when you're not there. The less stress your iguana is feeling, the better are his chances of eating while you're gone, of pooping when he should (or at least daily), and of maintaining a regular thermoregulatory pattern — doing his usual basking and lounging throughout the day. Good sitters can be hard to find and should be compensated accordingly. Unless you will be trading babysitting services with another iguana keeper, consider paying a sitter for the trial run and actual sitting job just one of the ongoing expenses of keeping an iguana.

When You Get Back Home

Remember that sweet, tame, potty-trained, green angel who lived in your home and shared your life before you went on your trip? Well, don't be surprised to find his evil twin in residence when you return. He may initially resemble your own iguana, but after the initial greeting, you can expect Dr. Jekyll to rapidly disappear as Mr. Hyde emerges to let you know, in no uncertain terms, just how displeased he was with your absence.

Your iguana, who has always been a clean-plater, finishing off every last crumb of food, may now refuse to eat. He may totally ignore the food or poop in it or see how rapidly he can disperse it over the widest possible area. Did you used to spend some quality cuddle time every day? Expect to be whipped, see lots of dewlap, and perhaps be nipped for your efforts. Was your iguana potty-trained, with no accidents for you can't remember how long? Expect accidents to happen daily, often where they're least welcomed, like on those papers you brought home from the office or on your best shoes or on your recently reupholstered couch. Under the bedcovers is also a highly favored retaliatory pooping place.

In some cases, iguanas who have given their sitters a very difficult time may return to being their perfectly behaved selves once you return. Some are so glad to see their keepers (and daily routines restored) that they act normally for a day or two before it occurs to them to make you pay for leaving them behind. Whether your iguana acts out from the moment you return home or a couple of days after you return, you can expect this acting-out behavior, which may last for several weeks, before your iguana resumes his pretrip behavior. If you board your iguana while you're gone, you can expect to see this acting-out behavior once you bring him back home again. As with iguanas who are left at home with a sitter, the behavior may start as soon as the iguana sees you or once he has been back home for a day or so.

There's nothing you can do to avoid these behavioral shifts. You may need to revert to some of your early behavior yourself, from back in the days when you were starting to tame and socialize your iguana — reestablishing the daily routine, picking him up and handling him at times when he's trying to make you go away, and so on. If your iguana is otherwise in good health and well fleshed, his not eating for several days or a week shouldn't be a problem; once he has made you pay enough for your boarding him or going away, he'll start eating once again.

Finally, the more highly socialized an iguana is — the more he's used to spending time with other people in places other than his own home — the more easily he'll take to being boarded or having an iguana sitter. If you have a highly socialized iguana and you need to travel a lot without him, he may act out less overall, and although he'll still miss you, he won't be as stressed as a less socialized iguana or one who rarely spends time away from home or in the care of others.

Part V
Socializing Your Iguana

The 5th Wave   By Rich Tennant

"Darlene! I said you could bring your iguana to work as long as you check the tanning beds BEFORE you send a customer in there."

In this part . . .

What's the difference between untamed iguanas and socialized ones? Their reaction to their humans. The reaction of an untamed or barely tamed iguana to its keeper's contact is going to be "RUN! It's a human!" A well-socialized iguana, on the other hand, is unlikely to do more than cock an eye at its keeper, as if to say, "Oh, it's you again, huh? Yawn." A tame but unsocialized iguana will come to an alert state but won't thrash around. Much.

While previous chapters covered some aspects of iguana behavior and communication, this section goes into far more detail. From building trust to building interspecies communication bridges, the information and techniques covered in these chapters are useful when working with untamed or unsociable iguanas of all ages.

Chapter 16

Gettin' Iggy with It

In This Chapter

▶ Understanding how iguanas get along with each other and you

▶ Figuring out your place in iguana society

▶ Strategies for handling iguanas of all ages

*A*ll the work of setting up the proper environment and getting the diet all sorted out is the easy part. Perhaps you have noticed that your iguana has been less than thrilled with your messing around his enclosure. Less than impressed by your sacrificing several months of your entertainment budget to buy the super-duper food processor so his food is made just so. Are you getting splashed a bit more than you think a gratified iguana should splash when you lower him into his luxury bath? If so, congratulations: You have a normal iguana! Unless you were lucky enough to acquire an already tamed and socialized adult, you now get to spend the next nine months or so taming him.

Iguanas Are Social Animals

In the wild, iguanas hang out with iguanas, mate with iguanas, get territorial with iguanas, feed with iguanas, sleep with iguanas, bob at iguanas, fight with iguanas, and ignore iguanas. Although there may be some passing interactions with other species of animals who are not predators, a green iguana in the wild interacts primarily with other green iguanas.

By understanding how and why an iguana behaves the way it does, you can get a better understanding of your role in iguana society. And *that* information can help as you tame and socialize your iguana, as explained in Chapter 17.

Aggressive behavior: Hey, you, get offa my cloud!

Aggression runs the gamut of behavior from violent attacks to well-understood (by other iguanas) ritualized behavior sequences to relatively mild behaviors. (*Ritualized behavior* is a specific sequence of postures that may be used to avoid serious physical injury.) Iguanas may become aggressive for various reasons:

- **To protect their property.** Protecting property to an iguana can include establishing a new territory, displacing another iguana from his territory, expanding existing territory, reaffirming existing territory, and defending the existing territory from a real or perceived interloper.

- **To maintain their status within the social group.** To an iguana, status within the group can also be considered property, and an iguana may defend his status as aggressively as physical territory.

- **To gain (or maintain) access to as many choice mates as possible.** Because males try to mate with as many females as possible during the course of the relatively short breeding season, you're more likely to see aggressive behavior by males — related to their obtaining access to preferred females and keeping potential suitors away from those females — than to see aggressive, possessive behavior by females.

Violent attacks are not as common as you might think. When a subordinate (or *omega*) iguana is desperate or feels cornered with no other recourse, he may launch himself into an attack with the intent to inflict bodily harm. Most times, however, the physical contact is limited to head butting — with one iguana ramming his head into the neck or torso of the other iguana, with both of them pushing against one another. Head-to-head face-offs may also occur — with the iguanas hunched up to increase the height of their dorsal spikes, dewlaps flared, inching forward and back, looking for an opening, or trying to look big and tough enough to force the other iguana to back down.

Less physically harmful forms of aggression include scent marking (primarily males, who mark by dragging their femoral pore plugs along the surface they're walking on), posturing (see Figure 16-1), and bobbing.

Generally, an iguana who is lower in status attacks a higher status iguana. The higher the status, the less need there is to defend status and territory violently, because ritualized posturing and scent marking are usually enough to dissuade subordinate iguanas.

In captivity, when iguanas are too often kept in too small a space for their needs, aggressive acts may be initiated by the dominant male against other males, even females, due to the normal social stresses being compounded by the forced close proximity. Such attacks are also more likely to result in serious injury.

Figure 16-1:
Male posturing, although a less harmful form of aggression, still makes a point.

Photo by Melissa Kaplan

Appeasement behavior: Whatever you say, boss

Appeasement behavior signals defeat or is otherwise used to defuse another's real or threatened aggressive act. Appeasement behavior is also ritualized. With green iguanas, appeasement may be signaled by relaxing the muscles along the dorsal crest, which lowers the dorsal and nuchal spikes, as well as tucking the dewlap up toward the throat and neck. Another appeasement posture is for the appeaser to lower his head and body until they're touching the surface the iguana is standing on (see Figure 16-2). The bright scale colors signaling excitement may also fade, though it's not done consciously by the iguana.

Avoidance behavior: I am not here

Avoidance behavior lets iguanas side-step threatened aggression altogether. By closing his eyes, turning away, or walking away, an iguana can avoid a stressful situation, including another iguana who is acting in a threatening or intimidating way. Avoidance is not necessarily a submissive behavior; dominant iguanas will avoid subordinate iguanas who are behaving in an annoying manner, such as bobbing at them or trying to grab them by the neck and mount them.

Photo by Melissa Kaplan

Figure 16-2:
How *low*
can you go?
The
appease-
ment
posture.

Affiliative behavior: Can't we all just get along?

Many birds and mammals engage in *affiliative behaviors* that build and maintain social bonds. Behaviors such as grooming each other (feather grooming by parrots, for example, or primates cleaning a troop member's fur), feeding one another, playing with each other, and just plain lolling around physically with one or more members of the social group are all affiliative.

With wild iguanas, there are apparently no comparable behaviors. Iguanas have not been seen grooming each other (by picking off stubborn dorsal spike shed, for example), feeding each other, or playing with each other. The primary affiliative behavior seen in iguanas seems to be sharing a basking or sleeping area.

One of the things that many iguana keepers find fascinating is that, despite the apparent lack of affiliative behaviors among groups of wild iguanas, tame captive iguanas do respond favorably to some affiliative behaviors when initiated by their humans — things like petting, picking shed, being hand-fed treats, and being carried around by or lying on or next to the keeper.

Who's in Charge Here? Your Role in Iguana Society

So where do you fit into this society fraught with behavioral booby traps? You, in a sense, become an iguana. Accepting this fact will get you farther, faster, than trying to force your iguana to think and react like a human — or even like a dog or a cat. Thinking like an iguana, as well as viewing the world — and yourself — as an iguana sees it, helps you better understand why your iguana acts and reacts as he does and how to communicate with your iguana. This, in turn, helps you establish your social relationship with him.

If you're going to be an iguana, you'd better be the dominant iguana in your household. If other family members are going to be interacting or otherwise coming into contact with the iguana, they, too, have to be of higher status than the iguana, which means they have to be active participants in the taming process. The following sections tell you what kind of behavior you can expect from iguanas at various ages and how you should interact with them to make sure that you remain head of the iguana household.

There is no set definition of *hatchling, juvenile,* and *adult* iguana. Different iguana keepers, biologists, and veterinarians have defined them in different ways, using physical development, size, and behaviors as the determinants. In this book, I go by the following meanings:

- ✔ *Hatchlings* are iguanas ranging from just hatched to about 9–12 months of age. They are still small in size and would be very low status in the wild.

- ✔ *Juveniles* range from those who are just short of going through the developmental changes leading to sexual maturity through those going through their first breeding season, or to about two years of age.

- ✔ *Adults* range from young adults (two plus years) to more mature adults (five plus years).

- ✔ *Seniors* aren't that much different from mature adults, but health problems may start to creep up, affecting vision, locomotion, and other physiological processes. How the iguana has been cared for (including diet) determines this stage of growth and decline, which may start at seven years or not until well past the tenth year.

Start working to establish your status and social standing from the start, even if your iguana is a hatchling. Although older iguanas can be tamed and retrained, it's much easier to tame them properly from the outset instead of trying to get them to forget the fact that you used to be such a wimp.

Baby iguanas: More bark than bite

During the first week or more of your iguana's life with you, he'll be on guard all the time, keeping an eye on you, running away from you, and trying to figure you out. After a couple of weeks have gone by, he'll start feeling a bit more secure. Where before the iguana was fearful and reacted out of fear, he now starts watching you more closely and takes steps to test your mettle. This is a subtle, but important, difference. Essentially, he's testing to see who is boss. Tiny though it may be, your hatchling's dewlap will be flared at times, and the body may be presented broadside, laterally compressed to make him look bigger. Although you may think this looks incredibly adorable, the iguana is actually trying to make himself big and scary.

When you go to pick him up, he may still run away as he did before, but now the reason isn't so much fear. He's trying to escape you long enough for you to tire and go away and leave him alone. Right here is where most new iguana owners make their first mistake: They walk away or put the iguana down. True, some iguanas, left to their own devices and their own time frame (which can take years), may become comfortable and tame and accepting of humans. But most don't. Because there's no way of telling whether or not your iguana is one of the rare ones, take an active role in the taming and socializing rather than crossing your fingers and waiting.

When you do catch him, expect to be subjected to tail whippings and alligator rolls and maybe even some open-mouth threats. The iguana is going to be acting partly out of fear and partly out of seeing just how far he has to go until you put him down. You, of course, should not put him down. If you do put him down in response to this type of behavior or, worse, give up and walk away when trying to get him out of his enclosure, you have lost status and the iguana has gained it. This fact will make it even harder for you to catch him the next time, and once you do, you can expect more of a struggle as he tries to get you to put him down.

Most iguanas don't get any worse than a spirited thrashing, whipping, clawing, rolling, dewlap flaring, and generous display of their tongue and throat. Some, however, may feel compelled to go one step further and actually bite. Although hatchling iguanas have a full complement of teeth, being bitten on the hands or fingers (or nose, as has happened) by a hatchling is far preferable to being bitten by an adult. Their smaller jaws exert less pressure, and their tiny teeth penetrate less deeply into your skin. Nonetheless, a pretty parallel row of punctures or slashes may be left to mark this rite of passage.

When you go to pick up your iguana, don't come swooping in from overhead. Instead, move your hand in from the side or in front of the iguana. Predators fly overhead or strike from above. Even tame iguanas can startle and launch into flight or fight if suddenly and rapidly approached from above by an otherwise familiar human.

Juvenile iguanas: Bark and bite

Relax. It isn't that a juvenile is more likely to bite — just that it's going to hurt a lot more if he does.

A tame juvenile is comfortable with the daily routines of the household. He is growing increasingly comfortable with being handled and carried about, and he enjoys excursions out of the house. Still, you may encounter unexpected bouts of regression. It isn't unusual to wake up one morning to find, instead of the sweet, relaxed iguana you put to bed the night before, a hellion with flashing tail, claws, and teeth. Just carry on with your normal routines and interactions, knowing that you didn't do anything to make your iguana suddenly hate you or slip a gear into psychosis.

Think of this period as middle-late childhood turning into the teenage years. Raging hormones, rapid growth, and a changing world view result in some unpredictable behavioral shifts as the iguana tries to adapt to all the physical and physiological changes happening within him. It's also a time of trying to make change happen outside himself as he tries to increase his status within your social group. The best thing to do is to just roll with the punches (and scratches and tail-whips). Maintain your daily routines with the iguana, including spending time with him even though you might really want to send him to his room without dinner. Remember that you have a vested interest in being the head of the human-iguana social structure, and so reassert yourself as necessary in daily encounters.

Adult iguanas: An armful — literally

If you have worked diligently to tame and socialize your iguana and he is of the usual iguana temperament, you now have a big adult who is companionable throughout the year except, perhaps, during breeding season. Unless you move or make significant changes in his enclosure or free-roaming area, he knows his environment inside out and has created his own daily and seasonal routines.

While you won't be spending as much time as you did focused on taming and socialization, now is not the time to just ignore him, either. Keep up the daily encounters, spending time with him, talking to him, taking him on outings. The longer you leave some iguanas alone, other than to clean and feed, the more the chance that they will regress into being less tame and the higher the risk you may be "surprised" by "sudden" aggression.

Does my iguana hate me?

Whether your iguana was bred on a farm with tens of thousands of other iguanas or was caught in the wild, one of his earliest experiences was of huge bipedal creatures stomping around throwing food. These creatures then chased him, grabbed him none too gently, and crammed him into a cloth bag with dozens of other hatchlings who were similarly terrified and pooping all over one another. After a long, noisy, bumpy period of time, the iguana was dumped out of the bag into a huge cage with all the other iguanas . . . by another human. Other humans came around and maybe put some food in and took feces out . . . but maybe not. Soon enough, however, a human came along and started grabbing iguanas again, including your little fellow. Back into a bag and box and

back on the road again. Finally, the iguana was disgorged into a pet store's iguana tank.

You're probably beginning to see why your iguana may not initially be overly grateful for the fine enclosure and gourmet food you lovingly prepare for him every day. Iguanas, having not been treated particularly well by humans, are highly suspicious of all humans. For all they know, your good intentions are just a prelude to dinner — with the iguana as the entree. Certainly, up until now, humans have done nothing to make the iguana the least bit trusting or accepting of them.

So, no, he doesn't hate you, but it will be some time before he comes to trust you and understand his strange new life with you.

Senior citizens: The powerhouse continues

The senior iguana is much the same as he was in early and middle adulthood — set in his routines and generally comfortable and complacent with his humans and other long-term nonhuman members of the household. Slowly, however, some aging shows as little things start to go wrong. Visual acuity may fade, making moving around, climbing, even self-feeding, difficult. Joints may start to stiffen up, especially if the iguana is susceptible to the oxalates in his diet. The chronic dehydration of years past may begin to take its toll on the kidneys. Fighting off infections may be tougher for the senior.

Behaviorally, the senior acts much the same, though pain, discomfort, and confusion as a result of the physiological changes may cause restlessness or decreased activity — and occasional crankiness. As much as possible, maintaining your senior's daily routine is important, to reduce unintentional stress on him.

Chapter 17

No, They Don't Get Tame All by Themselves

*N*ew iguana keepers spend the first week or so with their new iguana in a sort of honeymoon fog. The iguana is generally quiet, often unresisting when the keeper goes to clean or feed, although there is usually some resistance when the keeper tries to pick up the iguana. Such iguana keepers, if they even think about it at all, think how lucky they are that they got a tame iguana.

After a week or so, that rosy haze starts to fade as the iguana starts acting, well, not so tame. The tail whipping increases in frequency, intensity, and accuracy. The iguana seems to have been training for the Olympics, beating his personal best in the 50-gallon dash. If the iguana keeper is lucky (or not, depending on the point of view), he or she may get his or her first sight of the inside of the iguana's throat and at the tiny dewlap. "Why does my iguana suddenly hate me?" is the question most often voiced by iguana keepers when they reach this stage. Fortunately, the behavior has nothing to do with hate — just fear and distrust, both motivations more easily changed than hate.

An untamed iguana is under a lot of stress every time it sees or is forced to interact with humans. Tamed iguanas are more relaxed and often beneficially stimulated by interactions with humans. Although the initial taming and training process is itself stressful, taming and acceptance are accomplished more quickly when you actively work with your iguana, resulting in less time overall under acute stress.

Building Trust

Grabbed and tossed about, gawked at and terrorized by humans from the time they hatched, and often stared at by predators housed in tanks all around them at the pet store, recognizing your good intentions and automatically trusting in you are the last things going through the iguana's small, wild, lizard brain. You can help him overcome the fear and distrust, however.

- ✔ Give your iguana a couple of weeks to settle in, to start feeding freely throughout the day, and to get used to the daily routine you establish as part of your regular care.

  Things to keep on schedule or in a routine include the time lights go on and off, bath time, feeding time, the food and water bowls used, the times you're likely to appear and interact with him, and even the times you just look at and talk to him. Modifications, fine-tuning, and spontaneity can happen later on, but when just starting out, make a schedule and stick to it.

- ✔ If you have children, dogs, cats, or other nosy pets, keep them quiet around the iguana and keep all of them away from the enclosure for prolonged periods of staring — especially the cats.

- ✔ During these early weeks, let your iguana see and hear you. Doing so helps him get used to and eventually recognize your voice, and it helps him get used to seeing you move around and do things.

- ✔ Individual iguanas learn to recognize their names as well as the names of other iguanas, family members, and pets. If you have a name picked out by the time you get him home, use it. If it takes you a few days to think of one, that's okay, especially if you use some words or phrases that you'll probably always use when talking to him — like "baby," "lizard face," or "monster man."

- ✔ Iguanas, like all animals, communicate using body language. They also have two main vocalizations — the hiss and a guttural click-hiss. Eventually, iguanas will learn to adapt their language to communicate things to you, like hunger, dislike, wanting to be left alone, time for a bath, and time for some attention. You need to make an effort to read and talk Iguana. In the early days, it's necessary to know what not to say as well as what to say. See Chapter 7 for details.

Taking Your Iguana in Hand

Handling an iguana generally includes approaching, grabbing/picking up, holding, and releasing the iguana. The biggest challenge most new iguana keepers face in handling is getting the iguana in hand to begin with, preferably without ending up staring in shock at the tail wriggling around several inches (or feet) from the rest of the iguana.

Approaching your iguana

Approach your iguana from the front and side so that he can see you coming. While you will still be scary, you will be a little less threatening coming in low rather than from on high. (Doing this, unfortunately, is almost impossible in an enclosure that opens only at the top.)

In the beginning, regardless of the direction and altitude of your approaches, your iguana isn't going to like any of them. Even though he has had a chance to watch and listen to you for a couple of weeks, and you've never made an ill-intentioned move toward him when you've entered his enclosure to feed and clean and arrange things, he doesn't trust you yet.

You need to overcome your own reticence and his and pick him up. You'll probably have to spend several minutes or more with your hand(s) futilely chasing him around his enclosure. Stick with it until you actually get your hand around him and lift him up. Once you get him in hand, keep him in hand for at least a minute, making it very clear that it's your decision to put him down, not anything he has done.

Before initiating a pickup session, make the area secure. Close the door to the room. Turn off any light fixtures resting on top of the enclosure and put them to one side. Move any other breakables to a safe place. Make sure that you have secure footing and can move around freely as you try to get your iguana. You won't be helping matters if you fall down with a yell or if things start falling and breaking into pieces when you lose your balance. Give yourself the best possible advantage by at least making safe an already difficult situation.

Picking up and putting down your iguana

One trick that often makes picking up your iguana easier is to distract him with one hand while your other hand swiftly comes in from another direction: Hold one hand a couple of inches in front and to the side of the iguana's face; with your other hand, come down and aim your fingers for the space under his belly on the other side of where your left hand is. When your fingers are under his belly, cup your hand and lift. With small iguanas, one hand is all that's needed to hold them safely. With larger iguanas, you may need to put your other hand under the iguana's lower belly/pelvis/upper-tail area to give the body full support.

Until you get used to doing it, picking up an iguana can be like rubbing your tummy while patting your head. You need to keep a number of things in your mind while your brain orders your hands to do different things: Approach from the front and side, don't grab the tail, watch out for the legs and toes, keep your hand moving trying to catch him, keep your balance, and keep your language family-oriented if your kids are within hearing distance. With practice, the task becomes less trying, though it may be awhile before your iguana becomes less intimidating.

Calming your iguana

So now you have this handful of thrashing, whipping, gaping iguana, and you're trying to figure out how you're going to support a body in constant, random motion. No problem. Let the iguana move in your hands, scrambling from one hand to the other, offering your free hand as he is ready to launch himself from your other one. If you have ever played with a small mammal like a guinea pig, or let a pet bird walk from hand to hand, you'll find that doing the same works for the iguana.

If the iguana is trying to spin out of your hold, performing a series of alligator rolls, let him roll. Cup both hands and let him spin within them, making sure that the tail is able to move freely without hitting anything. Once your iguana spins for a while and realizes that it isn't working, he may stop to catch a breath before trying to spring away from you again. At this point, cup the iguana in your hand, your palm under his belly, and lift him right up into the air, your arm straight up, the iguana held so that his body is parallel with the floor (see Figure 17-1). In just a moment or so, he should stop thrashing around and become still.

Taming an older iguana

An increasing number of iguana keepers are adopting juvenile and adult iguanas that are often given away because the original owner didn't know the fine points of taming or didn't have time to work with his or her iguana.

The good news is that taming an adult is very much like taming a hatchling. All the tricks that work with a baby work with an adult. In addition, many adults learn more quickly than hatchlings or even juveniles.

The main difference between taming a juvenile/adult and a hatchling is size — and strength. Some adults feel like they're wrapped in coarse sandpaper, and their tails feel like they're edged with a sharp knife. Their jaws are more powerful and teeth larger than a hatchling's, making bites potentially serious enough to land you in the

hospital's emergency room. Their claws can scratch deep enough to leave lasting scars after you finally conquer the infections that set in while the wounds are healing.

Put off by the idea of adopting a juvenile or an adult? Don't be. Just be prepared. Plan your daily getting-acquainted and taming sessions for when you're well rested and alert. Keep focused on the iguana and keep distractions at a minimum. Iguanas tell you that they're going to bite. You just have to be watchful and pay attention, making corrections or adjustments to the way you're holding them, as well as how close to your body you're holding them.

TIP

You can call me Jack-o

Since, as far as we know, iguanas don't use names among themselves, they have no concept of gender-linked names, like Mary for a girl and John for a boy. Don't worry if you pick out a strong, virile name like Spartacus only to find that your lizard grows into a sleek, delicate female. Spartacus really won't care, one way or the other. The important thing is, once you pick a name, stick with it. Suddenly calling your iguana by another name is going to leave him wondering who the heck you're talking to and why you aren't talking to *him* anymore. This name-change problem is something to keep in mind when adopting an older iguana who was named by his previous owner.

Figure 17-1:
Holding an iguana up over your head calms him down.

Photo by Melissa Kaplan

If you haven't already been talking softly to him, start doing so now. Baby talk works very well in this situation. Give him another moment or two up in the air and then slowly lower your arm, bringing him to just below eye level with your face. Shift him in your hand so that both hands are cupped around him, your thumbs under his belly, your fingers clasped loosely over his back. Keep talking to him.

If he hisses at you or gives you an open-mouth threat, give him a hiss or an open mouth back to let him know that you're not intimidated at all by him, as well as make him think twice about his status in relation to yours, since you have a louder hiss and a much bigger mouth.

Human straight-arming, hissing, and open-mouth threat-ing works with older iguanas, too, but care must be taken to ensure that their mouths can't reach your fingers, hands, or face. Adult iguanas who've in the past always been successful in training humans to stay away from them may fight all the more to try to force you to get away from them. That fight may include biting you.

Once the iguana settles down, the battle isn't over. Expect to go through the same frustrating steps — chasing him, picking him up, wrestling with him, and convincing him that you're indeed bigger than he is and (supposedly) less afraid of him than he is of you — every time you pick him up for some time to come.

Calming yourself

Keeping yourself calm and focused while you're trying to deal with your squirmy green monster is as important for your safety and well being as it is for your iguana's. Keeping your body and face relaxed, your breathing slow and regular, your movements slow and steady (whenever possible), and your voice quiet and relaxed helps calm the iguana. Hurried, jerky movements, a loud or screechy voice, and your face scrunched by tension are going to scare the iguana even more than he already is — or provide the motivation to increase the intensity of his struggle.

Handling with ease (eventually)

Work on picking up and holding your iguana several times a day, but vary the length of time and what you do when you have him in hand. Many iguanas start to calm down as you begin walking around the room or house. They start to forget about you and take an interest in seeing what the rest of their new world looks like. Talk to him while taking him on a tour of your house. Pause occasionally when he seems particularly interested in something.

At other times, put him back into his enclosure once he has calmed down. Just as iguanas learn that thrashing about can make you put them down, they can also learn that being calm gets them put down. As time goes on, the amount of thrashing time will decrease until one day you realize that once you have your iguana in hand, he's perfectly relaxed.

You also need to let your iguana know that you're not going to descend on him and spirit him away from the security of his enclosure *every* time you approach him. Sometimes, just walk up and talk to your iguana. Other times, reach in and pet him. (You may have to chase him and pick him up, holding him a couple of inches off the floor of the enclosure, using your free hand to pet him.) As time goes on, he'll eventually stop fleeing from your approaching hand.

Once you're easily able to approach and pick up your iguana without his thrashing you or running away, you'll see the change in his body language. When he is willing to be picked up, he'll remain at rest or lift himself to meet your hand. When he doesn't want to be bothered, you'll likely see a stiffening of the body, a head toss, or a dewlap flare. When he signals that he wants to be left alone, go ahead and leave him alone — after petting him for a bit. Or pick him up briefly, say a few words to him, maybe give a pet or two, and put him gently back down again.

Moodiness and squirmy "Put me down!" behavior may have some physiological causes. Iguana skin gets sensitive to the touch just before they shed and during the first several days of their shed. If they're full of food or need to poop, the last thing they want is someone mushing their lower abdomen around. Minor injuries can cause strains, sprains, or just plain soreness, leading to a desire to be left alone or, at the very least, petted but not picked up. If the moodiness or abnormally quiet behavior doesn't pass within a day or so or you can find no self-resolving reason for it, get your iguana checked out by your reptile vet.

Potty-Training

If you positively reinforce the desired behavior and pay attention to the iguana's daily biological cycles and natural inclination not to soil his environment, you can potty-train your iguana.

An iguana who eats every day poops at least once a day. Depending on temperatures, activity levels, quantity of food consumed, and fiber content, wastes may be eliminated two or three times a day.

The first poop is generally 1–1½ hours after the iguana warms up in the morning. You can work this situation to your advantage: Time the lights to go on with your leave-for-work or leave-for-school schedule. (Remember: The key to potty-training your iguana is to work with *his* daily cycle and reinforce it, not forcing him into a skewed daytime or nocturnal schedule.)

Setting a potty time and place

Inside or outside of enclosures, iguana keepers have designated various places at the potty place: piles of newspapers, tubs of water, plastic bins, kitty litter bins (but *never* with kitty litter) . . . I even know of one intrepid iguana keeper who has built a sort of perch that fits over her toilet so that her iguana can go there. In picking your iguana's potty place, keep these things in mind:

- ✔ Don't use litters (even reptile litters). Several types of kitty litters are toxic, but all litters can cause serious, even fatal, gut impactions when ingested (see the section on substrates in Chapter 8 for more information on particulate litters).

- ✔ If every morning at the same time you put your iguana in the tub, filled to the depth of the iguana's hips with warm water (about 85–90 degrees Fahrenheit/29–32 degrees Celsius), you will eventually train him to go shortly after he goes into the bath.

- ✔ You can use a shower stall instead of a tub. Place a rubber disk over the drain. The disadvantage is that you need to put your hand in the poopy water to remove the disk to let the water out. Wearing a disposable glove on that hand eliminates any health risk. Then again, some igs will go with the water streaming over them, rather than waiting for the water level to rise up under their belly.

Whatever area you choose — tub, litter bin, even toilet — the premise is the same: At the time of day that your iguana has to go, take him to that area. Once you establish the daily routine and the iguana gets used to it, he will come to expect it.

If you fail to take your iguana to his potty place when you should, some iguanas hold it for days. As wastes collect in an iguana's body, the iguana begins to exhibit signs of stress due to the discomfort, the disruption of his routine, and the potential harm due to the wastes collecting in the rectum and bladder, backing up the entire digestive system.

Dealing with retributive pooping

Poop painting is just one way that iguanas voice their displeasure — pooping on or in your bed or on your clothes, shoes, important papers, or your favorite place to unwind. Iguanas housed in enclosures can also get back at you. They may wait until you have just spent hours cleaning and disinfecting the enclosure and reinstalling all the fixtures, and then let loose as soon as you put them back.

Want to know how to reduce, if not completely eliminate, retributive pooping? Don't do anything to tick your iguana off. Changing your daily schedule so that his schedule is altered will annoy him. Going away on a business trip or on vacation counts as an altered schedule, and so does changing shifts at work, staying home on vacation, and doing things at different times than usual. Planning a wedding? Bringing home a new baby (human or animal)? Heading back to school after the long summer vacation? All are activities that

AAAAAGH!

If the unthinkable happens — your iguana's tail drops off during a taming session — don't panic. Ignore the dropped piece of tail flopping around on the floor (or put it down if it's still in your hand) and treat the injury (Chapter 20 tells you how). Once that's done, *then* you can scream and yell and kick yourself for being such a dolt. Once you have worked the hysterics out of your system, calm yourself down enough to tell yourself that accidents happen. Tail dropping is a natural defense mechanism for iguanas and many other lizards, and there may not have been anything you could have done differently.

Oh, and what to do with the tail? Save it for your kid's next show-and-tell day. Or wrap it in foil and place it in a plastic bag and stash it in the freezer where it will be close at hand the next time you want to amaze (or gross out) your family and friends.

can distress an iguana to the point where he gets back by getting even in one of the ways he can.

Bottom line? Be prepared to do what you can to help your iguana adjust and don't get unduly upset when your iguana speaks his mind in this way.

There are a few other reasons why an iguana may break his potty-training routine: An iguana's natural functions may be altered if he has an infection, is in pain, is in season, or, in the case of females, is gravid. Don't just assume your iguana has misbehaved until you check out all the possibilities.

When Your Iguana Doesn't Become a Barney

Once in a while, despite doing your best, your iguana doesn't become tame enough after a year or more of work with him to interact with you comfortably. Either the iguana gets highly stressed when interacted with, or he is still aggressive or defensive. Before you throw up your hands and swear that your iguana hates you, bring in some outside help. Contact your local herp society, reptile vet, or iguana or reptile rescue. Or check out the various iguana resources on the Internet and World Wide Web to find someone in your area who can visit you and your iguana and provide some pointers.

Another reason some iguanas don't become tame, or suddenly start acting aggressive, is that they're sick or in pain. If you haven't had your iguana checked out (or checked out since the behavior changed), make an appointment with your reptile vet. If the condition is medical, your iguana will be easier to work with once he is feeling better.

If nothing works out and you need to find a home for your iguana, contact any local herpetological society, reptile rescue, or iguana rescue. If you're able to keep him until one of those organizations can find a home for him, do so. Even if your iguana dislikes you or is not at ease in your home, change is very stressful. It's better for him in the long run if he moves directly from your home to his new home instead of from your home to a temporary foster home and then to a new home.

Some things you can't (or shouldn't) do include releasing your iguana into the wild (it's cruel); giving him to a zoo (zoos already have what they want); donating him to a school (the setting usually isn't conducive to iguana health); or putting an ad in the paper (you can't be sure the home he's going to is a good one). Chapter 4 gives more information on why these choices aren't good ones.

You make me feel like dancin'

When an iguana has to go, he does a little dance (called by some "the potty dance") to get into a comfortable position, squats a bit, lifts his tail, and goes. When he's done, he walks away with his tail still lifted to keep it from trailing in the feces and urates. Kept in too small a space, an iguana will walk through his mess, trail his tail through it, and, perhaps worst of all, poop paint his floor, walls, and roosts with it. Painting is most likely to happen when the iguana has become peeved with you for some reason; other times, it appears to be just something to do to liven up an otherwise boring day.

Central American iguana, showing vivid turquoise and reticulating patterning on the body, in addition to the usual bold stripes.

This light green color is common on iguanas in Central and parts of South America.

This spindly hatchling is getting ready to shed the skin off his back. Note the dewlap tucked up tightly under the chin, a common sight in nervous hatchlings.

The slender head on this iguana is typical of many females.

Another example of the reticulated (cryptic) patterning. When these iguanas get very warm, the brown patches along the back may turn a vivid bronze color.

This male has flared his dewlap, either at another iguana, a potential predator, or the annoying photographer.

Females tend to have smaller dewlaps and shorter dorsal spikes, but the males in some areas have smaller dewlaps and shorter spikes than females in other areas, making it difficult to accurately tell an iguana's sex by these characteristics.

These small, delicate hatchlings perched on the flowers give no indication of the size they will be in just a few short years, at which time these same flowers would be crushed by their weight and shredded by their claws.

Many iguanas get protective of their food, standing or laying in it to keep others from getting to it.

This iguana clinging to an already too-small branch may not be getting warm enough because his body is farther away from the overhead heat lamp at his head.

This hatchling exhibits some of the bright turquoise patches common to many hatchlings, colors that are often lost once the juvenile and adult colors emerge during their first year.

Hibiscus flowers and leaves are favorite treats.

Iguanas often view their humans as nice, warm trees, while their humans learn that claw trimming and a layer of clothing help protect their skin.

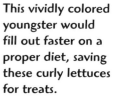

This vividly colored youngster would fill out faster on a proper diet, saving these curly lettuces for treats.

This trio may be getting along well now, but there is no guarantee that they will when they get older. While hatchlings know that there's saftey in numbers, most adults are less accommodating when it comes to sharing their living space.

Shredded orange vegetables, like squash or carrots, are a nutritious part of the diet and a healthy treat.

This spiny-tailed iguana not only looks a lot different from the green iguana with whom he shares habitat, but the spiny-tailed's temperament and diet are different too.

This gloriously vivid Fiji banded iguana is on of the two specias of Fijan iguanas, both of whom are considered to be endangered species.

Desert iguanas, native to the southwestern deserts, are partially omnivorous, eating a variety of carrion and insects in addition to vegetation, including cactus flowers.

Some of these Carribean iguanas reach a much larger size, overall, than green iguanas, growing and maturing at a much slower rate.

Chapter 18

Integrating Iguanas into Your Life

A major part of caring for any pet is developing a routine that incorporates the pet's daily and less regular care needs. Care includes making and serving food and water as well as cleaning and maintaining the pet's environment. It also includes playtime — time set aside for you to interact on a personal level with the pet, doing activities that are healthful, both mentally and physically, for that animal — as well as supervised time during which the pet is nominally on his own but outside of his enclosure or usual environment.

Routines may sound like drudgery (and, truthfully, some of them are), but they can also provide a measure of familiarity and security, especially for your green iguana. Because iguanas are thrown into an alien environment where everything is strange and new, routines help them learn what to expect and when, which in turn helps lessen their stress levels. The less stressed iguanas are, the healthier they will be.

Establishing a Daily Routine

The trick to establishing a daily routine for your iguana is to make a list of what you need to do for yourself (and family) and what you need to do for your iguana. Compare the two, paying close attention to the times of day that iguanas need things done, and then start working out the changes to your schedule. See? It's easy.

Why do you have to be the one to make changes in your schedule? Because you have taken this wild, tropical, diurnal lizard into your care. The timing of his lights and heat, feeding time, bedtime, activity time, and even his potty time (if you're going to work on potty-training) need to happen when they're biologically appropriate for him. Unfortunately, this biologically appropriate time may not be a time that's convenient for you.

Planning key tasks

Daily activities include those related to the iguana's environment and to the iguana himself. To keep track of these tasks, make a schedule (see Figure 18-1).

Time of Day	Weekday	Time of Day	Weekend
6 a.m.	Night heat off; UVB & day heat on	6 a.m.	Night heat off; UVB & day heat on
7-7:15 a.m.	Bath	7-8 a.m.	Bath and general hanging out
7:15-7:30 a.m.	Hang out while getting ready		
7:30 a.m.	Put yesterday's bowls in sink to soak; serve out today's salad, greens, and fresh water	7:30-8:00 a.m.	Remove yesterday's bowls for washing; serve today's salad, greens, and fresh water
7:35 a.m.	Check equipment to make sure everything's working properly before leaving for work. Refill humidifier or drip bottle	8 a.m.-6 p.m.	Clean and disinfect the enclosure; refill humidifier or drip bottle. Snacks. Supervised out time, field trip, playtime and/or alone time
6:15-6:30 p.m.	Clean tank if necessary. If shedding, spray or bathe. Offer treats or greens		Supervised out time, playtime, or alone time. Good time for claw trim
6:30 p.m.	Day lights off, night heat on	6:30 p.m.	Day lights off, night heat on
7-9 p.m.	Spend 30 minute or so holding or lying quietly with sleepy iguana then return to sleeping spot	7-9 p.m.	If anyone has any energy left, some quiet reading or TV time

Figure 18-1: A sample schedule of daily activities.

The heat and UVB lights need to go on and off at the proper times. Any humidifiers or drip bottles need to be refilled — possibly cleaned first. The enclosure may need spot cleaning if the iguana pooped or had a food fight with himself. Lighting and heating equipment should be checked to make sure that everything is in good working order — bulbs seated tightly, no frays in the cords, and no punctures in the heat pad.

Check climbing apparatus to make sure that it's still secure. Water any plants and check hanging plants to make sure the hangers are still securely attached to the pot and the ceiling. If you leave a soaking tub of water in the enclosure, it should be dumped, cleaned, and refilled; disinfect it at least once a week and whenever it's been pooped in. Clean and disinfect the previous day's food and water bowls. You can leave them soaking in the sink while you're at work; just use your second set of bowls for the current day's food and water.

Make a shopping list for any foods, replacement equipment, or supplies you need to stop for on the way home. Or save the trips to the pet and hardware stores for the weekend and make those trips an outing with your iguana.

Radical changes in your schedule, such as taking a vacation, having house-guests, having an illness in the family, changing roommates, and having your children come to stay for the summer, all cause your iguana great stress. To find out the signs of stress, how it affects your iguana, and what you can do about it, head to Chapter 19.

Together time

Even when you can't focus 100 percent of your attention on your iguana, you can still spend time together. Early morning time can be quite beneficial for taming and socializing. At that time of day, you have an opportunity to be together even though you're not in direct physical contact with him. You can chat with the iguana and give the iguana a chance to observe you and to check out things around your bathroom and bedroom (see Figure 18-2).

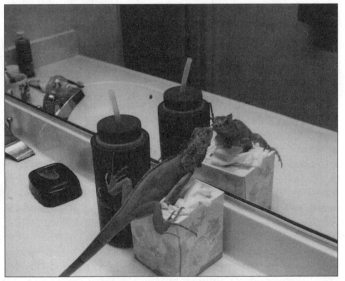

Figure 18-2:
Having your iguana with you as you go through the day's mundane tasks is one of the most effective ways to train him.

Photo by Melissa Kaplan

This early morning example sounds wonderfully easy, but when you're first starting out with an untamed iguana, it's a lot more nerve-wracking and time-consuming than it appears on paper. Keep at it, however, and within several

Nocturnal humans

Many people work the swing, or graveyard (third), shift and do their sleeping during most or all of the daytime hours. This sleeping schedule is a problem because iguanas who are forced to a reversed schedule (their "day" is at night, and night when it's daylight outside) simply don't fare as well. These iguanas are smaller, are more stressed, and tend to have more behavior and health problems.

If you're a night worker, you need to find ways to accommodate your iguana's diurnal schedule. You may have to find someone else to do the caretaking and socialization during the day, with you getting involved as much as possible during your off-work hours when they coincide with the iguana's normal daytime hours. Or you may need to alter your own wake and sleep schedule to fit in feeding, cleaning, and playtime during the iguana's day.

months to a year, you'll probably find that you can reset your alarm clock to give yourself a couple more minutes of sleep in the mornings.

Together time can also include your iguana's bath time. If he's taking his bath while you're using the bathroom to get ready for school or work, you can talk to and look in on him. Some iguana keepers take showers with their iguanas, with the larger iguanas sitting in the tub away from the flow of soap and shampoo and the small iguanas hanging on a towel attached to the side wall or to a perch set up on the top shower door track.

 If your iguana is used to pooping in the tub, you should poop him first; then disinfect the tub before you get in for your bath or shower. Given the design of the exterior human anatomy, I suggest that you don't take a bath with an iguana. Stick to showers if you feel the need to share this activity together.

More together time can be spent when you're eating breakfast, preparing and packing lunch for you or the kids, and when preparing your iguana's food. Smaller iguanas come to enjoy riding around on your shoulder, and larger iguanas can watch you from the floor or a comfy roosting place, such as a warming window sill.

Afternoons (after work) are usually the times when iguanas are let out for some exercise, maybe another bath, more food or hand-fed treats, and free time hanging out while their human puts together the human's evening meal. Many iguanas put themselves to bed around sunset, or between 5:00 to 7:00 in the evening. Some are amenable to being picked up and carried to a comfortable place where they can lie snoozing for a half-hour or so next to you (or, better, on you, as you're much warmer than the sofa cushion).

Weekends can be varied a bit. Iguanas usually adapt to a slightly different week-end schedule, accepting that you get up a bit later and holding the potty urge until you get them out to poop. They usually don't mind eating a little later. Spending time with you during the day can also be a welcome break, especially for iguanas who spend the weekdays stuck in their enclosures.

Providing quality time

Iguana keepers find great pleasure in spending time with their iguanas. While the word *playing* may be stretching it, this quality time can be thought of as constructive play and sharing time, much like you'd spend with a young child. During this time spent together, the iguana continues to learn new things about you and your shared environment as you learn more about him and about iguanas in general. This time is also important for reinforcing taming and socialization, especially if the time together involves interacting with other humans.

Bird watching, watching television, and visiting with a friend are all ways for you and your iguana to spend time together. So is having your iguana with you when you're working (or playing) on the computer or doing more mun-dane tasks, such as paying bills or folding the laundry. While you're watching or talking, you can be petting the iguana and talking to him. This is a calm, relaxed time that also gives you the opportunity to check him over thor-oughly — including all the toes, foot pads, individual spikes, and dewlap and tail — to ensure that everything is as it should be. As the iguana relaxes under your touch, you'll find that he comes to enjoy these sessions. With some iguanas, you may find that the iguana actually solicits this type of close contact and time with you.

Bodyguarding Your Iguana

Whether your iguana is inside or out, alone or with others, you need to make sure that he is safe. One problem that occurs when he feels comfortable in his environment (your home) and with you (preventer of all that's evil, provider of all that's good) is that your iguana may get a little too cocky for his own good.

Part of it isn't his fault. In the wild, when an iguana takes a flying leap, he has a reasonable expectation of snagging a thicket of leaves or vines or of landing on a nice, thick, bouncy branch. If worse comes to terrible, he may belly flop in deep leaf litter or a river. Nowhere in the wild have iguanas encountered a concrete slab, a hardwood subfloor covered with carpet or linoleum, or the edge of a coffee table. Fortunately, as long as he is in good structural health (good bone density) and nothing falls on him, a captive iguana has a reasonable chance of emerging from a 6-foot drop to the floor with little more than a bruised ego. If he hits something on his way down, such as a table or other hard object, there's a slightly increased risk in injury, significantly so if the iguana is a gravid female.

Expect your iguana to do the unexpected, whether at home or when he's out. If your iguana has a choice between a nice sturdy climber and a solid shelf to sun himself on, he'll at least once decide that climbing your expensive lace curtains and leaping to your fragile bric-a-brac shelf displaying several priceless figurines is going to be much more fun. Did you leave the miniblinds raised several inches so that your iguana can sun himself on the window sill? Then expect to see him threaded between a dozen slats of the blind.

When you're out and about, keep a hand on him. If you're taking a walk, assume that he is going to try to jump or grab a passing bush or tree. If you're in a store, remember that shelves are highly attractive as climbers — and that innocent customers may be viewed as stepping stones to be leapt on to get from you to something far more interesting.

All dogs and children may not be as benign as they seem. Your iguana, who may accept your own dog and children, may not accept others. Ultimately, your iguana's safety, your safety, and that of other people in the vicinity depend on your being alert to all that's going on around you and being able to keep control of your iguana if he has other ideas.

If your iguana injures someone, that person may sue you for damages. Always control encounters with strangers. Don't assume that they know how to approach and pet an iguana and be prepared to say "No, not today," if you're iguana isn't in the mood to be an ambassador. Being in complete control of the situation is especially important when you are around children. Kids tend to put their faces perilously close to your iguana's feet, mouth, and sharp dorsal tail ridge, something that could be a major problem if the iguana kicks, snaps, or whips.

Part VI
Health and Well-Being

The 5th Wave   By Rich Tennant

@RICHTENNANT

"Don't worry — Dr. Payton is one of the finest reptile veterinarians in the countrg."

In this part . . .

*L*earning about the normal abnormalities, such as those skin and behavioral changes associated with healthy shedding, and what the abnormalities are that indicate a health problem, can mean the difference between life and death for your iguana and peace of mind or enormous veterinary bills for you. You also need to know about human health concerns, what to do if your iguana isn't as tame as you want him to be, and what kinds of research and decisions need to be made if his quality of life is severely compromised.

Chapter 19

Healthy Is As Healthy Does

. . . .

In This Chapter

▶ Recognizing an iguana's normal "abnormalities"

▶ Understanding the signs and effects of stress

▶ Protecting your iguana from toxic plants in his environment

▶ Treating wounds and giving medication

▶ Finding a vet

. . . .

*W*hoever coined the phrase "It's a dog's life" clearly never lived with a healthy, well-socialized iguana. The iguana eats better than his humans, has elaborate indoor and outdoor areas designed solely for his use, is carried around and taken for rides, and has his every move (and bowel movement) fawned over and analyzed and discussed endlessly with other iguana owners. He gets warm baths every day, his keepers often plant a garden solely to provide him with tasty and colorful treats, and, as every seasoned iguana keeper will tell you, the iguana, not the human, is the master of the house.

Much of this fawning and peering and poking-around stuff, however, has a very important purpose: It helps you keep up with the dizzying number of changes that happen so quickly with a rapidly growing lizard. Throughout the course of a year, an iguana goes through a number of normal, healthy changes in appearance and behavior. But some of these changes may also be seen in a sick iguana. As an iguana keeper, you need to be able to recognize normal temporary changes from those that indicate the iguana is sick. You can do a couple of other things to keep your iguana healthy: Make sure that he doesn't have access to toxic plants, and find a reptile vet. This chapter covers all this stuff.

Normal Temporary Abnormalities

In the normal course of events, your healthy, well-adjusted iguana is going to periodically look unhealthy and act maladjusted. Once you know what's going on, your mind will be eased and your iguana will be less bugged as you let him get on with what he needs to be getting on with.

PMS: Pre-monthly shedding

Every four to six weeks, except possibly during the winter, your iguana will shed his skin. This process begins when your iguana hatches and continues throughout his life. The actual start of shedding, when the skin starts to break and peel off, is preceded by a syndrome known unaffectionately by iguana keepers as pre-monthly shedding, or PMS.

First, they darken

This period begins with skin color changes. Your iguana's skin starts to get dull and then darkens. The change happens gradually over the course of a week or so. During this time, his appetite may taper off, and he may not bask as long as he usually does. As the skin gets darker still, your iguana typically stays someplace cool, far cooler than you'd like. The iguana may want to stay in that place, or a similarly cool place, during the day and night. He may not want to move for a day or so.

When touched during this period, your iguana may be uncharacteristically cranky, pushing you away or slapping your hand with one of his feet. You may get the evil eye cocked at you. He may lie there, his head on his front feet, not stirring other than to hiss quietly at you.

Then they get white patches

A couple of weeks or so after the color and behavior changes occur, another color change comes about that is equally freaky to the new iguana keeper. Used to the dark color, the iguana keeper becomes alarmed one morning when he or she wakes up to find that one of the iguana's hands, and possibly an arm, has turned white. The rest of the skin on the body looks the same . . . but white? The worst possible thoughts flit through the iguana keeper's mind — cancer, fungus, the kids have found the water-color paints. Fortunately, it isn't anything to be concerned about. It's just a sign of the area that is about to shed within the next two to four days. Other white patches appear on the body as different areas get ready to shed.

The spikes stiffen and get spotted

The iguana's spikes lighten as well as start to get stiff. They may also look funny, with small blotches of dark color on them. This is normal, especially if the spikes have been injured by being broken or bent. As the skin at the base of the spikes starts to loosen, it will ready the skin on the spikes to start loosening and shed off as well.

Breeding season

Breeding season brings with it a host of abnormal normal behaviors —
behaviors that vary between male and female iguanas. The behavioral and
physical changes, including going off food, restlessness, color changes in
males (and some females), temporary suspension of shedding, change in the
appearance and frequency of defecation, the color and consistency of the
urates, and minor weight loss, are discussed at length in Chapter 24.

Winter blues

In the wild, the winter is the dry season, the time of year when less food is
available and the food that is available is of very poor nutritional quality.
Iguanas conserve their fat stores, created when they pigged out during the
lush summer months, by greatly reducing their activity levels. They may also
reduce the number of hours a day spent basking.

During winter, expect to see reduced activity and appetite, reduced volume
and frequency of defecation, and possibly a dulling of color and suspension
of shedding. Once the days start to lengthen again in late winter/early spring,
you'll see your iguana start to perk up again, eat more, poop more, thermoregulate based on his usual schedule, and start to shed once again.

Other Things Not to Worry About: Sneezing and Salty Deposits

Sneezing is a natural biological process, the way the iguana gets rid of salts.
This doesn't mean that if you don't see your iguana sneezing, you should be
adding salt to his diet, nor does it mean that the foods you're feeding him are
too high in salt. All foods have salts of different kinds, and those not required
for metabolic and other physiologic processes are voided by the body.
Iguanas get rid of theirs by sneezing.

If salt deposits collect around the nostrils, just gently wipe them away with
your fingers or a facial tissue. You may, however, need a razor blade or putty
knife to scrape the deposits off the glass of the tank and other surfaces.

If you start feeding a new food to your iguana regularly for one or more weeks
and then realize that your iguana is sneezing (sometimes called "snorting")
more than he did before that food became a staple, then you may want to
stop feeding that food for several weeks to see whether that makes a
difference. If it does, you can feed the food item again but make it an occasional
food rather than a staple.

Sometimes, instead of the iguana sneezing to clear the *salt glands* (the reservoirs that collect the fluid until a sneeze expels it), the fluid just sort of dribbles out of the iguana's nostrils. You may see it glisten on the bottom rim of the nostril or feel the wetness on his nose or chin. It may dry to a fine, salty film that coats the scales under the nostrils and around the mouth opening and farther down the outside of the lower jaw. Just as with the sneezed-out deposits, this salty film is nothing to worry about. Wet a cotton-tipped swab or dampen a facial tissue and gently wipe it away if it bothers you. Chances are, it doesn't bother your iguana at all.

Stress and Your Iguana's Health

Shedding, breeding season, and winter are normal *stressors* (stress events) in the life of an iguana. Encounters with other iguanas during the course of his daily activities are also normal stressors. Living in captivity, no matter how well cared for he is, is an abnormal stressor. Living in a relatively (to an iguana) small area is a stressor, too — more so if he is forced to share a small area with one or more other iguanas.

Stressed-out iguanas may look fine on the outside, but inside a host of malfunctions and impairments may be caused by the stresses set in motion the day they hatched from their eggs at a farm or were grabbed in the wild and thrown into shipping containers.

Stress can lead to shedding problems, failure to thermoregulate properly, prolonged hiding, cranky or aggressive responses toward other iguanas and humans, and repetitive injurious behaviors, such as constant digging or nose-banging. Stress can also lead to increases in the populations of gut flora — the organisms that break down the iguana's food — to the point where the levels of these otherwise beneficial parasites become injurious to the iguana's health. Stress also impairs the immune function, resulting in systemic and localized infections.

Signs of illness and stress

Assessing stress and illness in your iguana means looking at the iguana himself as well as his immediate physical environment (enclosure and equipment) and the room in which the enclosure resides.

Check the iguana's overall appearance:

- Are the lateral folds normal for your iguana or bigger/deeper than usual? Are there more folds than usual?
- Has there been a change in color? Is the color of the skin dulling or darkening, for example?

When your iguana's color changes to dark gray, dark brown, black, or yellow to brown, it's a sign of serious stress. When an iguana is stressed, the color change begins on the head, upper body, tail, and legs, spreading around the torso to the belly. The belly may remain green or yellow for some time after the rest of the body has grayed or browned out.

Check for changes in feeding habits:

- ✔ Has food intake dropped off or increased?
- ✔ Have the food choices changed?
- ✔ Is he selecting foods with higher moisture content?

Look for changes in the appearance, consistency, and amount of feces and urates:

- ✔ Are there less urates?
- ✔ Are the urates thicker and more viscous?
- ✔ Are fecal masses smaller, harder, and drier? Looser and wetter?
- ✔ Is he defecating less often? More often?

Check for any changes in behavior:

- ✔ Is the iguana lethargic?
- ✔ Is he spending more time in hiding or in the cooler places in his room or enclosure?
- ✔ Is he spending more time in the basking area?
- ✔ Is he soaking for prolonged periods in the water bowl?
- ✔ Is he more active, especially at odd times?
- ✔ Is he spending a lot of time digging or scratching at the door, floor, wall, or other surface, or head-banging?
- ✔ Is he doing more or less tongue-flicking than usual when handled or the enclosure is opened?

Check for changes in shedding:

- ✔ Has the shed schedule become erratic?
- ✔ Are sheds taking much longer than usual to complete?
- ✔ Are there areas that have not shed or will not shed without assistance?

Check for physical signs of illness and injury:

- ✔ Is the iguana *gaping* (sitting with an open mouth) for long periods of time?
- ✔ Has the saliva increased or thickened?

✔ Have the tissues inside his mouth turned pale pink or gray?

✔ Is he having a prolonged eversion of the hemipenes or cloacal tissue after defecation?

✔ Is he limping?

✔ Have digits, the tail, a limb, the back, or the jaw swelled?

✔ Is he having a loss in muscle tone/strength?

✔ Is he having tremors or shakiness?

✔ Is he climbing less or failing to climb?

✔ Is he having difficulty raising his body off the ground?

✔ Is he having difficulty righting himself when turned over — or failing to right himself at all?

✔ Is he showing clumsiness or uncoordinated movements, and is he toppling over when turning around?

✔ Are there any lumps, bumps, or bruised areas?

✔ Are there any scabs or blisters?

Finding the cause

If any signs of illness or stress occur, you must check the iguana's actual environment to make sure that he is getting what he needs. Any problems in temperature, humidity, layout, or cagemates must be corrected. If the physical and social environments inside the enclosure are not the problem, then you need to evaluate the room(s) the iguana spends his time in:

✔ Has the placement of the enclosure been changed (to a different room or different part of the original room)?

✔ Are children or pets annoying or scaring the iguana? (Think food chain/predator-prey relationships here as well as the annoyance factor of noisy, active children.)

✔ Have you moved your household? Had to evacuate due to a natural disaster?

✔ Have you had the in-laws over for the week, totally disrupting your usual animal maintenance (and playtime) schedule?

✔ Have you been away on vacation?

✔ Have you put up holiday decorations or redecorated the room the iguana is in?

All these things may seem like they wouldn't intrude on the life of your iguana, but they most definitely do. Some of these things you can change, like keeping kids and perceived predators away from the iguana. Other things you just need to give time so your iguana can adjust (like getting used to a new place or schedule). And some things you may need to play around with a bit, to see what exactly is causing the stress. You may find that a particular Christmas decoration, a new stuffed animal toy, or the new neighbor's cat who's decided that staring at your iguana is wonderfully entertaining has lead to stress that's severe and prolonged enough to cause obvious reactions.

Treating stress

In some cases, you can relieve your iguana's stress by placing the iguana in a new room (or home) where he won't be subjected to other animals, iguanas, or human stressors. In other cases, the iguana improves once the environmental conditions improve.

All stressed iguanas should be checked by a reptile vet. Prolonged stress hampers immune functioning, and these iguanas easily get sick. Mouth rot (stomatitis) and abscesses are common in highly or chronically stressed iguanas. (See Chapter 20 for information on these and other conditions.)

Protecting Your Iguana from Toxic Plants

In the wild, an iguana knows which plants to eat and which to avoid. In your home, thousands of miles away, he doesn't. If a wild iguana makes a mistake and becomes ill, he won't eat that plant again. If he eats a plant that kills him, well, he clearly won't be eating it again. The fact that the leading cause of death in the wild is not from eating toxic plants indicates that iguanas either learn their lessons well by observing older iguanas or are hatched with a sort of genetic field guide to edible plants. Once you remove an iguana from his environment, however, that internal field guide is rendered useless.

How plants cause injury

The toxic chemicals in plants are passed to an animal in one of two ways: by eating the plant or by coming into physical contact with it (if you've ever had poison oak or ivy, you're already familiar with the second method). Plants can cause injury in other ways, such as lacerating or causing puncture wounds to the body, eyes, mouth, or digestive tract. They may cause ulcers, lesions, and abscesses on the skin, or they may cause the skin or eyes to become hypersensitive to light. Some plants may have indigestible pieces that can lodge in the gut, causing intestinal impaction.

Some plants are completely toxic; others have only certain parts that are toxic, like the leaves or the flowers. Some plants contain toxins strong enough to very quickly kill the iguana; others can make iguanas seriously ill and may lead to death. Still others may just make iguanas wish they were dead. For a list of toxic plants and to find out which parts are toxic, head to Appendix A.

If your iguana eats something he shouldn't

If your iguana does ingest something he shouldn't have, watch carefully for signs of distress. Signs may include respiratory changes (the rate of breathing increases or decreases, breaths become shallower or deeper, breathing becomes labored or difficult), increased salivation, dry heaves, vomiting, lethargy, restlessness, rubbing the mouth on the ground or other surfaces, scratching at the face or mouth, and diarrhea or another alteration of the feces.

Don't wait to see if the signs will abate. Call your regular reptile vet or an emergency reptile vet (have these numbers and locations on hand before you need them) and let the vet know what the animal ate, what the signs are, and that you're on your way.

Identify your plants *before* you expose your iguana to them, not after a plant has been ingested and you're trying to find out whether or not it'll kill him. (For help on identifying your plants, check out Chapter 26.)

Wound-Management Basics

New iguana keepers should always take their iguanas to a reptile veterinarian to have wounds checked out and treated. As you gain experience, you may be able to care for minor wounds at home and also perform the necessary home care on more serious wounds that were initially treated by the vet, following the vet's instructions.

- ✔ Because even minor wounds can lead to serious local and systemic infections, you shouldn't treat them lightly; don't delay appropriate evaluation and treatment.

- ✔ Bites, lacerations, and puncture wounds can be flushed with dilute (0.5 percent) chlorhexidine diacetate or povidone-iodine. Topical antibiotics, such as a triple antibiotic ointment and silver sulfadiazine, may be used alone or with a dressing.

✔ Take care not to damage or forcibly remove scales when removing dressings. Gauze dressings should first be secured by paper tape, which is a light, low-tack adhesive tape made for sensitive skin. The paper tape itself can be overwrapped with regular adhesive tape, which prevents the paper tape from loosening. Vetrap and Coban are light, elastic, outer bandaging that you can apply over the tape and gauze dressing. You can use Vetrap and Coban to cover and extend beyond the dressing to prevent it from becoming soiled; they're also mildly water resistant.

✔ Don't let your bandaged or stitched iguana soak for prolonged periods of time in a bath or water bowls. They can be quite adept at working off saturated dressings using only one foot and a rostrum. Soaking may also cause infection or prolong the healing of an existing wound or surgical incision.

Once a reptile has been treated, you must provide a supportive environment to promote rapid, uncomplicated recovery:

✔ Provide temperatures toward the higher end of the iguana's thermal gradient, especially for iguanas on systemic antibiotics.

✔ Make sure that good nutrition and adequate food intake are maintained; nutritional deficiencies, such as insufficient protein and calcium, delay the healing process, with the latter affecting the healing of broken or weakened bones.

✔ Keep the environment as clean as possible during recovery to ensure the least amount of contamination of the wound sites. Keeping the enclosure uncluttered, while still providing his favorite hide box and climbers, will make it easier to clean and disinfect while still letting him feel like it's "his" home.

Giving Your Iguana Medication

The time may come when your iguana gets sick enough to require medication. The medicine may be given by injection or by mouth. Vets realize that giving medications to iguanas isn't easy, especially if the keeper is nervous about doing it. Most vets make every effort to teach you how to give the drug. If you aren't sure how to do it, or are nervous, ask for a guided demonstration.

When your iguana is being given an antibiotic, the most commonly prescribed medication, giving your iguana *all* of it is imperative, even if he starts looking and feeling better when you're part of the way through the 10–14 days you're supposed to give the antibiotic to him. If you don't give the full course of medication, the remaining microorganisms become resistant to the medication. They can continue to reproduce, once again causing infection and illness. The next time you go to use the antibiotic, it won't work as well. And eventually, it won't work at all.

Giving injections

Your veterinarian should show you how to draw up the medication into the syringe, hold the iguana, and actually give the injection. If the vet, or veterinary technician, doesn't automatically teach or offer to teach you how to do it, don't be shy: *Ask.* Giving injections to iguanas is hard enough as it is. Trying to find skin thin enough to slide the needle into — at the correct angle, while trying to hold a protesting iguana still enough so that the needle doesn't pop out or, worse, break in half — is a big enough challenge. The more comfortable you become with the mechanics, the easier the process will go. (Well, that's the theory, anyway.)

Types of injections

Three types of injections are available: One type is in the muscle (*intramuscular,* or *IM*), another is under the skin *(subcutaneous,* or *SQ,* or *Sub-q),* and the third is in the abdominal cavity *(intracoelomic,* or *IC* — or *IP* for *intraperitoneal).*

- ✔ The easiest area to give an intramuscular injection is often the fleshy area on the back of the arm.

- ✔ You need to give subcutaneous injections where there's enough room between the skin and the underlying muscle tissue to expand to hold the fluid. Due to the pain that occurs if too much fluid is given in one SQ injection site, either several different injection sites have to be used or the vet may recommend that you do an *intracoelomic* (abdominal cavity) injection instead.

- ✔ The intracoelomic injection is by far the scariest of all injections, but the IC injection is worth it if it means you're able to get 20 cc's or more of fluid into a seriously dehydrated iguana.

The skin on a very young iguana is soft all over, making it easy to pick and use an injection site. However, as the iguana gets older and the scales get bigger and thicker, finding an injection site can be quite a challenge.

Injections are usually given in the front half of the body (from the neck to the midsection). The reason is that many reptile vets are concerned that drugs injected into the back half (from the hind legs down through the tail) will first circulate through the kidneys before circulating through the rest of the body. Because iguanas' kidneys seem to be highly susceptible to disease and failure, reducing the strain on them as much as possible is important.

Giving the injection

Unless your iguana is very small and very sick, you'll likely need two hands to hold the iguana and another hand to hold and use the syringe. Unless you have three hands, it's helpful to have someone else hold the iguana while you steady yourself and give the injection. You can wrap the iguana in a towel, exposing only the injection site area, if you're working alone or with a handler who isn't used to holding iguanas or if you're working with an iguana whose scale surface texture could easily be used to grind down concrete.

Giving oral medication

Oral medication generally comes in two forms: pill and liquid. Although giving oral medication to an iguana would seem to be easier than giving an injection, many antibiotic-bedecked iguana keepers will tell you it ain't always so. Iguanas can be quite determined not to let you get something into their mouths that they don't want in their mouths and quite skilled at getting it out of their mouths much faster than you got it in there to begin with. Here are some things to try:

- ✔ To get small pills into large iguanas, hide the pill in a piece of food. Bite-sized pieces of banana are especially good for this purpose, and so are grape halves, pieces of papaya or mango, or even a bit of melon or bread. Mix liquids and crushed pills in a little mashed banana or another favorite fruit.

- ✔ If your fingers are at risk, serve the laced mashed fruit on top of the iguana's food, or make a green burrito out of it by wrapping the mashed fruit in a piece of leafy green. You can also spread it on a small piece of bread.

To get oral medication directly into your iguana's mouth without benefit of subterfuge, you need to get the mouth opened first. The best way is to pull down firmly on the dewlap with one hand while having the other hand ready to insert the pill or hub of the dosing syringe into the mouth opening. If you're giving liquid medication, be prepared to have it go flying from your iguana's mouth as he spits or flings it out when shaking his head. Another common occurrence is when most of the liquid ends up decorating your iguana's face and dewlap after you miss getting the syringe tip into his mouth or after your iguana moves his head just as you start pushing on the syringe's plunger. Another favorite with iguana keepers is when they get the syringe into the side of the mouth but push the plunger too hard or too fast, which results in all the medication flying out the other side of the mouth.

Most reptile vets understand the difficulties iguana keepers have administering oral medication. If you ask them, they may be able to come up with a more pleasant-tasting drug that your iguana will be more willing to lap off the syringe or eyedropper. If all else fails, you can try adding a little maple or corn syrup to the oral medication in the syringe or eyedropper before offering it to your iguana. The less you dilute the drug with food, however, the better it will work.

Finding a Reptile Vet

If you're new to keeping iguanas — and that includes those of you who haven't been able to keep other iguanas alive for more than a year or two — and the iguana's problem is more than can be fixed by simply tweaking the environment and diet, do both of you a favor and take him to a reptile vet. Until you have several years and various crises under your belt, you're probably not the best judge of whether your iguana needs stitches, lab work, surgery, or antibiotics. Your reptile vet is.

Although many vets list their specialties in their phone book ads, that doesn't mean they're the only vets in the area working with those species. Not all reptile vets advertise themselves as such. As many iguana and other reptile owners have found, sometimes the best vets are those who don't advertise themselves. Word of mouth is the best way to find a reputable reptile vet. Join the local herpetology society and talk with other iguana keepers. Check out the Web sites that list reptile veterinarians. Join e-mail discussion lists for iguana keepers.

Another source of information on local reptile vets is your local wildlife and bird rehabilitators. These are people and organizations who are licensed by the state to take in and rehabilitate injured native wildlife. Because they have to work with the local exotics veterinarians, they know who is working with reptiles. If you can't find a listing for a wildlife center, contact the local agency in charge of animal control and regulation: the city or county department of animal regulation, the local chapter of the Society for the Prevention of Cruelty to Animals (SPCA), or the Humane Society. These numbers can be found in your phone book's Yellow Pages.

As a last resort, check with your reference librarian for the list of nonprofit societies in your area (to find herp societies and wildlife rehab centers) and check with the local zoo's reptile curator or veterinary office (for leads to societies and vets).

There's no alternative to necessary veterinary care. If you truly can't provide the required care, including the veterinary care, especially when your iguana is sick, then do the best thing for your iguana and find a home for him where he'll be provided with what he needs.

When Nothing Else Can Be Done

Sometimes, the hardest decision of all must be made — that of euthanizing a terminally ill pet. What often happens, though, is that the iguana keeper delays making an objective evaluation of the iguana's quality of life (or lack thereof) and so doesn't make the decision to euthanize him, and all the while the poor iguana continues to decline and eventually dies in pain. Proper euthanization, by lethal injection by a capable veterinarian, is far less painful and frightening.

A fee is charged for proper euthanization, but it's a fee well worth the peace of mind you get knowing that your iguana has not suffered any more.

As hard as it may be, consider having a *necropsy* done by your vet or research institution. In a necropsy, the organs and tissues are examined in an attempt to determine exactly why the iguana died, as well as to see what effects the care and environment may have had on the iguana's body and internal systems. Vets usually charge for a necropsy (because they in turn are charged by the laboratories who do most of the examination and analyses), but it's a charge worth paying based on the information we may learn from it.

"But how much will it cost?"

There's no easy answer to that question. Fees for veterinary services — physical exams, lab work and x-rays, medications, surgery, and follow-up care — vary not only geographically but also dramatically within a single city or metropolitan area. Just as the most expensive veterinarian may not be the best one, clinically speaking, the cheapest vet may be a poor deal in the long run if it turns out the vet doesn't know what he or she is doing.

Many people call around to try to find someone — a herpetology society or reptile rescue — who will treat their iguana; unfortunately, it is illegal for nonveterinarians to treat other people's pets, administer prescription medication, perform surgical procedures, and so on. Besides, herp societies are nonprofit, volunteer-run organizations, while reptile rescues are generally individuals doing reptile rescue in their homes, paying for it out of their own pockets. It's one thing for them to take on the full responsibility for an iguana who needs a new home but quite another to cover someone else's veterinary bills while having to cover their own, pay the rent, and raise their kids.

The bottom line is that your iguana's welfare has to come before your own feelings of attachment or ego. If you can't come up with or borrow the money you need or negotiate a payment plan with your vet, a family member, or a friend, then give your iguana to someone who can. Please don't get another iguana until you know you have the financial cushion to provide everything an iguana needs.

Chapter 20

Common Injuries: What to Look for and How to Treat Them

In This Chapter

▶ Common injuries and their causes

▶ Assessing whether to treat the injury yourself or to use a vet

▶ What the treatment entails

An iguana can be injured several ways. Sometimes the injury is obvious; sometimes it's not. When the injuries are minor, you can often treat the injury yourself, but knowing whether an injury is minor — or knowing when it goes from being a minor problem to a major one — is the tricky part. This chapter tells you what you can do, what signs to look for to gauge whether the problem is getting better or worse, and at what point you need to call in the vet. If your iguana is sick, head to Chapter 21 for information on common diseases and disorders and what you should do about those.

If you're new to iguanas, or you've never encountered and dealt properly with the condition before, don't fiddle around with it. Take your iguana to a vet immediately. The longer you wait before taking your iguana to the vet, the bigger the risk to his health.

Abscesses

Abscesses are pockets of infection containing solid pus (see Figure 20-1). They commonly occur as a result of injury to tails, toes, necks, and legs, especially when two iguanas are kept together and one gets bitten. Rostral abscesses occur when an iguana repeatedly injures its nose or snout by banging it into hard surfaces. However, abscesses don't necessarily occur at the site of an injury or immediately after an injury. In fact, they may occur months after an injury or when there has been no injury.

Abscesses need to be treated by a veterinarian, who may recommend administering a course of antibiotics first and then surgically removing the abscess.

Figure 20-1:
An abscess
in a toe.

Despite being removed and being treated with antibiotics, abscesses can form again in the same place within a very short time during the recovery period. As a result, two or more treatments may be necessary.

Burns

Burns are most frequently caused by heat sources: hot rocks, under-the-tank heating pads when used without a substrate layer, human heating pads when they're the only source of heat, and overhead heat lights and ceramic heating elements. The burns may be mild, with just a small blister, or they may be severe enough to cause death by the time the keeper notices them.

Although you can treat minor blistering and burns at home by soaking them daily in povidone-iodine and applying a burn ointment, it's best not to guess at the severity. Even with moderate burns, the iguana must be seen by a vet. Serious burns destroy skin, result in heavy fluid loss, and leave the iguana highly susceptible to invading bacteria. This, in turn, can lead to a raging, possibly lethal, systemic infection.

You know the saying "Once burned, twice shy"? In the case of burn victims, it's "Once burned, forever susceptible to burns." If the burn is on the iguana's belly or pelvis, do away with all bottom heat sources for the duration of the recovery period. Once the burn is healed, you can use a human heating pad in conjunction with overhead or other radiant heat sources, but the pad will have to be covered with a thick terry cloth towel.

Iguanas require a warm environment, not just a hot surface, to successfully and safely thermoregulate their core body temperatures. If your iguana is found hugging a light or light fixture, or if it never leaves its pad or rock, that's a sure sign that the enclosure is too cold and that you're watching a burn about to happen. Fix the situation before it becomes a problem.

Claws — Broken or Torn Off

Iguanas climb using their claws as well as their toes. When walking, climbing, or jumping, they may jerk their toes instead of disengaging them, resulting in a broken toe, a ripped-out claw, or both. The same may happen if the claw is trapped in a tiny hole or fissure in a piece of wood.

Sometimes the claw may still be attached to the fingertip by the underlying fleshy structure or a tiny shred of skin. Removing the claw at this point is best. If just a tiny shred of tissue is holding the claw on, you can quickly pull it off; otherwise, you should take your iguana to the reptile vet to have the claw cut off. If the claw is gone, dip the toe tip in warm diluted povidone-iodine and let it soak for several minutes. Top the tip with antibiotic ointment. For the next couple of days, repeat the medicated soaks and apply the antibiotic ointment to the tip at night. Depending on how much of the nail matrix is left, the claw may or may not grow back. If it does grow back, the initial regrowth will be slow.

Keeping the iguana's claws neatly trimmed and reducing or eliminating the fissures and small holes in climbing and basking branches that can trap claws will help prevent future occurrences. Trimming off the ultra-sharp tip projecting off the main claw won't hinder his ability to climb. See Chapter 12 for instructions on trimming your iguana's claws.

Crusty Mouth

Sometimes, usually in the morning, you may find a mixture of serous fluid and saliva encrusted around the edges of your iguana's mouth. It may be thick and hard enough to have glued your iguana's mouth shut. The cause is usually a minor injury to the gums, as from the stem of a leafy green or a small chunk of squash. Biting cage wire, thin branches, your favorite ballpoint pen, another iguana's tail, and other hard objects can also cause minor mouth tissue injuries.

Remove these deposits by wetting a cotton-tipped swab in warm water and then twirling it against the deposit to gently loosen and move it away from the mouth. Then check inside the mouth, looking for signs of *petechia* (tiny red lines indicating bleeding in the tissue) or *plaques* (patches of tissue that may be yellowish, whitish, or greenish in color). If you see no signs of the plaques or petechial hemorrhaging, then there's nothing to worry about.

You may have to remove the crusts a couple of times a day for a few days, but the injured tissue heals quickly in a healthy iguana, and you don't need to treat the area with any topical antiseptic. Stubborn, recurring crusty sores on the rim of the mouth may mean an infection. If so, your iguana needs to visit a vet for evaluation.

Petechia, plaques, and regularly occurring crustiness may indicate a more serious underlying injury or infection, so you should see your reptile vet before the infection gets worse or spreads.

Dried food deposits look like crusty mouth deposits and are just as easily taken care of with a wet cotton-tipped swab. Iguanas generally grab and gulp their food, smearing food and juices on their face and dewlap. The result can, at first glance, look like your iguana's been bleeding or has other injuries. You can relax once you realize that your iguana is wearing the day's strawberries, raspberries, or blueberries. Because iguanas also walk in their food, check their toes daily and remove any bits of food found stuck on them.

Dry Gangrene of Tail and Toes

An iguana may injure his tail or toes in such a way that amputation is the only solution. Fortunately, iguanas do very well minus a few toes (or an entire foot or leg, if necessary) or several inches of tail. They're still able to climb and jump and do other iguana things. Quite often, removing the source of infection speeds overall recovery.

Mouth rot

Several conditions can affect the interior and exterior of the mouth. They're often incorrectly called *mouth rot,* which is the colloquial name for a serious condition called *ulcerative stomatitis,* or just *stomatitis.* Stomatitis is a secondary infection, appearing in the mouth, caused by an underlying systemic infection. For information on mouth rot, see Chapter 21.

The key to avoiding amputation, of course, is recognizing the condition before it's too late. Check the toes and tail frequently, especially after bathing the iguana, during sheds, and when trimming the claw tips every two weeks or so. Such regular checking ensures that nothing gets trapped around the toes or tail long enough to cause any damage to the underlying tissue.

The injured tail

When the tail has been crushed or caught in something, like in a closing door or between the shelf and the wall of the basking area, the tissue, starting at the end of the tail, may begin to die due to an infection known as *dry gangrene*. The tail turns dark brown or black, becomes very hard and brittle, shrinks inward, and collapses in on itself.

Sometimes the injury or infection may occur toward the middle of the length of the tail, turning it mushy, even oozy. As the infection spreads, the blood and nerve supply are disrupted in this area, causing the end of the tail to start dying; eventually, dry gangrene will set in. The infected tail must be dealt with by your veterinarian, usually by amputation, long before it gets to the point of the end dying and becoming brittle.

The dead, brittle section may be knocked off when the iguana whips its tail against something. Waiting for detachment to happen on its own, or ripping it off yourself, is not a good idea. If all the infected tissue is not surgically amputated, the infection will continue to spread farther up the tail. It may spread rapidly, in a matter of days or weeks, or slowly, over the course of several months. The saddest thing to see is an iguana with no tail or hemipenes left because the keeper kept waiting for things to get better on their own.

Injured toes

Toes may also be seriously injured due to a crush or twist trauma. The injured toe may look healthy, green, and filled out, but it may flop around uncontrollably when the iguana moves it. In other cases, the toe may start looking like the tail as described in the preceding section — turning black, brittle, or hard. The injured toe should be amputated, both to prevent the spread of any infection and to eliminate the risk of the toe being caught in something and being literally ripped off.

Poisons and Other Toxic Substances

The effects of ingesting toxic plants and chemicals (cleaning solutions, drugs, cigarette butts, medications, and so on) vary based on the size of the iguana, how much of the toxic substance he ate, how much food and water he's already had that day, his metabolic rate, and his general health. If your iguana has ingested or come into contact with a toxic substance or plant, watch for any changes in color (of the skin and in his mouth) and respiration, excessive salivation or dryness, diarrhea, heaving, vomiting, extreme restlessness, face rubbing, or lethargy.

Keep the number and address of your regular and any emergency reptile veterinarians handy at all times. Regularly weigh and measure (snout-tail length and snout-vent length) your iguana so that you can tell the vet or poison control center this information when you call. Don't try to induce vomiting or force purgatives or neutralizers without first consulting a reptile veterinarian or an animal poison control center.

Here are a couple of important phone numbers to have:

- Poison Control Center: 1-800-523-2222.

    This number is mainly for humans, not so much for animals. The call is free.

- National Animal Poison Control Center (NAPCC), University of Illinois School of Veterinary Medicine: 1-900-680-0000 ($45 per case, billed to your phone) and 888-4AN-HELP, or 888-426-4435 ($45 per case, billed to a credit card [VISA, MasterCard, Discover, or American Express]).

    NAPCC's case charge covers any necessary follow-up calls.

Make sure that you never have to find out how knowledgeable your reptile vet, your local poison control hotline, or the National Animal Poison Control Center is about poisoned iguanas: Keep toxic substances, including toxic house plants, away from your iguana (see Appendix A for a list of toxic plants).

Tail Breaks

An injury may occur that breaks, but does not sever, the tail. Instead of breaking off, or if the reflex that causes it to drop isn't triggered, there may be a separation of skin and underlying muscle that doesn't go down to the bone. This type of broken, but not severed, tail can generally be saved, but only if you get the iguana to a vet and have stitches put in within 24 hours of the break — the sooner the better to reduce the risk of infection or tissue death.

Many vets, even reptile vets, don't think to do stitches in this instance, so you may need to explain to them that it's been done successfully before. Some iguana keepers have tried to bandage the tail but have little success because iguanas are very good at removing bandages. Even if the bandage is secured with regular adhesive tape, you or the iguana may put enough pressure on the tail that it may sever completely.

If the break is through the bone but not all the way through the tail, or the stump becomes infected, removing the tail just above the break is best. Many reptile vets carve out a little bone and muscle and then pull the skin flaps over the stump, stitching them in place. Doing so helps reduce the risk of infection. It does *not* prevent the tail from regenerating: If the tail's going to grow back, it will grow through the sutured stump (see Figure 20-2).

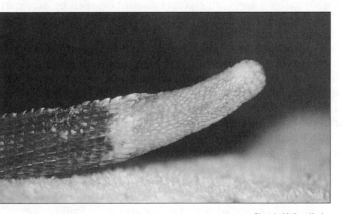

Figure 20-2:
This iguana's tail, caught in a car door, did not regrow to its previous length.

Photo by Melissa Kaplan

Tail Drops

The loss of the tail (called *autotomy*) may be natural, but it can be stressful, especially in a rescued or new baby iguana who is in less than good health. If your iguana drops his tail, there isn't much you can do other than to make sure to take care of the iguana properly, keeping his enclosure clean and warm, and him well fed. The less additional stress the iguana has to deal with, the faster the stump will heal, and if the tail is going to regenerate (they don't always do so), it will do so fairly rapidly.

When faced with a suddenly shortened tail, follow these steps:

1. **Soak the iguana in warm, chest-deep water to which you've added enough povidone-iodine to make the water the color of medium-dark tea.**

2. **Leave the iguana in the tub for 15–20 minutes, refreshing the warm water as necessary.**

   If he poops in the tub, empty it out, thoroughly flush the tail stump and set the iguana aside. After cleaning and disinfecting the tub, start the soak all over again.

3. **Remove the iguana from the tub and flush the wound with some dilute povidone-iodine.**

4. **At night, put triple antibiotic ointment on the stump.**

5. **Repeat the povidone-iodine and antibiotic application for a week or until the wound is healing over.**

If you see any sign of swelling at the end of the stump or just above it that doesn't abate after a week, the iguana should be seen by an experienced reptile vet.

In the weeks after the tail loss, be sure to maintain good nutrition and adequate food and fluid intake. Feel free to offer more food and let your iguana eat as much as he wants. Treats of bananas, grapes, and figs are nice at this time. Not only are they tasty, but they're high in calories, too. Also be sure to keep his environment as clean as possible during recovery to ensure the least amount of contamination of the wound sites.

Don't be surprised to find that your formerly agile iguana is now a bit clumsy when climbing up and down. It will take him a couple of weeks to find his new center of gravity.

Work with the tail as part of your taming and socializing process: Handle it, move it around, hold it, and pet it. The more an iguana is used to having his tail touched and manipulated, the less likely he will be to drop it defensively.

Chapter 21

Common Diseases and Disorders

In This Chapter

▶ Recognizing the signs and symptoms of common reptile diseases

▶ Making the appropriate treatment choices

*S*everal diseases and disorders commonly occur with iguanas, and this chapter can help you identify what is or may be wrong. There's no substitute for a good reptile veterinarian, however. Although some conditions or early states of some conditions may be reversed by correcting the problems causing them or by performing some minor home treatment, other conditions are serious enough to require veterinary care immediately.

I've said it before, and I'll say it again: If you're new to iguanas or you've never encountered and dealt properly with a condition before, take your iguana to a vet immediately. Waiting and hoping that things get better on their own or experimenting with over-the-counter medications that someone told you about further jeopardizes your iguana's health and, possibly, life.

Black Spots

Many iguanas have black markings, including stripes, spots, and skin showing between the scales. As a hatchling grows during his first year, his vivid green will change to his adult colors. Usually green, adults may have various markings and patches that help them blend in with their environment. All of these changes are normal. What isn't normal, however, are small, isolated black spots, which may be a fungal or bacterial infection.

✔ Fungal infections typically have a furry look (but not feel) to them and usually appear in circular patches, with two to three small circular patches clustered together.

✔ Bacterial infections may be crusty to the touch and may or may not be slightly swollen. (Small lumps may be bacteria or parasites.)

Both types of infections look very different from the normal or emerging natural black markings.

The topical and systemic drugs used to treat fungal infections are different from those used to treat bacterial infections. If you don't know which type of infection your iguana has, you won't be able to treat it yourself effectively.

One of the dangers of mistreating fungal infections on the skin is that if they're not treated fast enough with the right medication, they can penetrate through the skin into the bloodstream. Systemic fungal infections are very difficult to treat and are often not caught in time to save the iguana.

Blackening Skin Syndrome

Blackening skin syndrome is a generic name for a skin condition that has many causes. The condition itself may range from the relatively benign (corrected by proper diet, heat, and environment) to potentially lethal (advanced skin and systemic infections).

✔ An all-over black and crusty skin may be found on iguanas who have been housed in filthy or otherwise inappropriate conditions (too cold or overcrowded, for example). Once such an iguana is housed and fed properly, and soaked daily in warm povidone-iodine/water baths, the first shed can be startling, with the black scabby skin splitting apart to reveal the new, brilliant-green skin below.

✔ Iguanas housed in overcrowded enclosures get scratched and bitten by other iguanas. When they're left in this condition and in a poor environment, the wounds heal slowly, if at all. The result is an iguana webbed in crusty scabs. Proper diet, care, and daily povidone-iodine/water baths help the wounds heal. The scabs fall off and are replaced by gray scars or green scales. A veterinarian should be consulted about the use of systemic or topical antibiotics.

When adding povidone-iodine to soaking water, add enough of the antiseptic to change the color of the water to that of medium-dark tea. If you pour the povidone-iodine under the stream of incoming water, a lot of bubbly foam is produced, so pour it in farther away from the incoming water so that you don't scare or obscure your iguana. If your iguana does end up in a povidone-iodine bubble bath, he'll be fine — other than looking a bit ludicrous.

✔ Heavy infestations of mites may lead to areas of crusty, scabby, or oozing patches on the body, especially where the scales are smaller and thinner: around the head, neck, dewlap, and armpits. For information on getting rid of reptile mites, head to Chapter 22.

If not caught in time or not treated properly, skin infections may spread to the blood and organs and result in the iguana's death.

Constipation

An iguana who eats daily should be pooping daily. If he doesn't, there's a problem. The longer he goes without pooping, the more serious the situation is. As wastes back up in the iguana's system, illness and organ failure may occur.

If your iguana has never gone daily, check your enclosure temperatures. Chances are, they've always been too low throughout the day and possibly at night.

Due to minor conditions or blockage

Most often, constipation is due to the environmental temperatures being too low. During the winter, it's not uncommon for the temperatures to drop in the enclosure or iguana's room without the keeper being aware of it. Always double-check the day and night temperatures to make sure that they're where they need to be, and install additional equipment as necessary.

After a prolonged period of no pooping, bathing and massaging are required (along with correcting the temperature problem) to get things moving along again. Note that iguanas who are suffering from mild metabolic bone disease or paralysis benefit from bath and massage treatments, too, because pooping is difficult for iguanas with those conditions.

1. **Bathe the iguana in warm water (80–85 degrees Fahrenheit/26.5–29 degrees Celsius) for 10–15 minutes.**

2. **Gently massage the iguana's belly, in smooth stokes from sternum to vent, for 5 minutes or so while he is still in the water.**

3. **Let the iguana stay in the warm water (refreshing as necessary to maintain the proper temperatures) for at least another 10–15 minutes.**

The iguana should poop within 24 hours if the blockage is due to being too cool, a very small piece or two of ingested substrate, or a very mild case of internal parasites or metabolic bone disease. If he doesn't, get him to the vet.

If the urates are greatly reduced in quantity, very thick, and yellow or rusty, either the iguana is in breeding season, is dehydrated, or has another problem that may require a vet's attention. Rusty red urates of otherwise normal consistency usually mean the iguana has eaten a harmless food that temporarily colors the urates. If the urates and feces are rusty colored and there's a strong smell, the iguana likely has a protozoan infection and needs to visit the vet with a fecal sample to be tested.

Due to serious conditions or blockage

If the blockage is due to heavy parasite infestation, a clump of ingested human or pet hair, or several pieces of substrate or other foreign objects, then bathing, massage, and increased heat won't work. You need to get the iguana to the vet for further diagnostic work and treatment.

The use of laxatives is not recommended without a vet's supervision and thorough evaluation of the iguana's health and environment. The wrong type of laxative may cause other health problems, and if the blockage is due to a foreign object, the wrong type of laxative may further damage the intestines.

Diarrhea

Prolonged diarrhea can be caused by parasite infections, especially if accompanied by reddish urates or a strong odor. Get a fecal sample and your iguana to a reptile vet for immediate examination and treatment.

A proper microscopic examination of the fecal sample is required to determine what organism is causing the problem. Once that's known, the right medication can be prescribed. Doses are based on weight and size, so a vet needs to have an accurate weight to determine the proper dose. Follow the vet's directions for the initial and subsequent doses of medication. Have the feces rechecked a couple of weeks after the last dose to determine whether an additional dose is required.

Don't try to treat parasites and protozoan infections with pet store remedies. Even if you happen to get lucky and it's the right drug for the parasite that's causing the problem, the product is unlikely to be strong enough to work or can't be dosed properly without an accurate weight. When using such over-the-counter remedies instead of having your iguana properly diagnosed and treated by the reptile vet, you end up with a still-sick lizard and very healthy parasites who may now be resistant to the drug.

To get a fecal mass from the iguana's enclosure to your vet, turn a plastic self-sealing bag inside out over your hand. With your plastic-encased fingers, grab the feces (leave the urates behind) and use your other hand to pull the bag right-side out over your bagged hand. Seal the bag up, use a felt pen to write your iguana's name and the date on it, and then bag it in a second bag. You can store the bag in the refrigerator for up to four hours before taking it to the vet.

Psychological upset can also cause temporary diarrhea, and so can a radical change in diet or eating a food item that doesn't agree with the lizard's digestive system. If the diarrhea persists for more than a couple of days, however, the iguana needs to be seen by a vet.

Hibernation

Iguanas don't hibernate. Tropical animals don't hibernate. If your iguana appears to be hibernating (sleeping a lot, hard to rouse, staying in the cool side of the enclosure, not eating, not basking, or not doing much of anything), it's sick, not hibernating. You need to check to make sure the environment is set up properly, making all the necessary changes. You need to correct the diet if it isn't appropriate for the iguana. You also need to get your iguana to a reptile vet to be thoroughly checked out, including blood tests to check for systemic infection, metabolic bone disease, and kidney disease.

Although healthy iguanas are less active and eat less during the winter, they don't behave like they're hibernating — not if their enclosures or free-roaming areas are heated and lit properly. They remain alert, interact with their humans, eat and defecate regularly, thermoregulate their body temperature, and maintain a regular daily schedule of activity.

Hypercalcemia

Hypercalcemia, a condition in which there's a high level of calcium in the blood, is uncommon in captive iguanas. When it occurs, due to adding too much calcium to the diet, it can cause cardiac, gut, kidney, and other serious health problems. You won't see many visible signs of these problems, other than reduced activity and changes in urates if the kidneys are affected. The only time mild hypercalcemia is good is if your iguana is gravid. Having a little too much calcium at this time means that she not only has enough calcium to keep her own body strong and healthy but also has enough for the developing embryos (which can number from 12 to over 60) *and* their shells.

Hypocalcemia — calcium deficiency — is all too common in gravid iguanas. It can result in the iguana not being able to lay her eggs (dystocia) and may also cause her death if it's not caught and treated in time. See the section "Metabolic Bone Disease" for information on the other dangers of calcium deficiency.

Hypervitaminosis

Hypervitaminosis is the condition caused by excess administration or absorption of vitamins, which results in high levels of the vitamin or mineral in the blood (serum). Hypervitaminosis A is excess vitamin A, for example, and hypervitaminosis D is excess vitamin D.

High levels of vitamins and minerals can be just as dangerous as levels that are too low. There are few visible signs of vitamin overdose, a condition generally found when the vet is doing an examination and blood work. Fortunately, hypervitaminosis is rarely a problem with properly cared for captive iguanas. If you are careful with the vitamin supplementation, you won't have this problem.

Kidney Failure

Kidney failure and metabolic bone disease (covered in the next section) are the leading killers of iguanas in captivity. Signs of kidney failure may be subtle, so much so that you may not notice any significant changes until it's too late. Signs include weight loss despite eating, followed by anorexia; lethargy; a swollen or distended abdomen; frequent drinking or voiding; a grossly swollen neck (*not* the normal jowls of the sexually mature male) and/or dewlap.

Some iguanas may exhibit mineralization of the tissues due to the buildup of uric acid crystals (due to animal protein or lack of sufficient hydration to effect proper digestion and waste removal), which may be visible or felt as hard lumpy clusters around the joints of the legs and feet. Urates are thicker and yellowish, and small crystals may be seen in them.

The eyes themselves may become swollen. This swelling is very different from the puffy eyelids associated with a normal shed. The eyeballs swell and the lower lids droop, making the eyes look somewhat like a bloodhound's eyes.

During the final one- to two-week period, the signs start piling up on one another. There may also be reduced thermoregulatory behavior, or you may see a complete failure to thermoregulate as the iguana gets too weak to move. The iguana sleeps more. There's extremely rapid weight loss, inconsistent with past periods of reduced or no food intake. Loss of muscle tone, lack of deep pain responses, and gross reduction in interactive (animal/animal and animal/human) responses are noted as systems get toxic and start to shut down.

Your veterinarian and lab work will diagnose this condition and let you know if any treatment is possible. If the condition is caught early enough, treatment includes complete diet and environment overhaul, phosphate binders, and regular hydration via IV or IC injection. Iguanas who survive one bout of kidney disease are always susceptible to it and must be watched carefully in the future.

Metabolic Bone Disease

Signs of metabolic bone disease (MBD) include hard knobs in the long bones of the legs; thickened, "buff" thighs; bumps or swellings along the vertebral column of the back and tail; and a noticeable softening or hard swelling of the jaw (see Figure 21-1). Many of these signs can be felt before they can be seen, making a careful physical exam an important part of the keeper's routine. Signs of moderate to severe MBD include jerky gait when walking, tremors and twitches in the limbs and muscles of the legs and toes when at rest, and a shakiness when being held. Advanced cases of MBD include all the preceding signs plus constipation, anorexia, and fractured bones. Severely deficient reptiles tend to be lethargic and may only be able to drag themselves along the ground.

Figure 21-1:
A lower jaw swollen on both sides is a sign that your iguana is suffering from a metabolic bone disease.

Photo by Melissa Kaplan

You can successfully treat very mild cases — if caught early enough, when the signs are barely felt or visible — by providing the proper environment, including ultraviolet B, proper diet, and a temporary boost in calcium supplement. Moderate and severe cases of MBD require all of the above, as well as a more powerful calcium supplement than those found in pet stores.

Unless you have successfully dealt with metabolic bone disease before, however, it's always best to consult a reptile veterinarian instead of trying to determine for yourself the severity of the disorder and appropriate treatment. Your iguana's life depends on proper diagnosis and treatment.

Paralysis

If you're reading this section because your iguana is paralyzed and you have not yet seen a veterinarian about it, drop the book, carefully grab your iguana, and get to the vet *now*. Paralysis is not a normal physical condition and should be treated as a medical emergency.

Although a few cases of partial (lower abdomen and/or hind quarters and tail) paralysis are caused by an accident, such as a heavy object falling on the iguana's spine, the majority of cases are due to metabolic bone disease (see the section "Metabolic Bone Disease").

If the underlying condition is resolved, there's a chance that normal, or near normal, functioning will be restored. There may be some change in gait and residual deformity of the spine or tail, but, overall, the iguana should recover most of his former mobility and agility. Recovery doesn't happen all by itself, though. You *must* get veterinary attention for your iguana, as well as make the necessary changes to the diet and environment.

A permanently paralyzed iguana may require help moving around and, most importantly, defecating. You need to give him daily baths and massages to get the feces and urates expelled. If he's a quadriplegic, you may need to move him from the basking area to the sleeping area to the feeding area. (Paraplegic iguanas can often drag themselves around using just their fore-arms, though their climbing ability is severely, if not completely, impaired.)

In many cases, however, survival is relatively short, even with the most attentive of keepers. The iguana goes into both a physical and mental decline. Ultimately, the keeper is faced with having to address the iguana's quality of life versus euthanasia. When addressing this situation, it's important for the keeper to remove his or her personal feelings. The keeper needs to make an *objective* assessment of the iguana's day-to-day life. If the decision is delayed too long, the iguana continues to decline, eventually dying a prolonged, probably painful, death. (Refer to Chapter 19 for important information about euthanasia.)

Prolapses

A *prolapse* is the eversion (intrusion or forced protrusion) of tissue into an area where it shouldn't be. In iguanas, three types of prolapses may occur that can be seen by the keeper: cloacal, intestinal, or hemipenal. They're potentially very serious, and if they don't correct themselves within a very short period of time, the iguana must be seen by a reptile vet.

- ✔ If the iguana is constipated, the strain of trying to poop may result in either a section of the intestine, cloacal tissue, or one or both hemipenes being everted through the vent.

- ✔ Severe parasite infestation and *dystocia* (egg binding in gravid iguanas) may also result in prolapsed tissue. In these cases, or if the iguana is already weakened by the underlying condition, he or she may not be able to retract the tissue.

- ✔ When pooping, the male's hemipenes may be everted and then quickly retracted. During breeding season, the hemipenes may be briefly everted in conjunction with depositing some seminal material, especially when being greeted by their female keeper. If a hemipenes prolapses for too long, however, the tissue starts to die.

In all cases, if left outside the body, the everted tissue may become contaminated with feces, urates, food, or other matter, and start to dry out. If not properly cleaned and replaced, the tissue dies and requires amputation.

You can try soaking the iguana in a cool bath that you've added granulated sugar to. Heavy concentrations of sugar in the water draw out the fluids engorging the swollen everted tissue, which may reduce it enough to be inverted back into place by the lizard. If the soaking doesn't work, the iguana should be placed on a damp towel and taken to the vet right away.

Some lizards may repeatedly prolapse. If this is the case, the vet may need to suture the tissue to the body wall to try to prevent the tissue from prolapsing again.

Respiratory Infections

Respiratory infections are generally caused by prolonged periods of inadequate heat in the reptile's environment. They're not caused by catching human cold or flu viruses. (*Note:* The respiratory system may be affected by the ingestion or inhalation of toxic plants or substances. Refer to Chapter 20's section on poisons and other toxic substances for more information.)

Symptoms include listlessness; weight loss due to decreased appetite; a swollen or bloated body; gaping; and open-mouth breathing, often with audible exhalations when the infection is in an advanced state. You may hear wheezing or clicking noises while the iguana's breathing. Bubbly, stringy, or sheeting mucous appears in the mouth. The iguana may hold its head in a raised position to make breathing easier. Sneezing is *not* a sign of respiratory infection. (To find out what sneezing is about, head to Chapter 19.)

If your iguana has a respiratory infection, check the temperatures in his enclosure or area. If the day and night thermal gradients are not being met or

---

"But my iguana was so healthy!"

Generally speaking, right up until 1–2 weeks before they start to die — before their kidneys give out — most iguanas suffering from kidney disease may look as healthy as always, exhibiting normal behaviors in thermoregulating, feeding, and defecating. Feces and urates may look normal. The signs of renal failure can come on so suddenly and overlap those of many other conditions, that most owners don't even have time do anything about it before their iguana lapses into final shock. As iguana keepers become more knowledgeable about the signs of kidney disease, they're able to jump on the situation before it goes too far, and an increasing number of people have been able to save their iguanas' lives.

---

maintained, add whatever is needed to make sure that they are. If the signs of respiratory infection don't clear up within a day of correcting the environment, take your iguana to a reptile vet, who may prescribe antibiotics for the infection and fluid injections for the dehydration. During his convalescence, you need to keep the iguana in a draft-free but well-ventilated enclosure or area and maintain the proper thermal gradients. Doing so not only helps the iguana's own immune system function better but also increases the effectiveness of the antibiotics.

If your iguana isn't eating, you may need to hand-feed him or force-feed him by administering a slurry of pureed food (such as iguana salad liquefied in a blender) with a feeding syringe. Feel free to offer more of his favorite treats if that will help get him self-feeding. Once he shows signs of improvement and increased appetite, wean him back onto his usual diet.

Be careful when you're forcing fluids or food into a sick or weak iguana's mouth. At the back of their tongue, as it begins to curve into the throat, is the *glottis,* a valve leading into the trachea. The glottis has a flap of skin that keeps it closed when the iguana is eating or drinking. The glottis may remain open as the iguana struggles or is breathing with its mouth open, allowing food or fluid to pass into the trachea and then into the lungs instead of going down the esophagus.

Shedding Problems

A healthy iguana sheds every 4–6 weeks. During peak growing periods, such as spring and summer, one shed may start while the previous shed is still coming off. It's common for such growth to slow down during winter and breeding season. During these times of slowed growth and reduced food intake, iguanas often don't shed.

If your iguana is not shedding, and it's not winter or breeding season, then there's a problem. It may be that the environment is wrong, the diet is not nutritious enough to promote growth or normal skin-renewal processes, or your iguana is sick. The iguana may also be psychologically stressed. Check out the environment and diet and review any other factors that may affect how the iguana responds psychosocially to his environment. Slow growers should also be seen by a reptile vet to ensure that they're not suffering from bacterial or parasite infestations or any other medical problems. Even healthy iguanas have a little problem shedding now and then, due primarily to the captive environment not being humid enough.

If your iguana is shedding normally, you still have to be on the lookout for problem areas:

- ✔ Watch the shedding skin on his toes, spikes, and tail to make sure it all comes off. Small circles of skin left attached to these areas strangle the tissue beneath as the iguana continues to grow. The blood supply is cut off, leading to tissue death.

- ✔ If the skin on the spikes is stuck, you can help it off by first bathing the iguana and then rubbing some baby or mineral oil into the still-wet spikes. The oil traps the water, giving it time to work its way up the spikes between the layers of old and new skin. You may need to do this task for a couple of days until the rack of spike shed comes off.

- ✔ Sometimes the grommet-shaped pieces of skin around the nostrils may not come off, and as your iguana nears his next shed, you begin to hear a sort of distant whistling sound as he breathes. After the next bath, work at this area gently to remove any such retained shed. This whistling may also occur when the grommets are loosening inside the nose prior to a shed.

TIP

The best way to ensure complete shedding is to bathe your iguana regularly before and during the shed. Spraying with plain tap water several times a day is very helpful, especially during the winter and summer months.

TIP

Particularly resistant dorsal crest shed may need extra attention, especially on rescued iguanas who may have several layers of retained shed stuck to them. After a long, warm bath, bundle up the still-wet iguana in a warm, thick towel. Soak a washcloth in warm water. Expose a small area of the dorsal crest and place the damp washcloth on it, holding it for several minutes. Work at the old skin, loosening it with your fingers. Rewet the cloth in warm water and work your way down the spine, exposing an area of spikes, applying the compress, and fingering the old skin to loosen it. You may need to repeat this process for several days or more until all the old shed layers have been removed.

Stomatitis (Mouth Rot)

Stomatitis (frequently called *mouth rot*) is caused by a systemic bacterial infection. This underlying infection in the body creates abscesses in the mouth — in the gum, palate, or tongue tissue. It can't be effectively treated with over-the-counter preparations from the drugstore or with pet store remedies. It requires veterinary intervention, both to surgically remove the abscesses and to prescribe the proper systemic antibiotics. (For information on abscesses caused by injury, refer to Chapter 20.)

Signs of stomatitis include excessive salivation; thickened, sheeting, or ropy saliva; *petechia* (tiny burst capillaries visible in the gum, palate, or tongue tissue); or *plaques*, cheesy-looking patches of whitish, yellowish, or greenish material, which are actually the tops of the abscesses embedded in the surrounding tissue.

Sometimes the infection is persistent, with new plaques forming after the original plaques are removed. The vet may prescribe a second course of antibiotics or double the dose (which may safely be done with Baytril, the most commonly used antibiotic for stomatitis). If the infection still isn't resolved after a second course or doubled dose of antibiotic, a section of one of the abscesses has to be taken and cultured to determine the best antibiotic to use.

If your iguana has stomatitis, keep him quiet and warm. At night, keep the temperatures the same as the daytime temperatures (75–85 degrees Fahrenheit/23–29 degrees Celsius). A well-fleshed iguana may be able to go a couple of days without eating, but if the iguana has been sick for some time, he does need to eat. Since some may be reluctant to eat or drink because of the discomfort, you may need to hand- or force-feed fluids and food. Pedialyte, a pediatric electrolyte solution, or a 1:1 mix of Gatorade and water, may be used for oral fluids. If force-feeding is required, it's best if a slurry is administered by a tube attached to a large syringe. Iguanas may be encouraged to lap the slurry off the tip of the syringe itself. Once they realize that it doesn't hurt to eat it and that they can lap it up themselves, you can leave a bowl of the slurry for them to lap up when they're hungry. As the mouth heals, you can mix some iguana vegetable-alfalfa-fruit salad in with the bowl of slurry, gradually increasing the amount of salad and decreasing the amount of slurry until your iguana is feeding normally once again.

Infections occur as a result of an injury or a suppressed immune system. Immune suppression may be caused by many things: The iguana may have been subjected to incorrect temperatures; a sick new lizard or other pet may have been brought into the household without first being placed in quarantine; the enclosure and furnishings and equipment may have gone a little too long without being properly cleaned and disinfected; or the iguana has been under psychosocial stress. Once you figure out the cause and correct the situation, you reduce the risk of continued illness, stress, and reinfection.

TIP

Slurries for sick iguanas

You can offer two types of slurries to your iguana. The first is a pureed blend of alfalfa powder, baby food squash, baby food fruit, and multivitamin and calcium supplement, thinned with water or fruit juice. This slurry is good if your iguana was in generally good health before the infection set in and had been digesting his food well. Iguanas who have been sick a long time and who are severely underweight should be started off with a small amount of liquid acidophilus or nonfat yogurt with live bacteria. Then make a slurry with regular Ensure (a liquid human food supplement), banana or other fruit, and calcium, thinned with Pedialyte. Once the iguana has been fed this slurry for several days, start weaning him onto the alfalfa-vegetable-fruit slurry and then onto solid food.

Vesicular Dermatitis: Blister Disease

Vesicular dermatitis, sometimes called blister disease, scale rot, or necrotizing dermatitis, is commonly caused by housing reptiles in moist, dirty environments. As the animal is forced to lie on damp substrate saturated with water, rotting food, or feces and urates, the skin becomes infected. Watery blisters are the first sign. The infection may pass into the body, causing infection of the blood and then passing to internal organs. In small reptiles, or reptiles already severely weakened from illness, environmental stresses, or psychological stresses, infection may be rapid — and rapidly fatal. The skin may rot away from the initial blister, leaving the body more susceptible to bacterial and fungal invasion and thermal burns.

As with many illnesses and conditions, treatment must be two-fold. The iguana must be seen by a vet for evaluation and initiation of treatment (antibiotic therapy and surgical removal of the dead skin and tissue), and the iguana's environment must be thoroughly cleaned, disinfected, and set up properly to promote healing and growth, not disease.

- ✔ When small blisters are first noticed, you can soak the iguana in a povidone-iodine/water bath one or two times daily. Follow the soak with a dab of triple-antibiotic ointment on the blisters.

- ✔ During recovery, use a substrate that's easily changed and discarded or disinfected, like paper towels or clean terry-cloth towels. Also, all bottom heat should be suspended during this period; provide the necessary thermal gradients by overhead radiant heat sources.

- ✔ If the blisters don't resolve in a few days, or if they are large blisters or are spread out over a wide area, the iguana must be seen by a reptile vet. Blisters increase the fluid loss from the body, rapidly leading to dehydration.

Small blisters, crusting, or ulcerations of the skin may also be caused by exposure to toxic substances, such as residues from cleaning compounds and disinfectants, and exposure to toxic substrates, such as cedar wood or redwood used in cage construction or furnishings. If the condition is due to toxic substances, the substances need to be removed and discarded, and the contaminated surfaces of the enclosure or free-roaming areas must be washed with hot, soapy water to remove all oily or other chemical residues. After a thorough rinsing and disinfection, the enclosure may be outfitted with a proper substrate and furnishings.

Crusty blisters or oozing bumps may also be a form of topical salmonella. If you can't figure out what is causing the blisters or lumps, and a few days of topical antibiotic or antifungal medications don't result in visible signs of healing, your iguana must be seen by a vet for evaluation and proper treatment. If your iguana does indeed have salmonella, you or your family members can get it, too.

Chapter 22

Dealing with Reptile Mites

In This Chapter

▶ Knowing when you have an infestation

▶ Getting mites off your iguana

▶ Ridding the environment of mites

▶ Some safety issues

*M*ites, like ticks, are eight-legged blood-sucking creatures. They carry and transmit diseases from one reptile to another. (Fortunately, the mite species found infesting reptile hosts are unlikely to feed on nonreptilian hosts.) They are tiny, are very mobile, and may be found roaming around from place to place on the iguana and in the iguana's environment.

A captive iguana is especially vulnerable to mites. He's confined in a relatively small environment with rapidly replicating mites. The mite population explodes so dramatically that shedding for a captive iguana, unlike a wild iguana, doesn't provide any relief. As soon as a patch of new skin is exposed, it's colonized or traversed by mites looking for easy pickings through soft, new skin.

Mites can have a devastating impact on healthy iguanas because even well-adjusted iguanas suffer from chronic stress. Mites are such a big problem, in fact, that they merit their own chapter.

Recognizing an Infestation

On lizards, reptile mites can usually be found roaming the body — tucked under the edges of scales and congregating around the eyes, ears, tympanic membrane, and any place on the body where the scales are thinner. Other favorite places to look for them include the tiny spaces in between the dorsal crest and in the folds of soft skin around the armpits, neck, dewlap, and ears.

If you can see them from about three feet away, or your hand comes away with several mites on it, then you have a severe infestation. Reptiles who are moderately to severely debilitated may require fluids and nutrient supplementation to help restore fluid balance and provide energy for rapid recovery.

Depending on where they are in their life cycle, mites may be black, bright red/orange, or the color of old, dried blood. They're primarily nocturnal, so you can often best see them at night after the lights have been off for several hours: Check your iguana and his enclosure using a flashlight.

Effectively Killing Mites

The best way to get rid of mites is to never get them to begin with. Unfortunately, every time you visit a pet store, reptile expo, or herp society meeting, or interact with an infested herp, you risk unwittingly transporting mites into your iguana's environment.

Mites are a drag, plain and simple, and there's no easy way to get rid of them. You need to do a two-pronged attack: aggressively treat the environment as well as the iguana. You treat the environment with toxic pesticides after removing the iguana to a safe area. While the environment is being fumigated, you work on the lizard, using less toxic substances. If your iguana is a free-roamer, treating the environment may be an overwhelming proposition but one that must be undertaken — and undertaken aggressively.

Generally speaking, the mite treatment products available at pet stores are ineffective, and attempts to treat the environment with herbal or homeo-pathic remedies don't work. Many people appropriately try to reduce or avoid the use of toxic chemicals in their lives and the lives of their pets, but when it comes to ridding an environment of tenacious, hard-shelled pests who, in concentrations large enough, can kill your iguana, you must act quickly and aggressively. Finally, cleaning and disinfecting simply the enclosure/environment do *not* eradicate the mites. Doing those tasks gets rid of the loose feces and may wash away many of the exposed mites and eggs, killing any bacteria left behind where the mites were squashed or defecated. However, it's very unlikely that cleaning and disinfecting kill the nonfeeding morphs, larvae, and pregnant females hidden away in deep crevices.

Fortunately, the following methods have proven successful in ridding an envi-ronment and iguana of mites. Note that, because mite eggs and mites in non-feeding morphs are not affected by most of the chemicals that kill off the adults, you may have to repeat the treatment of both the environment and iguana at least once, possibly twice, within a two- to six-week period.

Treating the iguana

To get rid of mites on your iguana, you need povidone-iodine, a bathtub, clean towels, cotton-tipped swabs, and a warm holding area. With this stuff at hand, do the following:

1. **If the iguana is loaded with mites, give a plain, warm-water bath first.**

   Pour water over the iguana from a cup or pitcher. Doing so helps loosen and float off the majority of the mites, which can then be washed down the drain.

2. **Refill the tub with warm, shoulder-deep water (80–85 degrees Fahrenheit/26–29 degrees Celsius), this time adding the povidone-iodine (Betadine), and let the iguana soak.**

   Larger iguanas can be left to soak for a half hour or so, with fresh, warm water added as the original bath water cools. If the iguana is very small, remove him from the bath once he has been cleared of mites and continue with the rest of the treatment, which follows.

   Add enough povidone-iodine to the bath water to make it the color of medium-dark tea. Pour the bath water over the lizard, being careful around the eyes. The water flushes most of the mites off and drowns them; the Betadine, a topical antiseptic, helps treat all the mites' bites.

3. **When he's done soaking, remove the iguana and check him over carefully for any remaining mites.**

   You may still find mites in some of the areas where folds of skin are.

4. **Saturate a clean, soft cloth in diluted povidone-iodine and then run it around the joints between the iguana's legs and body and also through the folds of skin around the neck, jowls, and dewlap.**

5. **Use a cotton-tipped swab to apply the diluted povidone-iodine carefully around the eyes and nose.**

   If your iguana is very small, or you are a bit shaky, use plain water on the cotton-tipped swab when working around the eye area rather than risk getting any povidone-iodine in the eye itself.

   Don't put oil into the iguana's eyes. Unlike snakes, iguanas don't have a protective covering of skin over their eyes, and putting oil in the eyes can cause severe irritation or inflammation.

6. **Check between all of the neck, back, and tail spikes to see if any mites remain lodged in there.**

   If you find some, you can remove them with a moistened cotton-tipped swab.

7. **When you're done, place the iguana in a plain warm-water bath if he hasn't already defecated or if he just likes to soak.**

If the iguana is badly chewed up by mites (lots of scabby or oozy areas are on the body and neck), let him soak again in a fresh povidone-iodine bath. You should repeat these medicated baths once a day while the bites heal. If your iguana is trained to go potty in the tub, poop him first, clean out the tub, and then run the medicated bath for him.

While your iguana is soaking, or once he has been removed from the medicated bath and checked over for any remaining mites, leave him in a warm, secure area while you go to work on treating the enclosure (described in the very next section).

Treating the environment

Treating the environment includes removing the loose pieces (furnishings, substrates, and so on) and de-miting them, as well as working on the enclosure or room itself.

Removing the moveable bits

If you're using indoor/outdoor carpet for the substrate (or some other type of disposable or loose material), carefully remove and dispose of it by putting it in a plastic garbage bag and getting it out of the building. If your substrate is terry-cloth towels, place them in a plastic bag and take them directly to the washing machine. Set the water temperature to hot, set the water level to accommodate a large load, and set the machine to run an extra rinse cycle. Then add your usual amount of soap or detergent and some household bleach.

If you have heating pads inside the tank, unplug and gently shake them (to shake off as many mites as you can). Wipe the pads down with a damp cloth to remove any clinging mites and then remove the pads from the enclosure, placing them in a sink, tub, or receptacle outside the house (don't submerge the control switch in water). Clean the pads with soapy water, rinse, and then spray them down with disinfectant. Let them sit with the disinfectant on them for at least ten minutes; then rinse and set them aside.

If you have one of those self-adhesive reptile heating pads, check under it as best you can or, better yet, get rid of it entirely, replacing it with a human heating pad or infrared heat panel. Mites can crawl into the tiniest of spaces between the self-adhesive pads and the glass to await their next metamorphosis. If there's any doubt as to whether or not any mites are hiding under the self-adhesive pad, rip it off and throw it out.

Unplug all light fixtures and any other electrical fixtures and wipe them down with a damp cloth to remove any adventuresome mites and their feces.

You can bake wooden cage furnishings such as branches, caves, or rocks in the oven, set at 200–250 degrees Fahrenheit (93–121 degrees Celsius), for 2–3 hours (depending on the thickness of the wood and the temperature); check on them during this time to make sure that they don't start to scorch or burn. If you don't bake them, you need to soak them in a bleach-water solution.

Pieces that are too large to fit in the oven may be soaked in a 1:30 bleach-water solution (½ cup of bleach per gallon of water) in the bathtub or another receptacle for eight hours or so, giving time for the water and bleach to penetrate into all crevices. Rinse the pieces thoroughly, spraying fresh water into all the crevices until they're well saturated and flushed free of any bleach residue. Let the pieces dry thoroughly, preferably in the sun, before placing them back into the iguana's enclosure or area.

Rocks (*not* electric hot rocks) may be submerged in a pot of water and boiled for 20–30 minutes. Rocks too large to fit in your largest soup pot can be soaked in bleach water as described previously for large branches.

Wash all bowls with the bleach-water solution, rinse them well, and let them air dry.

Once the moveable contents of the enclosure have been removed and dealt with, vacuum the inside of the enclosure thoroughly, especially in the angles of the walls. If the tank is made of wood, or melamine that doesn't have a bead of grout running along the intersections of walls, ceiling, and floor, lightly scrape the inside angles with the edge of a blunt knife; then vacuum again. If your flooring is made of self-stick linoleum tiles, run the knife between any gaps between tiles. The knifing helps dislodge and bring to the surface dead mites, mite eggs, live mites, and mite feces hiding in those crevices. Vacuum up any dislodged debris.

If your tank is made of wood and wire, or PVC and wire, run your knife along every spot where the walls and floors of the enclosure come into contact with the frame. In addition, with PVC pipe, you have to check the insides of the pipe to see if mites may have found their way inside.

If your enclosure is glass or Plexiglas, wipe all surfaces down with hot, soapy water. Wooden and PVC enclosures may be sprayed with soapy water. Remove all soap residues.

For good measure, take the time to thoroughly disinfect tanks by swabbing them down with a 1:30 bleach-water solution (½ cup of bleach per gallon of water). Let the solution sit for ten minutes and then thoroughly rinse out the bleach residue. Disinfecting doesn't kill the mites; it kills potentially harmful organisms that may be spread around by the mites. But depending on how much of the disinfecting solution you apply, it may drown the mites you missed during the cleaning step.

Killing the remaining mites

Squeeze a pest strip or cat flea collar out of the inner envelope it was packed in and put it onto a piece of aluminum foil. (Leave a bit of the strip or collar inside the packaging so that you can easily slide it back in without touching it when done.) Lay the foil on the floor of the enclosure.

If the enclosure is a large one, you may need to set out several strips or collars, placing them in different locations. If you're using a flea collar, stretch it out so that more of its surface area is exposed (and chemicals released). You may need to cut them into pieces to prevent them from curling up again when you let go of the ends; if so, use a disposable razor blade and cut them on several layers of cardboard, disposing of the blade and cardboard when you're done.

Close the enclosure doors and seal the enclosure up as air-tight as possible to keep the toxic pesticide fumes inside the tank where they're needed. Cover large mesh or screened areas, ventilation panels, and holes with waste paper or plastic, taping it in place with masking tape. Use masking tape over the seams and any gaps between the doors and tank. (Masking tape works well because it seals tightly but comes off easily, doesn't leave a tacky residue, and doesn't rip paint off of painted surfaces.)

Leave the sealed enclosure alone for three hours — longer for large enclosures. During this time, you can vacuum the floors and the nearby upholstered furniture and drapes, and clean all surrounding surfaces. Check the drapes carefully; if they're heavily infested, they may need to be sent out for professional cleaning. Remember to wipe down the table and chair legs and other smooth vertical surfaces with a damp cloth: Because mites can walk on glass, your laminated or wooden bookcase is going to be a piece of cake for them. Once you're done vacuuming, take the vacuum bag out and dispose of it outside the building.

With all the Disposing of Things That Crawleth with Mites that'll be going on during your eradication process, you may want to plan your de-miting day to be the day before your garbage is due to be picked up. If you live in an apartment building, take the bags down to the dumpster and place them where they won't be smashed and broken open by other people's garbage falling on top of them.

When the time is up, unseal the tank, putting all the paper and tape into a plastic bag for immediate disposal into the trash. Push the pest strip or flea collar back into its original packaging, place it in a zipper type of bag, and then store it in a safe place for future use if needed.

Leave the tank open to air it out for several hours. If possible, open a window in the room and turn on a fan to help get rid of the fumes. A portable fan may even be placed inside the enclosure or positioned so that it's blowing into the enclosure to speed the air circulation. The fumes may be undetectable to you, but they can still affect your reptile, so you want them flushed completely out of the reptile's environment.

Put new substrate and any new furnishings into the enclosure. Simple substrates, such as paper towels, are best for the next couple of weeks. They enable you to easily see if additional mites have hatched or migrated into the tank from the surrounding area. Place the water bowl and hide box into the tank. Reinstall and turn on the heating and lighting, warm the tank back up, and place the iguana back inside.

After you're finished

Keep a close eye on the iguana and the enclosure for the next month. If you see any reappearance of mites or traces of mites (such as their ashy feces), repeat the preceding procedures. If you see no reappearance, you still may want to repeat the procedure in six weeks just to make sure that you have caught all the eggs, especially in a wooden tank.

Alternative Methods and Substances

Here are some other options and products iguana keepers have used in their battle against mites (read this stuff carefully, though, because some of them work, some don't, and some are downright dangerous):

- **Heat:** You can use high heat to kill mites in an enclosure. Glass or other enclosures may be sealed up and placed in the sun (obviously, the animal should be housed elsewhere while this is being done). Do this option on days when the outside temperatures are in the mid 80s–90s (29–32 degrees Celsius) so that the temperature inside the enclosure reaches or exceeds 131 degrees Fahrenheit (55 degrees Celsius) for the several hours required to kill the mites.

- **Ivermectin (Ivomec):** Although some vets recommend injecting a reptile with ivermectin (a cattle and sheep wormer) as a way to get rid of mites, the drug is highly toxic. Even the drug's manufacturer strongly advises against injecting it into reptiles for any reason, including for worming. Another way to use this drug, however, is externally, in a spray made by mixing ivermectin and water. Mix 0.5 cc (5 mg) of injectable ivermectin per quart of water. Shake or stir vigorously and use it immediately to wipe down or spray the entire inside of the enclosure and the iguana (being sure to avoid his eyes and mouth).

- **Pest strips:** Although this product has historically been recommended to be used in the tank *while the reptile is in residence,* an increasing number of reptile keepers and vets recommend against doing so due to the often fatal incidents of poisoning from the fumes that comes off of these strips. Some reptiles may die right away, but exposed animals may take months to sicken and die — so long from the exposure event that the exposure isn't remembered or associated with the "sudden" illness (and the reptile is said to have died "mysteriously" or "for no reason").

If you're planning to use the more "natural" pyrethrin and permithrin products, keep in mind that these plant-derived pesticides are still highly toxic. Research is finding that even the supposedly innocuous inert ingredients in these products are highly toxic.

✔ **Pet trade reptile mite sprays:** Any spray-on-the-reptile product is going to be worthless unless the environment is treated as well, and plain water washes off most mites just as well. Avian mite sprays, which generally contain permithrins or pyrethrins, are also generally ineffective on mites but pose a problem if your iguana comes into contact with them or their residues. One spray product that does seem to work is Provent-A-Mite, available through ads in reptile magazines or its Web site at www.pro-products.com.

✔ **Trichlorfan:** Trichlorfan, a cattle insecticide, has been reported as useful, but it has also been reported as fatal to geckos. The recommended procedure for using it includes keeping the reptile in the chemical's residues and without water for 24 hours. This is not recommended for iguanas. The residues of this chemical are also toxic to humans, making cleaning and removing the residues a problem.

A Word on Safety

Working with pesticides — internal and external products alike — always involves some risk. An animal may be oversensitive to a product or to a particular component in a product. In a group of animals being treated, one may suffer while the others remain apparently unaffected. This situation could be due to an extreme sensitivity or an unknown underlying physiological condition.

Even using nontoxic materials, such as coating the body with olive oil or soaking in diluted Listerine mouthwash, are not necessarily safe. A severely debilitated animal may suffer unanticipated consequences, including death, if these substances are not used carefully.

Although the saying "If some is good, more is better" works well when applied to something like chocolate, it usually causes problems when applied to using any substance, toxic or nontoxic, in a manner not specifically tested for or approved by the manufacturer. More is not necessarily better, and less is often smarter (except for prescribed antibiotics). The practice of self-treating animals always carries the potential for harm, even death. If you have any questions about procedures or products, discuss them with an experienced reptile veterinarian.

Chapter 23

Human Health Concerns

In This Chapter

▶ Knowing how to protect yourself from infection

▶ Handling the health risks of having your iguana in public

*T*alking about an animal's dark side may seem like an odd thing in a book on pet care, but it's a very important part of responsible pet care, regardless of the species. When talking about reptiles, especially iguanas, issues and problems arise that have little to no comparison with the issues and problems of more traditional pets.

For example, when a cockatoo tries to mate with your hand, you won't end up in the emergency room. But when an iguana decides to mate with you, chances are that at least once you'll see an ER doctor's look of bemusement and horror as you explain why you won't be getting rid of the "monster" that did this to you. An over-amorous dog annoying your houseguests is quite a bit different from an iguana who stalks and leaps on them, trying to grab their neck or other accessible body parts with his 116 razor-sharp teeth.

Fortunately, breeding season comes but once a year. Other problems, however, may arise throughout the year, year in and year out, or may start suddenly after an initial period in which these behaviors were never displayed. Knowing what you're up against before you're nursing wounds or dissolving friendships is always a better, if not less stressful, way to go.

Infections

Salmonella has been the most publicized of diseases passed from reptile to human. But iguanas carry other diseases as well, such as E. coli and streptococcus, that can be passed to humans. The following sections explain the methods of transmission and how you can protect yourself. (For information on protecting yourself while cleaning and disinfecting your iguana and his enclosure, head to Chapter 12.)

Fecal-oral

Bacteria is usually transmitted by the fecal-oral route. For example, if feces-contaminated water is splashed on the floor or counter and you don't thoroughly clean that area, organisms in the feces are left on that surface where they can be picked up by food, cooking utensils, or your hands. Or, if you don't wash your hands after cleaning up your iguana's mess, you can inadvertently transfer those organisms to the next thing you touch. Fecal-oral contamination may also occur if you touch contaminated superficial scratches and then touch food or your mouth with the same fingers before washing them.

One way to guard against transmitting bacteria and other organisms from your iguana to you via this route is to wash your hands frequently, but especially after touching him or anything in his environment, and clean your iguana and disinfect his enclosure using the guidelines outlined in Chapter 12.

Scratches

If the iguana's claws are contaminated with any potentially harmful organisms, they can be transferred into your bloodstream when the iguana scratches your arm deep enough to draw blood. Whenever you get scratched, take a moment to clean the scratch with soapy water, even if the scratch doesn't penetrate deep enough to draw blood. If blood is drawn, you should follow the cleaning with a topical antiseptic, such as povidone-iodine. If the scratch becomes infected, the wound may remain puckered, swollen, and crusty. The skin around it will be inflamed. You should consult your physician to see if he or she wants you to do something other than continue to clean it and apply antiseptic and topical antibiotic.

It's often recommended to keep bites and scratches exposed to the air instead of bandaging them. But if you're doing a task that may result in caustic or contaminated substances coming into contact with your open wound (cleaning enclosures or preparing raw poultry or beef), cover the wound for the duration of the task and remove the bandage when you're done.

The best way to avoid serious scratches is to keep your iguana's claws trimmed. See Chapter 12 for details.

Bites

Iguanas, like all animals, have a wide range of organisms living in their mouths. Some of these organisms are beneficial to the iguana, keeping harmful bacteria and other microorganism populations down. Others aren't so useful but are kept under control by the iguana's immune system and biochemistry.

When these microorganisms are transferred to another animal — including you — they may not be so benign. If you get bitten by your iguana, bacteria from his mouth are inserted into the punctures and lacerations made by his teeth. How your body responds to these bacteria depends on the type of bacteria, how much of it enters the wound or your bloodstream, and what shape your own immune system is in.

Iguanas will communicate to you when they're going to bite. You need to watch their body posture, color, body tension, and eyes (see Chapter 16 for information on how to read your iguana's moods and behavior).

If you get bitten, flush the wound. Doing so helps remove some of the bacteria inserted by the iguana's mouth as well as any bits of your own skin that were jammed down into the wound. You can flush minor wounds by holding them under running water for several minutes. More serious bites should be treated by medical personnel, who may remove bite debris by *power flushing,* using a large syringe to squirt sterile saline into the wound. Because serious wounds may become infected, some doctors prescribe a precautionary course of systemic antibiotics; others may take a wait-and-see stance, prescribing systemic antibiotics only after signs of infection appear.

Many doctors are not well acquainted with reptile bites, so they may not be aware that your wound may be infected with two types of bacteria. These bacteria are classified on the basis of how they respond to staining when prepared for viewing under a microscope: *Gram positive* and *Gram negative.* Letting your doctor know about the potential presence of both in the wound ensures that you're given a prescription for an antibiotic that's effective against both types of organisms.

When treating wounds at home, be sure to include daily soaks in hot water that you've added povidone-iodine or chlorhexidine gluconate to. The antiseptic cleanses the wound while the heat increases the blood flow to the site, bringing with it your immune system's own infection-fighting cells and any systemic antibiotics you may be taking.

Iguanas and the Public

One of the joys of taming and socializing your iguana is that you'll be able to share him with others. There's some risk, however, in taking your iguana out into the public arena.

Your iguana may be at risk if you're inattentive to him and what's going on around him. You need to pay attention to the people who are actively touching him or in close proximity to him. Not all people show common sense when it comes to interacting with animals they've never met before (or with animals *period*). People may yank on the tail or dewlap or stick their fingers in the iguana's eyes, nose, or mouth, and otherwise annoy the heck out of him.

Depending on how tolerant your iguana is overall and how he is feeling that particular day or moment, he may do nothing more than close his eyes, move his head away, or slap the person's hand away with a foot. If your iguana isn't used to or tolerant of such rude human behavior, or is having a particularly cranky day, audience members may end up with scratches or bites. And in our litigious society, someone could slap you with a lawsuit.

Because some organisms can be spread by touch, you may want to ask people to wash their hands before they touch your iguana. And ask them to wash their hands afterward, too, stressing that they should do so after touching *any* animal — especially if they're going to be eating afterward.

Some iguana keepers bring antibacterial products with them. In case of potty accidents, a roll of paper towels and a bag for garbage, as well as a spray bottle of disinfectant spray (such as chlorhexidine diacetate), are part of the kit of supplies. Chlorhexidine diacetate can be sprayed on people's hands, as well. Some herp keepers bring towelettes (hand wipes or baby diaper wipes) into which they previously poured a bactericide such as chlorhexidine diacetate or rubbing alcohol. People can be given a towelette before touching your iguana and another one afterward, if you want to be really on top of things. Commercial hand sanitizers such as Purell are also effective but quite a bit more expensive to supply to all the folks who may come into contact with your iguana.

Read up on the issue of salmonella and reptiles, animal-to-human disease transmission, and precautions in general because you will get a lot of questions about them. The information you supply is often particularly welcomed by pregnant women and families with very young children.

Part VII
Breeding and Reproduction

The 5th Wave   By Rich Tennant

ROBERT LOSES ANOTHER FRIDAY NIGHT STARING MATCH WITH HIS IGUANA, LOU

Dang!

RING

In this part . . .

The biological imperative to reproduce is strong in all animal species, including the green iguanas. Seasonal changes in hormones and hormone levels play a key role in iguana behavior, both for males and females. Knowing what goes on before it happens will make the transition into sexual maturity and the first breeding season a little easier.

Even though it is typical of many animals, iguana owners are frequently stunned to find out that their unmated, solitary female iguana has not only entered her annual breeding, but she is *gravid,* the egg-layer's equivalent of being pregnant. Being prepared ahead of time by making some changes to her diet and environment will help ensure an easy passage through a time that has in the past claimed the lives of too many iguanas whose owners were ill-prepared to help them through what in the wild would be a relatively easy, natural process.

Chapter 24

Caught in the Act

- -

- -

Simply speaking, put a male and female iguana together and you get 12–60 or so baby iguanas. Of course, as you've probably already figured out, very few things are simple with iguanas.

Even if you just have one iguana, you need to know how to recognize the signs of breeding season. Some iguanas get through the season rather uneventfully, while others become difficult — even dangerous — to live with. Knowing what to expect and how to deal with what comes will get you both through the season, maybe even in one piece.

Love Is in the Air . . .

Well, not love, perhaps, but hormones. Breeding season is triggered by hormonal changes within the body that were themselves triggered by the ambient light, temperature, and/or humidity levels. Despite being kept in static daily photoperiods during the year in captivity, iguanas still go into season at the same time every year.

Although iguanas generally go through one breeding season a year, there have been reports of captive males going through two breeding seasons in a year, as well as a few females who apparently double-clutched, that is, developed eggs twice in a year. These double seasons appear to be related to the weather — two distinct dry and wet seasons. Regardless of whether your iguana has one or two seasons a year, the behavioral changes will be the same.

It's so easy to fall in love — not really

Is it true that, as many iguana care books and articles say, iguanas don't breed in captivity? No, but a captive iguana definitely faces some obstacles that a wild one doesn't when it comes to reproducing. As you have probably figured out by now, just as overall health is affected by the physical and psychosocial environment, so, too, is sexual maturity. A malnourished or sick iguana, or one kept in an environment where the temperatures are always lower or higher than they should be, will not grow or mature at the same rate as an iguana who is healthy and cared for properly. Instead of reaching sexual maturity at 18 months of age as healthy wild and captive iguanas do, a malnourished or environmentally deprived iguana may not reach sexual maturity until he or she is three to six years of age.

Since most improperly cared for iguanas usually die by six to nine years of age due to metabolic bone disease, kidney failure, or other captivity-induced health disorders, this also tends to affect reproductive success. Another reason there's been little spontaneous breeding in captivity is because iguanas are being imported from several countries throughout the iguana native range. In the wild, breeding season occurs at slightly different times of year throughout the range. In captivity, iguanas start their breeding season about the same time of year as they would have if they were still in the wild. So even when you have a male and female who are sexually mature, if the female is from a different country than the male, or from a distant part of the same country, nothing will happen if they're not in the actual mating part of their breeding season at the same time.

Physical Changes

In many iguana populations, the changes occur inside the body as well as outside. The initial changes occur when hormones, triggered by one or more of the factors mentioned in the preceding section, are produced by the brain, pituitary gland, and germ cells.

On the outside

While the hormones are coursing through the body, the outside of the body may undergo some color change (see Figure 24-1). Depending on where the iguana is from, the normal color may turn orange or red or may be washed over by a rusty orange color.

Color changes occur most often in males, although females may also change color. The color change happens gradually, usually starting on the face and neck, the arms and legs, and then the body and tail. Some iguanas get only patches of color, but others have the orange or red covering almost all of their body and tail.

Figure 24-1:
The pronounced markings on this male indicate either breeding season or a male dominance display.

Photo by Melissa Kaplan

The color change associated with the onset of breeding season often occurs outside of breeding season. These color changes occur in dominant iguanas, especially males, whether they are dominant over their humans or over other iguanas — or over the dog or cat. When a female turns orange or red, she's usually in an environment without any other iguanas; in many such instances, the female is dominant over her human family.

Iguana keepers who have several male iguanas find that the omega (subordinate) males are their usual green when in the presence of the alpha male. But once the omegas are away from the alpha male, or at night when they're all asleep, the omega males' colors change to the oranges, reds, and rusts reflective of breeding season or social status in relation to the other omega iguanas or humans.

The color change usually happens at the time the iguanas enter their first breeding season, at about 18 months of age. Although the total body area covered and the intensity of the color may diminish and fade once the breeding season is over, some color remains year-round and may increase in intensity and body coverage if a new iguana is introduced into the environment.

Hemipenal envy

Iguana testes comprise 1 percent of the male iguana's body mass. By comparison, the great apes have testes ranging in size from 0.017 percent to 0.269 percent. The great apes, then, have one-fourth as much testicular tissue, relatively speaking, as green iguanas. (Human males come in somewhere in the great apes range, with a 6-foot, 180-pound human male having testes weighing in at about 0.041 percent of his body weight.) Iguana keepers who have had occasion to clean up iguana ejaculate are not surprised by this data.

Which came first — the iguana or the egg?

That question isn't any easier to answer for iguanas than it is for chickens. Female iguanas are born with the germ cells in their ovaries that grow into eggs. The eggs start growing during breeding season, getting large enough to break through the ovarian walls. From there they spill into the abdominal cavity where they keep growing. When the time comes, they pass through the oviduct where they meet up with sperm (if the female was mated) and are coated with the shell.

On the inside

Germ cells, formed while the iguana is still an embryo in the egg, ultimately become either *ova* (eggs) or *spermatozoa* (sperm), depending on the sex of the iguana. During breeding season, the testes of the male iguana, already larger in relation to body mass than those of other animals, begin to enlarge as sperm is produced and stored.

In females, the almost insignificant dark gray mass that is the ovaries, nestled up against the dorsal wall of the body cavity, undergoes a change. The tiny germ cells in the ovaries begin to enlarge. Estrogen triggers the liver to start converting lipids in the stored body fat to vitellogenin. As the vitellogenin is circulated through the bloodstream, the enlarging egg follicles absorb the vitellogenin, which is stored in the ova as yolk.

Behavioral Changes

In captivity, in-season males and females both get very restless. If they're kept caged, they spend hours scratching at the walls and trying to dig through the floor; often times they keep it up even though they have scraped at the surfaces so much that their toes are bleeding and snout is bruised or torn. If your iguanas are free-roaming some or all of the time, the restlessness is better satisfied, but not fully resolved, by their being able to range throughout as much of the house as you can let them roam in.

If the breeding season hits during a time when you normally have screened windows and doors open, don't have them open now. Iguana claws can slice through most screens when given enough time to claw and claw and claw at them, and determined iguana bodies pushing at the screen in repeated attempts to get outside will loosen the mesh from its frame. Iguana males want to get out and display and patrol their territory, and iguana females want to get out to start checking possible nesting sites.

This restlessness may last for a month as the season heads into the copulatory period. During the copulatory period, both continue to be restless but the incessant digging and scratching is significantly reduced. The season overall lasts longer for captive males than it does for captive females.

Males

It doesn't matter if you have one or more female iguanas for your male. It doesn't matter if you have any other males. Your sweet, adorable male iguana is going to act differently during breeding season. If you're lucky, he'll just drive you crazy with his restlessness, his loss of appetite (which is quite normal and nothing to worry about), and the resultant change in the appearance, frequency, and quantity of feces and urates. Did I mention the restlessness?

You may see some other behavioral changes during the breeding season: hanging around the female keeper longer than usual, staying in closer physical proximity to the female keeper, following the female keeper around, soliciting physical contact (being picked up, held, petted, carried around) more often than usual, or staying in such contact for longer periods of time. Some of these nonaggressive behaviors may be quite unlike the normal behavior of the otherwise tame iguana outside of the season.

Aggression

If you're not so lucky, you may find yourself under attack. If you're female, your iguana may try to mate with you, trying to grab whatever part of your anatomy is the closest (see the sidebar "When breeding seasons collide"). If you're a male, whether or not you're the primary caretaker, you may be considered to be competition, an intruding male. As such, you may or may not be warned of an impending attack prior to being charged or leapt on by a male iguana.

Iguanas see colors. Males who are aggressive during breeding season seem to consider humans who are wearing blue, green, purple, or a bluish pink to be other iguanas. Whether you're male or female, wearing these colors is more likely to result in your being attacked by your iguana. Retire that favorite pair of blue jeans, green flannel shirt, or pink and purple tank top. You'll look much better wearing them without all the scratches and scars they'll otherwise get you during the season.

When breeding seasons collide

Male iguanas can tell when human females are ovulating and menstruating, and attacks on human females often happen during menstruation. Attacks during ovulation are less common, but some female iguana keepers report that their male iguana acts differently toward them during ovulation, exhibiting some of the nonaggressive behaviors described in this chapter.

Being a human female who has had a hysterectomy is not necessarily protection against the predations of a sexually mature male iguana. Whether or not you still have your ovaries, your body is still producing hormones that continue to fluctuate on the same schedule they always have, enough of which can lead to altered male behaviors during breeding season.

Even if a human female is not the primary caretaker, she may be at risk. Some of the early veterinary literature that published articles about this phenomenon reported that it happened to female primary caretakers who had raised their iguana from hatchlinghood, slept with the iguana, fed it from their plate, and otherwise spoiled it. This is not completely true, as my wrists and hands can attest, decorated as they are with several interesting and curvaceous scars from an iguana I rescued when he was 6 years old. Raised by men, he had been languishing in a pet store, in less than healthy conditions, for well over a year before I got him. He knew my cycles better than I did (I didn't need to mark a calendar when he was around), and he kept a close eye on me, waiting for me to be slowed by fatigue or otherwise distracted. When I was, he would launch himself at me, sinking his teeth into me at least once per breeding season.

Can anything be done to stop the aggression?

You can do some things to reduce or deflect the aggression toward humans. They may or may not be effective for your male, or for all of your males:

- ✔ Reduce the number of hours the UVB-producing light is on. If your iguana is in good overall health and has been getting plenty of UVB through the rest of the year, he can go without any UVB lighting for a couple of weeks or more during the breeding season.

- ✔ If your day heat light is on more than ten hours, reduce it to eight hours or so, allowing the iguana to have a natural sunrise and sunset, leaving the lights out in his room after the sun goes down. Use non-light sources of heat to attain and maintain the necessary temperatures.

- ✔ If your iguana is super aggressive, try keeping him in a darkened room for a couple of days. Provide the necessary heat and thermal gradient but don't turn on the UVB fluorescent or the white daytime light. The objective is to trick his hormones into thinking that the season is over.

  When you resume the regular lighting again, keep the number of hours the lighting is on down to six to eight hours during the day, giving him a natural sunrise and sunset. Provide heat through non-light heat sources.

- Provide your iguana with something other than you to ply his amorous and competitive attentions on. Give up your favorite sweatshirt, towel, or other article that's appropriately colored (blue, purple, green, pink) and smells like you. Try giving it to him when he starts going after you or leave it where he can easily get it.

- Some iguana keepers have had success deflecting their iguana's attention by giving him a "sex toy." Choose an object such as a stuffed animal (skip ones with small pieces that can be detached and swallowed), a sturdy leather glove, or another item that can withstand the repeated attention of a hundred or more sharp iguana teeth.

- Make a Luv Sock. Take two green (or another color attractive to your iguana) men's athletic socks and insert one inside the other. Fill the sock with regular, uncooked rice so that the sock is firm yet pliable but not rigid. Securely stitch the opening closed. Heat the sock in the microwave oven to heat up the rice; you want it warm, not hot. Give it to the iguana. Clean it between uses by removing any secretions (the smell is less than pleasant if they remain on the sock the next time it's heated).

If none of these suggestions work (and do give them some time to work), talk to your vet about pharmaceutical possibilities. Some experimenting has been done with the use of hormones or tranquilizers to reduce seasonal stress in a variety of animals.

What about neutering?

One option that really isn't an option is neutering your iguana by removing his testes. Neutering the sexually mature males of some species has been effective in reducing aggression and some of the other behaviors associated with breeding season. Up until the late 1990s, neutering was being recommended and done on male iguanas. One top reptile vet decided to survey the owners of iguanas he neutered and found that in fact neutering made very little difference in the level of aggression or intensity of other behaviors. Because aggression is caused by more than the hormones produced in the testes, removing the testes of an already sexually mature male who has demonstrated aggressive behavior addresses only part of the overall aggression matrix.

Neutering to prevent aggression would be most effective when done prior to the onset of sexual maturity (12 months of age), but by the time males are identifiable as such, about six months before the onset of their first breeding season, many of the hormone changes have already occurred. Neutering is a surgical procedure requiring your iguana to be anesthetized, and, like all such procedures, risks are associated with the surgery and anesthesia. Neutering an iguana without knowing whether or not he'll need it or benefit from it is considered by most iguana keepers and vets to be inappropriate.

Keep in mind that, despite the horror stories you'll undoubtedly hear from vets, on the evening news, and when you start meeting and talking with other iguana keepers, most male iguanas don't become dangerously aggressive during breeding season. Most male iguanas can be managed by your being alert, reinforcing your dominance, giving them more alone time (similar to the time-outs recommended when working with children), providing them with a sex toy of some sort, and watching your back and the trigger colors you wear on it.

Females

An interesting behavioral change occurs in many female iguanas. Females who are tame and sociable out of breeding season often become cranky and temperamental during the season. On the other hand, females iguanas who are usually cranky and unresponsive to attempts to cuddle and socialize out of breeding season become cuddly and sociable during the season.

Needless to say, extra caution and attention to what your iguana is doing and how the season is affecting his or her behavior are required throughout the breeding season, regardless of the sex of your iguana.

The Deed

Copulation takes place a short time before the eggs will be laid. Generally, females are receptive to the males' sexual advances for seven to ten days or so.

When the female accepts the male, he mounts her from the rear, using his mouth and teeth to hold onto one side of her neck where the pointy projecting scales will help protect her skin (see Figure 24-2). She lifts her tail to give him room to bring his vent in close proximity to hers. He then everts the hemipene lobe on the side closest to her vent and inserts it into her vent (called *intromission*).

Figure 24-2:
Male and female iguanas during intromission (sex).

Photo by Melissa Kaplan

I think of you as a friend

Female iguanas don't accept every male who approaches them. Although there's some forced copulation, female iguanas can be quite dissuasive when it comes to discouraging males. Behaviors used to dissuade an amorous male include waving or slapping at him with one of her feet, hunching her body, twitching or lashing her tail, head bobbing, confronting the male face to face, biting his face (or neck, if he is trying to mount her), and running away. Males try to catch females, grabbing at the females with their mouths and teeth, trying to force them to stay still long enough to mount and connect.

Intromission may last between 5–15 minutes, during which time you'll see a sort of rhythmic pulsing in the male's body, including compressions of the abdomen and pulsing in the upper tail. It's assumed that these pulses are moving the sperm from his testes through the groove in the hemipenal lobe inserted into the female and forcing it into her. With their large testes, iguana males can produce a lot of sperm, taking some time to complete the mating. Once the male is done, he withdraws from the female. In a moment or two, the retractor muscles begin to pull the lobe back into its normal position in the tail. During the actual mating, the female may lie still or she may walk slowly around.

Once she is no longer receptive, the female undergoes another hormone change. The male can tell that she is no longer receptive. If she is the only female around, he may still bug her for a while, trying to mate with her, but eventually gives up, especially if convinced to do so by being bitten soundly on the jowl or snout.

Should You Let Your Iguanas Mate?

This is a difficult subject for many iguana keepers. As much as they love their iguanas and would like to have their offspring, you can't escape the fact that female iguanas lay lots of eggs and that there's a limit as to how many iguanas any one person can keep, given iguanas' space and environmental needs.

The other factor to consider is that iguanas have too often been impulse buys for many people — people who got them because they were cheap and cute and who found them less cute once they realized how expensive and complicated they were to care for properly. Too many of these people give their iguanas away. Added to this population of iguanas in need of proper homes are the following:

✔ All those untamed iguanas whose owners give up trying to tame them.

✔ The sick iguanas whose owners don't want to or can't afford to get them treated properly and make the necessary environmental and dietary changes.

✔ Those iguanas whose owners are going through life changes or have health problems that require them to find homes for their iguanas.

Every year in the United States, and increasingly in other countries such as Japan, England, and Canada, tens of thousands of iguanas are being given to reptile rescues and herp societies. These organizations are having an increasingly difficult time finding homes for all of them. Because most of the people doing iguana rescue and providing foster care and veterinary care are paying for it out of their own pockets, there's a limit to the number of iguanas that can be received from owners who don't want them or can't keep them. The question is, then, how can an iguana keeper justify breeding his or her iguanas and producing any offspring when there are so many literally dying while waiting to get into a proper, caring home?

There's one way to change this situation: Ban imports of farmed and wild-caught iguanas. By drastically reducing the numbers of iguanas imported, domestically bred iguanas can be sold for higher prices. This price will more accurately reflect the care and nurturing of the parent iguanas and their offspring. The higher price will eliminate impulse buys (purchases made because imported iguanas are so cheap) and help ensure that people who do buy iguanas are more willing to make the significant financial commitment to caring for them properly. The only way to ban iguana imports is to get the change made at the federal level, one that may take years of concerted effort by concerned iguana keepers and rescuers.

Think very carefully before deciding to breed your iguanas with the intent to produce offspring. If your iguanas do breed before you have a chance to take steps to keep them apart during the breeding season, you can still keep from adding to the overpopulation of iguanas: Don't incubate the eggs (see Chapter 25 for info about that).

Chapter 25

Eggs, Eggs, and More Eggs

· ·

In This Chapter

▶ Telling whether your iguana is gravid

▶ Setting up a nesting box

▶ Caring for your iguana and knowing when to call the vet

▶ Deciding whether or not to incubate the eggs

▶ Taking care of your hatchlings

· ·

You've worked hard to raise your female iguana properly, lavishing your attention on every detail of her environment, diet, and taming. She has turned into a wonderful, highly socialized lizard who enjoys spending time with you, going places, and entertaining you with her antics. Then you wake up one morning and realize that your formerly green girl is, well, a little rusty around the edges of her dewlap, spikes, and eyelids, and along her arms and back.

Before you have a chance to be concerned about that — or remember that it's a sign of sexual maturity or the onset of breeding season — your sweet girl is exhibiting every sign of being Mrs. Hyde. She's crabby, antisocial, restless, and just generally not a lot of fun to be around. Or you find that your normally crabby, antisocial, and generally not-a-lot-of-fun-to-be-around female is cuddly and friendly and can't be held and petted enough.

Who, you scratch your head in wonder, stole your iguana and put this stranger in her place?

Before You Panic

In case you started panicking about having a female iguana the moment you sexed your iguana and determined that she was a she, there are a few important things to remember about female iguanas that may (or may not) reduce your stress levels:

✔ Healthy iguanas can (and most do) become sexually mature around 18 months of age. This is 6 months or so after you can first sex them (see Chapter 6 for information on sexing iguanas). So you have 6 months to prepare by reviewing the signs of the onset of breeding season and gravidity (*gravid* is the egg-layer's equivalent of being pregnant) and preparing your female for the most anxiety-producing scenario (she actually becomes gravid) by boosting the calcium in her diet starting around 16–17 months of age.

✔ Female iguanas don't need to mate with a male to develop and lay eggs. Just like chickens, iguanas can develop and lay unfertilized eggs. The fact that your female hasn't seen or been in the company of a sexually mature male since you got her when she was a month old is no longer a source of comfort to you.

✔ Your sexually mature female who has shown clear signs of being in season may in fact not develop or lay eggs. Nonproduction of eggs may occur whether or not she has mated with a male. A variation on this point is that she may develop eggs but resorb them instead of carrying them to term or laying them.

So, just as not all male iguanas become crazed psychos and attack every human in sight during their breeding season, not all females become gravid. Or, if they do become gravid, not all females carry their eggs to term and lay them.

See? And you thought iguanas were complicated!

A *gravid iguana* is one who is carrying eggs that have started developing, building stores of yolk within their individual membranes. The eggs may or may not end up being fertilized by a male's sperm. Some gravid females *resorb* their eggs, absorbing the nutrients back into their bodies or excreting the material with their waste products.

How Do I Tell If She's Gravid?

Most of the physical and behavioral changes associated with breeding season were covered in Chapter 24. One of the major differences between males and females in season is that, while the male hardly eats at all, females eat more than ever.

Starting a month or so before the onset of their season and continuing through the first month, their food and water intake increases tremendously. They eat and eat and seemingly gain no weight. What they're doing is building up their fat stores and packing away enough to sustain themselves as well as their developing eggs. If they don't become gravid, their appetite tapers off to their normal intake.

During this time, defecation may take place more often than usual while they're eating heartily. An iguana who previously went once a day, depositing a prodigious amount, may defecate two or more times a day, with smaller than usual amounts each time. The color and consistency of the urates change, too, becoming yellowish or rusty and very thick. Tiny, hard, crystalline bits may be in the urates.

If the female actually develops eggs, you will see some changes in the second month. At that time, the eggs inside are getting larger and starting to compress her intestines. This forces her to eat less, to the point where she is able to just nibble on some greens or a bit of salad every other day or so. The frequency of defecation declines, with often no more than a tiny bit of fecal matter in a mass of thick, yellow, viscous urates coming out.

Timing is everything

When it comes to healthy iguanas, timing is important. From the time when you can sex them when they reach a year of age, to the possible onset of their first breeding season around 18 months of age, to the time of year breeding season starts every year, the iguana (and iguana keeper) lives by a sort of biological clock. Gravid iguanas have their own 60-day (8-week) timetable, which goes something like this:

Weeks	Typical Changes and Signs
1 – 4	The appetite remains normal or nearly so.
	Behaviorally, she shows increased restlessness. Or restlessness continues if it started before egg development.
4 – 5	The appetite starts to falter as eggs begin to compress the intestines and other organs. She may start taking in only small amounts every couple of days or so.
	Water intake increases.
	Feces become very small and may appear the day or two after the last food intake.
	Urates may become thicker, more yellow. Small, whitish grains may appear.
	She becomes quieter during this period, basking more. Previously standoffish females may be more receptive to petting/attention, and tame females may become touchier about physical contact.
	Iguana keepers, build the nest box now if you haven't already done so. A veterinary checkup is also a good idea if you haven't done so already.

(continued)

(continued)

Weeks	Typical Changes and Signs
5 – 6	She eats intermittently, with only small amounts taken in.
	She drinks deeply daily or every other day.
	Urates and feces are affected accordingly (thicker, smaller, less frequent).
	Despite the reduced food intake, there's no apparent loss of weight in the body because the eggs are taking up some of the space formerly filled by the well-stocked but now shrinking fat pads. The base of the tail and hip area may start to look thinner about now.
$6\frac{1}{2} - 7$	When stroking the iguana along the sides of her abdomen, you may begin to feel two soft swellings, one in front of the other (as you stroke from the ribs toward the back where the hind legs join the body), on each side of her body. These are just four of the dozen or more eggs inside of her.
$7\frac{1}{2} - 8+$	Her hips and tail are getting thinner and bonier.
	Her body is still broad across the abdominal area, filled with the developing eggs.
	Around week 8, the bulges previously felt when stroking the sides may now be seen to cause small outward bulges along the sides. It's usually 5–7 days after you can see the eggs bulging from the sides that she is ready to lay her eggs.

What to Do If She Is

If your iguana starts eating like a pig and her urates and feces change, you need to take a few steps to ensure that she's getting enough fluids and calcium.

Fluids are important because she needs plenty to keep her own body going as well as to make yolk for all the eggs, which, depending on the iguana's age, may range from 12 to over 60 eggs. Being insufficiently hydrated can cause health problems and make laying the eggs more difficult.

Boosting her calcium intake is equally important. During her period of gravidity, an iguana whose serum calcium tests within the normal range is actually deficient in calcium. Not only does she need enough calcium to keep her own bones strong and to keep her heart and other systems functioning well, but she also needs enough calcium to supply to her developing eggs and their shells. A gravid iguana should test out in the hypercalcemic range — a level that's considered borderline or problematically high for an iguana outside of breeding season. Once your slightly hypercalcemic gravid iguana lays or resorbs her eggs and she resumes eating normally, her serum calcium levels will return to normal.

Boosting fluids

If your iguana is already freely drinking from her water bowl, you probably don't need to do anything other than to make sure her bowl is cleaned and refilled with fresh water daily, or more often if needed. If your iguana drinks better when in a bath, give her daily baths if you aren't already doing so. Setting up an ice cube or dripper bottle over her water bowl may also stimulate her to drink.

If she enjoys taking treats from your hands, you can dip leafy greens in water or juice and hand-feed them to her, feeding her several such treats a day. If she doesn't normally take treats from your hand, try it while she's gravid, especially when she's in the latter stages of her gravidity and isn't eating more than a mouthful or so at a time; iguanas often overcome their reticence to taking hand-fed treats at this time. Some females spend most of their time basking or lying in their egging place and won't rouse themselves to walk to their food bowl, but they will take offerings from your hand.

Another way to boost the fluid intake is to spray or sprinkle her pile of leafy greens with water. You can also mix a little water or fruit juice into her salad.

Some iguanas lap up or accept into their mouths the stream of water from a spray bottle. If your iguana is a bottle baby, spray her several times a day so that she gets fluids this way. Some iguana keepers use a feeding syringe or eyedropper to get water right into their iguana's mouth.

Given the long-term kidney problems that are common in otherwise healthy captive iguanas, don't take too lightly periodic stresses on the kidneys, such as when your girl is gravid or receiving antibiotics. Get fluids into your female any way you can. If keeping her in a humidified environment and hand-feeding her fluids still isn't enough, talk to the vet about giving her subcutaneous fluid injections during this time.

If your female has previously had metabolic bone disease (MBD), get her checked by a reptile vet early in the season and closely monitor her throughout her season. Doing so helps ensure that she doesn't develop MBD related to her being gravid and that any residual skeletal deformities are not causing her problems in developing and laying eggs.

Boosting calcium

Generally speaking, adding additional calcium carbonate to the salad five to six times a week should be sufficient for gravid iguanas, assuming that they started the season with a strong serum calcium level. If you see any sign of calcium deficiency (reduced activity, tremors in the toes or legs, swelling of the leg bones or the lower jaw, or bumps felt along the spinal column), you need to boost the calcium even more.

Because being gravid can be so stressful to an iguana, take her to the reptile vet as soon as you notice that the season has started and her appetite has increased. Ask the vet to check her serum calcium and, depending on the findings, discuss the best way to supplement calcium.

Talk to your vet

If you suspect that your iguana is gravid, and you either have never had a gravid iguana before or suspect that laying eggs will be difficult for her (she's calcium deficient, for example, or she's been sick lately), talk to your vet. He or she may want to see your iguana just to check things out.

Because emergencies often happen after hours, discuss with your regular reptile vet what course of action to take if the problem emerges in the evening or on weekends, after regular office hours. Your vet may have you call him or her or may have an on-call vet working backup who is capable of handling such problems. You should also discuss with your vet what to do if your iguana has difficulty laying her eggs and you notice the problem outside of office hours.

If you have any suspicion that your iguana may have calcium deficiency problems (she tested within normal serum calcium range late in her gravidity or has a prior history of MBD), talk with your vet about having some NeoCalglucon (a liquid calcium product frequently used in treating moderate to severe MBD and dystocia) on hand to administer to her if problems develop after hours.

Making the Maternity Ward

Did you think you were done with your construction projects once you completed your iguana's palace? Keepers of female iguanas have one more major project: a nesting, or egg-laying, box.

In the wild, gravid iguanas dig burrows two to three feet underground, excavating a chamber into which the eggs are laid. The female then climbs out and backfills the burrow, burying her eggs. In captivity, unless you have a very deep planter box, or your iguana lives in a greenhouse with specimen-sized trees and you don't mind her digging around the roots, you need to provide her a sort of bogus burrowing place.

The nesting box

Any large, sturdy, moisture- and claw-proof box will do. Objects iguana keepers have used include

- A large, covered kitty-litter enclosure (see Figure 25-1)
- Two large kitty-litter bins (one inverted over the other to form an enclosed space)
- A large garbage can (the size you use to put the household garbage in for the weekly garbage pickup, not the size that fits under your kitchen sink)
- A large plastic storage bin with a lid
- A large plastic bin with a board fitted to form a lid
- A wooden box constructed for this purpose
- A rectangular doghouse, inverted

If the container or object you're using for your nest box doesn't already have one, you need to carve an access hole for your iguana. This is an opening she'll crawl through and then start digging downward, which means that the opening you create needs to be positioned in the upper part or on top of the nest box.

If the objects you're using for your nest box are composed of two pieces, you need to secure them together so that the unit can be moved when filled with the nesting media. Because you don't want your iguana disassembling it while in the throes of vigorous digging, the pieces need to be fastened together in such a way that they can be taken apart again so you can clean the insides of both pieces before and after use.

When using two large kitty-litter bins inverted together, cut the opening in the short end of one of them. Depending on the rigidity of the litter box material, the equipment at hand, and your upper arm strength, cutting the opening, a sort of doorway, can be difficult. You can use a soldering iron to burn in a series of holes outlining the shape of the opening and then use the soldering iron to burn through the connecting pieces (or use a small saw to cut through them). You also can use a saw or heavy-duty shears to cut the opening; the soldering iron can be used to smooth the edges once the piece is removed. To secure the two bins together, you can use duct tape to tape them tightly together, or you can drill a series of holes through the rims and use nuts and bolts to fasten them together.

You can use the same cutting-out process when using garbage cans and lidded storage bins. The garbage can will be laid on its side, so cut the access hole in the part of the lid that will be exposed on top. As with the inverted litter boxes, you need to tape or otherwise semipermanently fasten the boxes together. Figure 25-2 shows a nest box.

Figure 25-1:
A litter
box makes
a good
nesting box.

Photo by Melissa Kaplan

Figure 25-2:
A nest box
all set up
and in place
may look
ungainly but
still be just
what your
female
needs.

Photo by Melissa Kaplan

Using something that you can break down into easily stored pieces is helpful, especially if storage space is rather limited. This may dictate the choice of materials you use to create the nest box. Keep in mind, however, that unless your iguana is full grown, she is going to be getting bigger every year, so make a nest box large enough that you can reuse it for at least three to four years, saving yourself a little work.

The nesting dirt

Making diggable soil that won't collapse on your iguana while she's digging is kind of like making mud pies or building sand castles: You have to play with the consistency until it feels right. Here is a good basic recipe to start with:

> 14 quarts potting soil (free of chemicals and perlite)
>
> 1 quart dry sand
>
> 9 cups warm water

1. **Mix up your soil and sand.**

2. **Start adding water, about 6 cups to start with.**

   Mix it into the soil/sand mixture.

3. **Keep adding more water as necessary until the mixture is easy to push and dig through but firm enough to stay in place once you remove your hand.**

   If you pour in too much water, add some more soil or sand.

4. **Fill your nest box nearly to the top with the soil/sand mixture, leaving enough room for your iguana to get in and push the soil around.**

Finding a place for the nesting box

If you're placing the nest box in your iguana's enclosure, place it at the warm end so that the temperature in the top part of the box is around 85 degrees Fahrenheit (29 degrees Celsius). If your iguana is a free-roamer, place the box in a warm, quiet room. If need be, place the nest box about ½ inch above a heating pad or securely mount a heat light above and to one side of the nest box. The top part of the box should be warm, with the temperature inside the box getting cooler as the iguana digs toward the bottom.

Once the soil/sand mixture is mixed up and the nest box is put in its place, check the consistency periodically, mixing in more warm water as needed to maintain consistency.

Who made this big mess?

The sense of wonder the iguana keeper experiences when contemplating the displacement power of those long, thin, iguana toes is soon replaced by amazement at just how far those toes can throw the nesting media out of the nesting box.

Assume from the start that your iguana will transfer a significant amount of soil/sand mixture from the inside of the box to the outside of the box. To reduce the amount and type of cleanup work required to get that dirt back into the box, place the box on a drop cloth so that the soil mixture ends up on the cloth and not all over your carpet or other flooring. The box can be lifted up and the cloth gathered together to enable you to pour the sand/soil back into the box.

Lights! Camera! Action!

Okay. The nesting medium is perfect. You have placed the box in a warm, quiet area. Everything is secured against accidents. You bring your iguana over to the nest box, burbling about how perfect it is. She takes one look at it and walks away. You stand there, crestfallen, watching her green spiky back waddle away from you.

You really didn't think this was going to be easy, did you?

Unfortunately, there's no way of telling what your iguana will do before you spend the evening or weekend making the box and mixing the media. If your iguana is avoiding the nest box, play around with it to see if there's something she doesn't like that you can fix.

- ✔ Placement is one big factor in whether your iguana will like her nest box. You may think you have picked out the perfect place, but your iguana has very different ideas about what constitutes perfection. Try reorienting the box, turning it so that the access hole is facing a different direction.

- ✔ Try partially covering the access hole with a towel or blanket (remember to keep the heat lamp far enough away so you don't start a fire).

- ✔ If reorienting the box or covering the access hole doesn't work, try moving it to a different location.

- ✔ If your iguana has spent a considerable amount of time digging in one particular part of her enclosure or place in a room, try placing the nest box there for several days to see if she becomes interested in it there.

The egg hunt is on

Interesting places iguanas have laid their eggs include on computer keyboards, on their keepers' tummies and chests, in their favorite human's hand, under the covers (especially on heated water beds or warm electric blankets), on and under bed pillows, near the warm air blowing out from the bottom of a refrigerator, and in nooks and crannies around the house. One particularly sociable iguana laid hers while on top of her open enclosure door, right next to her humans and their human company while they were having an impromptu beer-and-pizza party.

You may have just jumped the gun by a week or two, setting up the nest box earlier than she is interested in using one. The key to your own sanity is not to get discouraged. Be flexible. Expect your iguana to do the unexpected, and you won't be disappointed.

The Laying

Your iguana may lay from 12 eggs (first breeding season, around 18 months of age) to 60 or more eggs (4 years and older).

A healthy iguana with good calcium levels (that is, one who is slightly hyper-calcemic), once settled into her nest box or other preferred laying area, should lay all of her eggs within 24 hours, with the majority of them deposited within the first 10–12 hours. She may leave her nest box or area at some point after most of the eggs are laid, returning to it to lay the last few. If this is the case with your iguana, then things are happening pretty much the way they should and you don't have much to worry about. However, there are some instances in which you should be extra vigilant:

- ✔ An iguana who has had little opportunity in her life to do a lot of strenuous climbing may be too weak to get the eggs out. Such iguanas are usually ones kept in enclosures that are too small or enclosures that don't permit much in the way of vertical climbs. This is another good reason why a proper environment is so important to an iguana's long-term health.

- ✔ An iguana who is calcium deficient (hypocalcemic) by the time she lays eggs will be weak, and her eggs' shells will be poorly formed. She may strain and strain, trying to get an egg to pass through, becoming weaker with every attempt. She also may develop dystocia.

Dystocia is also called *egg binding* and *egg retention*. It's a condition where one or more eggs can't be laid, due to a deformed or obstructed oviduct or pelvis or an oversized or deformed egg. If an egg ruptures (due to excessive pressure applied from the outside or trauma from a fall against an object), egg peritonitis usually sets in due to some of the yolk getting into the abdominal cavity, starting an infection. Iguanas with advanced dystocia will be depressed and lethargic rather than alert and may give up trying to nest. Since severe stress and dangerous physical decline happens rapidly in dystocia, the faster you react and get your iguana in to the veterinarian, the better her chances are of pulling through.

If your iguana is taking days to lay her eggs, is showing difficulty in laying (straining, growing weaker), or has other signs of calcium deficiency (jerky gait, tremors, twitching), she must be seen by a reptile vet right away.

After the Laying

After your iguana has laid her eggs, she is going to look half-dead. All that food she packed away over a month ago has gone to nourish her eggs, and the fat stores she has been living on are greatly depleted. Instead of the robust iguana who disappeared into her nest box, a skeleton covered in dry, baggy, dirt-covered skin emerges, dragging herself out of the nest box to collapse in a basking area.

Taking care of mama

After you finish shrieking upon seeing this ghastly apparition, get her some fresh water and a few favorite tidbits to eat, preferably tidbits high in calcium. A bit of fresh fig, leafy greens, and mashed banana mixed with some NeoCalglucon all work well.

Once she has had a day to rest, feel free to give her a bath to get the remaining soil off of her. Let the dirty water drain out and then refill the tub with warm water to let her soak for a while. This is especially important for iguanas who are more likely to drink large amounts when their bodies are in water than when they only have access to a drinking bowl. She is going to be weak and tired, so check on her frequently and don't run the water as deep as you usually do. Once she has regained her strength, you can resume her normal bath regime.

In the ensuing weeks, you can let her do what she wants. What she will most likely want to do is sleep, eat, bask, eat, sleep, and eat. Let her eat as much as she wants, whenever she wants. Keep the calcium boosted a bit for a month or so. You can increase her calorie intake by using higher calorie fruits, such as some mashed banana, rehydrated or fresh (or even canned) figs, and even a bit of avocado (without the skin) now and then if she likes it.

Your iguana should be well on her way to having regained all of her lost weight by the time a couple of months have passed. Her color and skin condition should have returned to normal, and normal behavioral patterns should be reestablished. If she isn't progressing in this way, get her checked out by the vet.

What to do with the eggs

Assuming that everything has gone well, you now have a pile of eggs. If your female wasn't mated, the eggs are not fertile and should be disposed of. Cold as it sounds, you can throw them away or bury them in the garden. If you aren't sure whether they're fertile, freeze or boil them first to prevent the eggs from hatching (in case your garden conditions are right for incubation and the eggs are indeed fertile).

If you have children and they have show-and-tell time at school, you can keep some eggs and boil them. Boiling them eliminates the risk of salmonella contamination if the eggs will be handled by children, by people who come into contact with young children, or by other at-risk individuals, as well as prevent messy accidents.

If your iguana's eggs are fertile, you have a serious issue to deal with, an issue you should have thought about before you reached the point of having a pile of eggs to dig out of the nest box:

- ✔ In the United States, over 15,000 iguanas a year are given away by people who don't want them anymore.

- ✔ If you are thinking about selling your hatchlings, keep in mind that with all those free iguanas being given way, there aren't many people who will pay more than the pet store prices for hatchlings.

- ✔ Until you can find homes for all of them, you're the one who will have to care for them, make their food, clean up their poop, bathe them, separate them into evermore enclosures as they get too big to live together, and tame them.

If you're set on having one of your adult's offspring, you can incubate just one egg. Keep in mind, however, that you ultimately may have to separate the youngster from his parents. Just because they're related doesn't mean they're automatically going to be best friends. Do you have the room to house them completely separately for the rest of their lives if need be? If you incubate more than one egg in case something happens and the one egg doesn't hatch, are you prepared to keep all the hatchlings until you can find homes for them, no matter how long it takes or how old they get?

Hatching

If you decide you want to hear the pitter patter of (lots of) little feet, you need to incubate the eggs. To properly incubate iguana eggs, you need an incubator. An *incubator* is a unit you place the eggs in that automatically controls the temperature and humidity. There are very big, expensive incubators and simple, relatively inexpensive incubators. Here are the three most commonly used incubators:

✔ Hova-Bator, a simple Styrofoam unit. The basic unit has a thermal wafer that can be set to maintain a specific temperature; the different models handle humidity in various ways, some more manually than others. The egg box or boxes holding the incubation medium and eggs will be set in the bottom of the unit.

✔ The aquarium incubator is made of a standard aquarium, a submersible aquarium heater, several inches of water to cover the heater, a sheet of glass to cover the aquarium, and a couple of bricks or other water-resistant objects to set on the bottom of the aquarium to keep the lidded plastic egg box holding the eggs and incubation medium above the water.

✔ In warm climates where the ambient room air temperature is consistently high enough to incubate the eggs, a plastic lidded box is partially filled with incubation medium — enough to securely seat the eggs and maintain sufficient moisture, with the eggs sitting low enough not to be touched by the lid.

Setting up the incubator

If you are going to incubate the eggs, the time to set up the incubator is when you see your female disappear into the nest box to start laying. The temperature inside needs to be between 86–87 degrees Fahrenheit (29–30 degrees Celsius). Any higher, and you'll cook the eggs; any lower, and the temperature may be too low to maintain embryo development.

The incubation medium most often recommended is equal parts (1:1), by weight, of vermiculite (available at plant nurseries, grocery store garden departments, and garden centers) and water. Breeders of green and *Cyclura* iguanas report better success using 1.5 parts water to 1 part vermiculite.

The incubation medium is placed inside the plastic egg box or boxes that will be placed inside the incubator. The eggs must be able to sit in shallow depressions in the medium, low enough not to come into contact with the lid when the box is closed. If the eggs sit too high, reduce the amount of medium in the box instead of burying the eggs in the medium.

Handling the eggs

Once your iguana has laid her eggs and headed back to her basking area, disassemble the nest box and begin carefully digging through the dirt to find the eggs. They will generally all be laid together in a pile; some will be buried under dirt that has other eggs on top. Wash and dry your hands before you start handling the eggs. Or wear disposable surgical-type gloves.

Carefully remove the eggs from the nest box. Normal eggs are slightly soft, the white shells leathery rather than hard like bird egg shells. Taking care not to turn them over, set them in the depression you have pressed into the incubation medium with your thumb or the back of a spoon. Set the eggs slightly apart from one another. If two or more eggs are stuck together, leave them stuck together if they don't easily come apart. Once the eggs have been placed on the incubation medium, put the lid on the box and place it into the preheated incubator.

Incubating the eggs

You waited out breeding season, counting the weeks, then the days, and then the hours until your iguana laid her eggs. Now you get to start another waiting period: from laying to hatching.

At 86–87 degrees Fahrenheit (29–30 degrees Celsius), iguana eggs take about 90–120 days to hatch. The earliest reported hatching at that temperature is 73 days using a tightly lidded egg box that had its lid lifted for 30 seconds every other day. Regardless of your method of incubation, you need to check the eggs at least every several days to monitor their progress.

Mother love? No, nest competition

Although most females collapse in their basking area and never return to their nest box, some females haunt their nest boxes. Presumably, these are females who originate in areas where there's fierce nest competition. Their lurking is not because they have an emotional attachment to the eggs but because they don't want any other female to disturb them.

If you will not be incubating the eggs, you can turn the heat off and leave them in the nest box.

Once your female finally stops lurking in the area, you can dismantle the nest box and dispose of the eggs. If your female deposited her eggs in several areas, or where it's not convenient to leave them (in your bed, on the computer keyboard, in your lap), you may want to remove most of them; leave one or two nearby for her and remove those once her alert period passes.

You can't tell, just by looking at them, whether an egg is fertile or not. You need an egg candler or small flashlight that shines a bright, focused light. In a darkened room, check 3- to 10-day-old eggs by holding the egg next to the light source so that the light passes through the shell and the inside of the egg can be seen. If the egg is fertile, you should be able to see a blood spot and vessels webbing the inside of the egg.

If any of the eggs collapse in on themselves, you may want to remove and discard them because they typically indicate infertile or "bad" eggs. Eggs that get moldy may also be infertile. You can, however, try to salvage moldy eggs by lightly brushing them with an antifungal powder, such as an athlete's foot product. You may want to move the moldy eggs away from the ones without mold, perhaps putting them into their own box. Some moldy eggs, when the mold is contained by repeated applications of the antifungal powder, hatch out normal hatchlings, so it's worth maintaining them throughout the incubation period if they otherwise remain turgid and appear viable. If an egg is moldy and mushy or collapsed, it's likely infertile or the embryo died.

Happy Hatchday!

The baby iguana, when it's getting ready to hatch, moves around in its shell and begins to pierce the shell with its *egg tooth,* a tiny projection on its rostrum that disappears soon after hatching. After the shell is pierced, the hatchling rests for a while before trying to make its way out of its shell.

The hatchling may emerge partway out of the egg and then rest. It's hard to know when to assist an iguana who is trying to pierce the shell enough to push through — or one who is too weak to pull itself all the way out. If you decide to assist, do so very carefully and be prepared to stop if you see that you're causing harm.

If a hatchling emerges with his yolk sac still attached, gently place him on damp towels in a warm "yolk tank" and leave him alone so that he can finish absorbing the rest of his yolk. Do not, under any circumstances, detach a yolk sac from an iguana. Iguanas continue to absorb the yolk until the sac is depleted. The sac then dries and shrivels up and falls off by itself. The "belly button" (where the sac was attached to the belly) heals over until a faint straight line between two rows of scales is all that remains.

Preparing the nursery tank

Around day 70, begin setting up your hatchling nursery tanks. They should be set up with the same heating, lighting, photoperiods, and so on, as described in Chapters 8 and 9. Because the nursery tanks will be housing several iguanas, you want to keep the substrate simple and have several climbing branches and hide boxes.

Hatchlings require slightly higher humidity than juveniles and adults, so be prepared with a misting system or keep a spray bottle of water handy and always refilled.

Raising Arizona and All Her Clutchmates

You need to keep an eye on the incubator, moving hatchlings from the incubator to the interim yolk tank if necessary or directly to the nursery tank if they emerge with their yolk absorbed. Make sure that you keep tabs on the hatchlings in the yolk tank and get those who have absorbed their yolks moved to the nursery tank. Make sure that the damp toweling in the bottom of the yolk tank stays damp as long as hatchlings are in there absorbing their yolk.

When the hatchlings are ready to go into the nursery tank, try to get a little nonfat yogurt with live cultures into them to help boost the iguanas' own gut bacteria. You can put a bit of fruit-flavored nonfat yogurt with live cultures in the nursery tank for several days for the hatchlings to lick up. Mixing the yogurt with some banana or a red- or orange-colored fruit may entice reluctant ones to lick at it.

Feeding iguanas yogurt with live cultures takes the place of feeding them adult iguana feces (referred to as *fecal inoculation*). Some people believe that hatchlings must ingest some adult feces to get their gut bacteria. Offering them yogurt is safer than giving them feces, which may be riddled with harmful parasites or salmonella.

Hatchlings will eat the same salad and greens that you feed your adults, with the exception that you may need to prepare their food in smaller pieces than you do for your adults. Use some clips to fasten larger pieces of the leafy greens at various places around the tank for them to tear at.

Water for drinking and soaking should be provided in a shallow bowl or dish. Some frozen food entrees for humans come packed on microwavable rigid plastic dishes that are perfect for this purpose.

Finally, you need to keep your eye on all the hatchlings to make sure that they're all eating, basking, pooping, and getting along together.

Investing in an ounce/gram food or postage scale comes in handy, as does a dressmaker's tape measure. By keeping track of each hatchling's weight and length, you can tell which iguanas aren't doing as well and thus may need to be moved into a different tank or fed separately to make sure that they're getting enough. If you're having trouble telling your iguanas apart, you may want to dab their heads with some edible vegetable food coloring, replacing it as it wears or is shed off.

To spay or not to spay?

Some people recommend spaying female iguanas as soon as they become gravid for the first time. Others urge restraint in this area, suggesting that the owner wait and see how the situation progresses first. If the female resorbs her eggs and does so year after year, surgery would be the riskier alternative. If she has an uneventful laying each time and bounces back rapidly, there's little justification for subjecting her to the risks of general surgery. The same holds true for females who never become gravid. On the other hand, the annual development and carrying of eggs, even if uneventful, is stressful on female iguanas.

Nonemergency spaying is an option iguana keepers should be aware of and think about. Talking things over with the veterinarian and other keepers of female iguanas may be helpful in making the decision to go ahead with a nonemergency spay. If spaying is done, on an emergency or other basis, talk to the vet about hormone replacement. We don't yet have enough data on the long-term health effects on spayed green iguanas or whether they live longer lives as a result of the spay. We do know that there are adverse health effects in females of other species, so it's not unreasonable to expect similar problems in spayed female iguanas.

Final Thoughts

When all is said and done, keeping iguanas is a big responsibility. With 600,000 to over 1 million iguanas still imported every year and tens of thousands looking for new homes, the decision to breed your iguanas or incubate the eggs is not one to be made lightly. If imports are ever stopped, and breeding iguanas is combined with educating prospective buyers about the proper care and treatment of iguanas, then that would be a good time to start thinking in the family way.

Part VIII
The Part of Tens

In this part . . .

Want to know where to go for more information about plants and whether they're safe or unsafe for you iguana? How about what games you can play to keep your iguana stimulated and active? Or a quick reminder of important training and socialization tips, as well as a list of situations that require veterinary care?

Then this part is for you. Here you can find helpful tips, pointers, and reminders about online resources you can use to research plants, the ways some iguanas play and how you can provide for their safety, the top tips for socializing your iguana, and a quick list of the critical reasons for getting your iguana to a reptile vet.

Chapter 26

Ten Plant Identification and Nutrition Web Sites

● ●

*T*he great thing about the World Wide Web is that new resources are constantly being added and old resources are frequently being updated. Still, trying to find what you want can be tricky unless you've already developed some good Web search skills. To make that process a little easier for you, I cover in this chapter ten (well, sixteen, actually) of my favorite sites used in researching plant information.

Vegetable and Fruit Names

Common names are anything but. They may vary geographically, and they certainly vary from country to country. If you live outside the United States, figuring out what Americans are talking about can be particularly difficult. This site gives the common names as used in the United States and in other countries, as well as the plant's botanical name.

www.sonic.net/melissk/vegetablenames.html

If you aren't sure what some of the foods are in my basic salad recipe, be sure to check out www.sonic.net/melissk/mksalad.html, the "MK Salad: An Illustrated Reference."

U.S. Department of Agriculture's Nutrient Database

This site has the nutrition breakdown of all foods commonly consumed by humans. To look up a plant, use the common name and then just select the proper entry from the list the database gives you. Once you make your selection and choose how you want it displayed (the default is 100-gram portions), you're shown the nutrition breakdown and the botanical name of the plant.

```
http://www.nal.usda.gov/fnic/cgi-bin/nut_search.pl
```

If accessing the database is too costly (in terms of your online time costs), you can download the (huge) database files onto your own computer and access them offline. Access won't be as easy as it is online, and you'll need an Adobe reader or relational database to be able to bring up the files. You can find more information on this form of the database at `www.nal.usda.gov/fnic/foodcomp/Data/SR13/sr13.html`.

Virtual Garden / Time-Life Plant Encyclopedia

Use the link at this Virtual Garden Web site to take you to the Time-Life Plant Encyclopedia. This site is useful for the pictures it has of the 3,000 primarily ornamental plants in its database and for the growing information if you want to get a little gardening in. The Virtual Garden site is loaded with information on planting, growing, and other resources.

```
www.vg.com
```

GardenWeb

At GardenWeb, you can access a plant glossary to figure out the meanings of various terms you come across at other plant sites. There's also a plant name and nomenclature database, which is useful for finding out the botanical names of plants as well as the plants they're directly related to (would you believe 55 listings for broccoli?). This site is useful for gardeners as well as those researching food name equivalents. Although the common names of plants change geographically, the botanical names are universal.

```
www.gardenweb.com
```

U.S. Agricultural Research Service's Phytochemical and Ethnobotanical Database

No nutritional data is provided, and some common plants (like broccoli) are oddly missing, but this site is useful if you're trying to determine whether any harmful or potentially harmful chemicals are in a plant. You can search by common name, botanical name, and chemical. You can opt to have the results shown with the chemical activities (a list of the actions of each of the chemicals in the plant) shown, and with or without all the literature references for the data displayed.

```
www.ars-grin.gov/duke/
```

Plants for a Future

This UK-based Web site (with a U.S. mirror site) contains a wealth of information on plants. Included is info on plant name synonyms and common names, as well as info on whether the plants are edible or medicinal or have other uses. Actual nutritional data is rare, but there are often indicators of what, if any, plant parts are toxic or harmful.

```
www.metalab.unc.edu/pfaf/
```

The Gatherer at Kippewa Gardens

This Web site is actually a meta search engine that automatically searches 11 different databases and includes another search engine that allows you to search an additional 15 sites. About the only thing it doesn't search is nutrition databases. Among the databases The Gatherer searches are the Plants for a Future and the ARS Phytochemical and Ethnobotanical databases.

```
www.kippewa-gardens.com/cgi-bin/Gatherer.pl
```

Plant Images

These two sites have photographs and drawings of plants, useful if you have no idea what a particular plant looks like.

AltaVista Images

Just head to this search engine's site and click on the IMAGES tab to go to the online images search engine. This Web-wide search engine lets you type in a noun for the object you want to see pictures of and retrieves them for you in pages of thumbnail photos. Note that the search engine is rather literal. For example, if you search for *chard*, you not only get gorgeous photos of chard plants, but you also get dozens of wine labels and winery graphics for Chardonnay.

```
www.altavista.com
```

Texas A & M University's Vascular Plants Image Gallery

With over 8,000 images, sorted by family, this site is a big one. Although the focus is on plants found in Texas, many of the plants are found throughout much of North America.

```
www.csdl.tamu.edu/FLORA/gallery.htm
```

Toxic and Safe Plant Lists

You can never have too much money or too many toxic plant information resources. Since databases tend to get updated at different times, if you come across a plant you aren't familiar with and it isn't listed on your favorite database, keep digging by checking out other databases to see if you can find any information on the plant. Some sites list only toxic plants; some have links to both safe and toxic lists.

University of California, Davis Safe Plant List
```
http://envhort.ucdavis.edu/ce/king/PoisPlant/SAFE-COM.htm
```

University of California, Davis Toxic Plant List
```
http://envhort.ucdavis.edu/ce/king/PoisPlant/Tox-COM.htm
```

U.S. Food & Drug Administration, Center for Food Safety & Applied Nutrition Vascular Plant List
```
http://vm.cfsan.fda.gov/~djw/plantnam.html
```

U.S. Army Center for Health Promotion and Preventive Medicine
```
http://chppm-www.apgea.army.mil/ento/PLANT.HTM
```

Cornell University Poisonous Plants
```
http://www.ansci.cornell.edu/plants/plants.html
```

Chapter 27

Ten Suggestions for Socializing Your Iguana

Untamed iguanas are more stressed than tamed ones because they never become comfortable with even the most basic daily activities, including cage cleaning, feeding, and claw trimming. This chapter provides ten suggestions you can use to help socialize your iguana. For more detailed information on taming and socializing, refer to Chapter 17.

Let Him Get Used to You

Your new iguana, no matter what his age is or where he came from, needs to have some time to start getting used to his new environment. Depending on the iguana, you can leave him more or less alone for several days or a couple of weeks. You still need to go into his enclosure or area every day to clean, feed, and check up on him, so don't hesitate in doing so. Part of the acclimation process will be his getting used to a new daily routine. By doing the same things at about the same time every day, you help him acclimate and get used to things — and to you.

Think Like an Iguana

Learn to read and understand your iguana's behaviors and postures. The more accurately you can read his language and understand the nuances based on the situation (context), the more fluent you will become. The more fluent you are, the better the two of you will begin to understand and build trust in each other. Iguana keepers with lots of experience with untamed or aggressive iguanas are cautious and respectful of such iguanas, but they understand that biting and scratching are natural behaviors that have served iguanas well for thousands of years in getting other organisms to leave them alone. New iguana keepers sometimes have to remind themselves that an iguana and keeper need to mesh into a sociable unit where, if there's going to be a dominant organism, it's going to be the human, not the iguana. Finding that fine line between being firm and persistent and letting your iguana be an iguana is a skill developed over time with regular practice. (See Chapter 17 for information and advice.)

Iguana-Proof the Training Area

As with a young child, you must iguana-proof the room or rooms your iguana is going to be allowed access to. To do so, you need to spend a bit of time on your back and knees, roll of duct tape in hand, covering up holes and openings under and inside cabinets in the bathroom and kitchen, under appliances, and between appliances and cabinets. Ensure that all window and door screens are made of strong material, free of rips and holes, and securely fitted. Remove all toxic houseplants (and nontoxic ones you don't want disappearing into a hungry iguana). Don't forget to check the underside of upholstered furniture to make sure that no rips are in the fabric that your iguana can secrete himself into. Make sure that fireplace dampers are closed and any large bags of trash or articles being given away are tightly secured against an iguana looking for a place to hide.

Clip Those Claws

You can and should trim your iguana's claws before you get into training sessions; even small iguanas can shred your arm or snag your clothing. Of course, you have to get enough control over each toe to hold it still enough to cut off just the tip of the claw — without taking off the entire toe (see Chapter 12 for details). You need to help your iguana get used to clippers and clipping even when he's too young to need it: Hold your iguana in one hand and the clippers in the other; let him see them, smell them, and feel them on his body. Playing with his toes gets him used to their being touched and manipulated, which is useful for when you need to clip claws and inspect toes for injuries and retained shed.

Pick Him Up

Don't let your iguana stop you from picking him up. If the iguana continues to elude you, dodging between the basking branches, hide box, and water bowl, remove as many furnishings as you need to in order to get a clean shot at him. Take away any places he can hide behind. Don't give up. If it's taking longer than you thought it would and you're getting to (or past) the point where you just don't care anymore, still don't give up. If you do, the iguana has won that encounter, and you will have reinforced the fact that he can indeed make you go away. Remember that you're supposed to be smarter than the iguana.

Assert Control — Gently

Once you're finally able to pick him up, hold him for at least a couple of minutes. The decision to put him down must be yours, not his. Even if he gets particularly wild — scratches, lashes, or bites you — don't put him down. If you do, you've reinforced the concept that scratching, lashing, or biting works.

Let him climb from hand to hand and roll freely within your hands. Talk gently to him, using his name often. Rock back and forth with him. Try holding him in your hand and extending your arm upright over your head. The iguana should start to settle down and stop writhing around. After a moment or two of calm, slowly bring him to your eye level. Support his body in both your hands, thumbs under the belly/chest area, his hind legs resting on your forearms, your fingers arched over his back, his face within a few inches of yours. (Do be sure to keep the iguana far enough from your face so that he can't reach your nose with his mouth.) Continue talking softly, using his name. At this point, the iguana should settle down for a few moments. The more often you do this procedure, the less preamble (fighting, lifting) you'll have to go through, and you'll both experience longer periods of calm. The iguana will learn that you won't put him down until he calms down, resulting in an iguana who settles down more quickly each time.

Include Him in Your Daily Routine

One of the fastest ways to tame your iguana, and the best way to ensure a mentally healthy iguana, is to give him as much time out of his enclosure as you can and include him in your daily routine. A plastic hook stuck on the tile wall of your shower with a washcloth securely hanging from it makes a nice place for your baby iguana to hang out while you shower. Or install one of those pet hammocks in a large shower. A shoulder or the back of a chair is a comfortable perch while you're eating meals, paying bills, working on the computer, or doing your homework. Hold your iguana and let him sit with you or explore the couch or chair while you talk on the phone or watch TV.

Also keep his routine interesting. Walk him into the kitchen for a leafy green or floral snack. Take him on a walking tour of the house, his head facing forward so he can see where you're going. Walk slowly, talking softly. You'll see the iguana start taking an interest in the sights around him, looking at things near the floor and on the wall and turning his head quickly when something captures his attention. Iguanas are alert, curious, and interested in their surroundings, eager to explore new spaces and find great places to bask, sleep, and, at least initially, hide.

Reinforce Good Behavior

Reinforcing the behaviors you want helps to train the iguana to exhibit those behaviors. Waiting until he calms down before putting him down is one example. Other behaviors you may want to reinforce are when he goes potty where you want him to (or at least doesn't go where you don't want him to) and when he responds to your "No!" and stops climbing on something you don't want him climbing on. Rewards may be giving food treats, petting him for a while in his favorite spot, and lavishing praise on him (when he begins to recognize your "I'm pleased" voice from your "Bad lizard!" voice).

Be Patient and Persistent

Regression happens. You may have gone to bed one night ecstatic about the progress you two have made only to find in the morning that your iguana's evil twin moved in overnight. If you are patient and take the time to do it right, you will be rewarded with a tame, if not actually socialized, iguana. Just as you spent a great deal of money and time setting up the iguana's environment and strive to provide him with the proper care and diet, use the same patience to work with your iguana. It'll take anywhere from six to eight months (or longer, depending on the individual's temperament) to reach the point where your iguana is comfortable in most situations. That's a short period of time when weighed against the total life of the iguana.

Get Help If You Need It

Sometimes we can't see what we are doing wrong. It may be one little thing, but that thing can make all the difference between your iguana understanding you or not. If you're having problems with taming your iguana, you want to find someone who knows iguanas and can work with you. Contact your local herp society, reptile rescue, or reptile veterinarian, or join one of the iguana groups on the Internet, to find someone in your area you can meet with.

Chapter 28

Ten Reasons to See a Veterinarian

· ·

*T*he more you know about your iguana and iguanas in general, the better able you will be in troubleshooting situations. Until then, and for situations requiring critical medical diagnosis and intervention, take your iguana to see a reptile vet. The following lists some of the reasons why an iguana should see a vet.

He's Lethargic

Lethargy is a symptom of many different illnesses and disorders. If his environment isn't causing the problem (the lighting is right, the temperature is where it should be, and so on), get your iguana to the reptile vet. You may be dealing with metabolic bone disease, gut obstruction, systemic fungal or bacterial infection, kidney failure, or dehydration — just to name a few conditions for which lethargy is a common symptom.

Signs of lethargy include not moving for very long periods of time; prolonged sleeping, including during the day; and a lack of interest in his surroundings, even when you move him or attempt to interact with him. Eyes may be closed or partially closed most of the time. If he drags himself or is placed at the food bowl, he may fall asleep rather than eat. If you press your fingernail into the sole of his foot, he shows little or no response (a healthy iguana jerks his foot away).

Lethargy during the winter is not a sign of hibernation. Iguanas and other tropical animals don't hibernate. Although reduced activity and appetite are common during the winter months, despite your maintaining the enclosure at the proper temperatures, iguanas in winter remain alert, thermoregulating properly and maintaining normal day and night schedules.

He's Hurt or Bleeding

Minor scratches that bleed for a very short time and then stop bleeding on their own can be treated at home, but wounds that won't stop bleeding need to be attended to properly and quickly. Reptiles don't have a lot of blood to lose, and so even apparently insignificant losses can have serious impacts.

Large wounds, whether from bites of other animals (including iguanas), punctures, or lacerations, need to be attended to properly. Any skin, scales, teeth, and tissue that get driven down into the wound will fester if not cleaned out, which leads to infections. Your veterinarian is equipped not only to flush the wound properly but also to close it up, either with stitches or bandages. Although a topical antibiotic may be fine to use on minor wounds, large or deep wounds typically require systemic antibiotics.

He's Paralyzed

Paralysis is most commonly associated with severe metabolic bone disease (MBD), which may or may not involve a fracture of the weakened vertebrae. Healthy iguanas may become paralyzed as a result of a serious injury to the spinal column. If you notice either complete or partial paralysis in your iguana, take him to the vet immediately. Once MBD reaches the point of paralyzing the iguana, more serious treatment is required. If the paralysis is due to an injury, the vet may be able to determine whether it's a fracture or an inflammation causing the paralysis, and he or she may prescribe medication to reduce inflammation, which in turn may lead to the restoration of movement.

His Limbs and Spine Are Swollen

Metabolic bone disease (MBD), bone fractures, and abscesses in the muscle tissue or bone can lead to swelling of the arms and legs, as well as the dorsal spine along the iguana's back and tail. Environmental and/or dietary corrections are required in cases of MBD, and so is veterinary care. The vet will be able to determine whether the swelling is a fracture that needs to be set or swollen tissue that will resolve with proper care, including calcium and/or vitamin D injections. Abscesses require antibiotic treatment and/or surgery.

He Has Problems with His Tail or Toes

Trauma to the tail, including bites, crushing, and thwacks (when the tail is hit against a hard surface, such as a wall), can lead to infections or to wet or dry gangrene. In wet gangrene, the area becomes puffy and mushy and starts oozing serous fluid as the skin stretches. If left untreated, it may continue to spread up into the body or may convert to dry gangrene. In dry gangrene, the infection kills the tissue, causing it to dry and shrivel up, making the tail (or toes, for that matter) look like they're shrinking in on themselves, turning hard and brown in color.

In the case of toes, swelling in one area may be an abscess. Left untreated, it may destroy the underlying tissue and bone. Once the toe begins to flop around, it may get caught in something and literally get ripped off if the iguana jerks his foot trying to free it.

Caught early enough, abscesses may be treated with antibiotics and/or surgery. Gangrene is generally best treated by the amputation of the tail or digit above the infected area.

His Feces Are Smelly or Runny

Some iguana keepers think even healthy iguana feces smell bad, but that's because they've never had the pleasure of smelling the feces of an iguana suffering a *Giardia* infection (a smell shared with *Giardia*-induced vomit, too). *Giardia* are parasites that love the water and live in many outdoor water sources. Other types of parasites and protozoans can make feces loose, runny, or smelly, and so can the ingestion of toxic substances, including many house plants. If loose feces last more than a day or two, get your iguana and a fecal sample to the reptile vet for testing. (Give it that day or two first, though, because it may just be due to a change in diet or overeating one particular food item.)

Feces and urates may be tinted by foods containing a lot of red or orange pigments, such as carrots, cactus pear, and berries. If your iguana pigs out on such foods, you may see reddish or orangey urates or feces that otherwise look normal or may be a little loose. As long as the color returns to normal within a day or so, you can safely ignore it.

His Neck and/or Dewlap Is Swollen

Abscesses may form in the dewlap or on the head or neck. They require veterinary attention. Abscesses are localized, forming a swelling in only one or more individual areas. Overall swelling of the dewlap or neck area is most often associated with kidney failure; iguanas need to be seen by the vet immediately to see whether or not the failure is reversible.

He's Bloated and Not Pooping

An iguana who eats every day should be pooping every day — or at least within 24–36 hours of eating. If your iguana isn't, then you need to do an environmental check to see if that holds the reason (insufficient UVB, calcium, or heat, or particulate substrates). If a warm bath and gentle massage don't get things moving along within 24 hours afterward, the iguana must be seen by a reptile vet. The vet may do radiographs to see if there's something stuck in the gut, and/or he or she may prescribe an appropriate treatment.

A gravid iguana looks quite large and lumpy toward the end of her two-month gestation period, despite having eaten little or nothing during the prior couple of weeks. She poops infrequently, and when she does, the feces are small in size and quantity. The same goes for a male during breeding season. These are normal changes. If the bloating and constipation occur outside of breeding season, you need to correct the environment and get to the vet.

He Has Rapid Weight Loss

Visible weight loss that happens within a day or two is a sign of a serious problem, such as gut obstruction or kidney failure. You need to take these iguanas to the reptile vet immediately to determine the reason and figure out what can and should be done.

He Has Seizures

Although iguanas occasionally exhibit a single, rapid jerk or spasm of the entire body, seizures resulting in the repetitive spasmodic jerking of the head and body are a sign of a serious underlying problem. Advanced metabolic bone disease, kidney failure, and head trauma may cause seizures. Your vet will be able to run tests to try to determine, or at least rule out, the cause of the seizures.

Part IX
Appendixes

The 5th Wave   By Rich Tennant

"Which one looks better with this shoulder bag, the Black Spiny-tailed or the Desert iguana?"

In this part . . .

There's a lot to know about iguanas. Some of this stuff is vital, some is helpful, and nearly all of it is interesting. The appendixes in this part give you resources you can use to care for your iguana: If you are having problems locating in your town some of the equipment and supplies you need, you will find a list of mail order suppliers who carry many of these items. If you need a vet, or want to join a society, subscribe to a magazine or do some more reading, you will find the information here to help you to find these resources, too. You'll also find a list of toxic and safe plants.

Appendix A

Toxic and Edible Plants

· ·

*T*able A-2 provides a list of plants that are safely edible — at least in small amounts — by reptiles. It's not an all-inclusive list, however.

Many junior colleges and university extension programs, and some parks departments and nature centers, offer short courses or day hikes (led by naturalists or botanists) that explore the edible wild plants growing in your area. Taking such a course can be invaluable if you have trouble translating the photos and text descriptions from books into what you see growing around you. Since some safely edible plants look very much like highly toxic plants, it's better to know exactly what you're dealing with rather than to guess and be wrong.

Organic gardeners take heed

Many people pride themselves on their organic garden or yard, where they never apply any herbicide, fungicide, pesticide, or chemical fertilizers. But what these people don't realize is that even if *they* don't use pesticides, herbicides, or fertilizers, if their neighbor does — or their neighbor's neighbors do — then some of those chemicals are going to end up in their yard.

Many plants purchased from nurseries and stores have been treated with topical pesticides and herbicides, or the soil they were grown in was treated with fertilizers. You should wash and repot these plants before using them.

Cut flowers from florists may also be a problem because they may have been sprayed with or stored in water that a chemical's been added to — a chemical that may be harmful to your iguana. It's best not to feed the petals or leaves from these plants to your iguana.

Harmful and Toxic Plants

If you are thinking about furnishing your iguana's enclosure or area with plants, or are considering letting him free-roam in your house or in an outdoor enclosure, you need to ensure that the plants in those areas are not toxic. The best way to protect your iguana is to positively identify all the plants in your home and get rid of all those that are toxic or harmful.

Although every captive iguana won't try to eat every plant he sees, there's no way of knowing which iguana will — or which iguana will after years of ignoring that particular plant.

The common names used in this appendix are those typically in use in the United States. Table A-1 uses the following symbols and abbreviations:

CAR	Affects cardiovascular function
CARn	May contain toxic levels of nitrates
CNS	Affects central nervous system
CP	Affects cardiopulmonary function
DERM	Affects skin
GI	Affects gastrointestinal tract
HAL	Contains hallucinogens
HEP	Affects liver (hepatoxic)
KID	Affects kidneys (nephrotoxic)
PHO	Causes photosensitivity
RES	Affects respiratory function
TOX	Has other toxic systemic effects
*	Can cause mechanical injury (such as thorns)
†	Is safe to eat in moderate amounts as part of a varied diet

If you can't identify plants from gardening or houseplant books — or from field guides to wild plants — take cuttings or clear, detailed photos to a plant nursery (a real nursery, not the plant section in the supermarket, Wal-Mart, Target, and such). Check your public library's community organizations listing to find the local horticultural society and contact the society to find someone who can help you identify a plant. The County Agricultural Extension office may also be helpful in identifying species that have stumped everyone else.

Table A-1		Toxic and Harmful Plants	
Plant	*Scientific Name*	*Poisonous Part*	*Note*
Ackee	*Blighia sapida*	Seed, seed covers	GI, CNS
Aconite, Monkshood	*Aconitum* spp.	Entire plant	CAR
Amaranth	*Amaranthus hybridus*	Entire plant	CARn; may contain toxic levels of nitrates
Amaryllis	*Amaryllis* spp.	Bulbs	GI
Anemone	*Anemone* spp. (includes *Pulsatilla* spp.)	Entire plant	GI, DERM, *
Angel Trumpet Tree	*Brugmansia x candida*	Entire plant, seeds	CNS, HAL
Anthurium	*Spathiphyllum* spp.	Entire plant	GI, DERM
Apples	*Malus* spp.	Seeds, entire plant	Cyanide
Apricots	*Prunus* spp.	Seeds, entire plant	Cyanide
Areca Palm	*Areca catechu*	Entire plant	TOX
Arnica	*Arnica montana*	Rhizomes, flowers	CAR, DERM, GI (***Note:*** Arnica creams and ointments are toxic when absorbed)
Arrowgrass	*Triglochin maritima*	Leaves	Cyanide
Autumn Crocus	*Colchicum autumnale*	Entire plant	GI, DERM
Azaleas	*Rhododendron* spp.	Leaves, nectar	CAR
Bagpod	*Sesbania* spp.	Seeds	GI
Bahia	*Bahia oppositifolia*	Entire plant	Cyanide
Balsam Apple	*Momordica balsamina*	Outer rind of ripe fruit, seeds	GI
Balsam Pear	*Momordica charantia*	Outer rind of ripe fruit, seeds	GI
Baneberry	*Actaea* spp.	Foliage, berries, roots	GI, CNS

(continued)

Table A-1 *(continued)*

Plant	Scientific Name	Poisonous Part	Note
Barilla	*Halogeton glomeratus*	Leaves, stems	TOX, oxalates
Barley, Wild Barley, Squirrel-Tail Grass	*Hordeum spp.*	N/A	*
Barnyard Grass	*Echinochloa crusgalli*	Entire plant	CARn
Bead Tree	*Melia azedarach*	Entire plant	Convulsants
Beggar-Tick	*Bidens frondosa*	Entire plant	CARn
Belladonna	*Atropa belladonna*	Entire plant	CNS
Bellyache Bush	*Jatropha gossypiifolia*	Seeds	GI, DERM
Bermuda Buttercup (also Bermuda Oxalis)	*Oxalis pes-caprae*	Leaves, entire plant	TOX
Betel Nut	*Areca catechu*	Entire plant	TOX
Bindweed	*Ipomea* spp.	Entire plant	CARn, HAL
Bird-Of-Paradise	*Caesalpinia gilliesii*	Seeds	GI
Birdsfoot trefoil	*Lotus corniculatus*	Entire plant	Cyanide
Bishop's Weed	*Ammi majus*	Entire plant	CARn
Bitter Gourd	*Momordica charantia*	Outer rind of ripe fruit, seeds	GI
Bittersweet	*Celastrus scandens*	Entire plant	Reputedly TOX
Bittersweet	*Solanum* spp.	Immature growths	CARn, GI, DERM; plant may also contain toxic levels of nitrates, *
Bitterweed	*Helenium* spp.	Entire plant	DERM

Plant	Scientific Name	Poisonous Part	Note
Black Brush (also Tarbush)	*Florensia cernua*	Fruit	GI
Black Bryony	*Tamus communis*	Entire plant	GI, DERM
Black Locust	*Robinia pseudoacacia*	Bark, seeds, leaves	GI
Bleeding Heart	*Dicentra formosa*	Entire plant	DERM, convulsants
Bloodroot	*Sanguinaria canadensis*	Juice, sap	DERM
Blue Rush	*Juncus inflexus*	Entire plant	Convulsants
Blue Taro	*Xanthosoma* spp.	Leaves	GI, DERM
Bluebonnets	*Lupinus* spp.	Leaves, seeds	TOX
Bouncing Bet	*Saponaria officinalis*	Seeds	GI
Box, Boxwood	*Buxus sempervirens*	Entire plant	GI, DERM
Bracken Fern (also Brake Fern)	*Pteridium* spp.	Fronds	Thiaminase
Broomcorn	*Sorghum* spp.	Leaves	CARn, cyanide
Buckeyes	*Aesculus* spp.	Nuts, immature growths	GI
Buckthorn	*Karwinskia humboldtiana*	Fruit	CNS; not to be confused with the mildly toxic *Rhamnus* spp. also called buckthorn
Buckthorn	*Rhamnus* spp.	Fruit, bark	GI (**Note:** See also *Karwinskia humboldtiana*)
Buckwheat	*Fagopyrum esculentum*	Entire plant	DERM, PHO
Buffalo Bur	*Solanum* sp.	Entire plant	CARn, GI, DERM
Bull Nettle	*Solanum* sp.	Immature growths	CARn, GI, DERM
Bunch-Grass	*Nolina texana*	Foliage	HEP

(continued)

Table A-1 (continued)

Plant	Scientific Name	Poisonous Part	Note
Bur Clover	Medicago denticulata	Entire plant	PHO, †
Burdock	Arctium lappe	Entire plant	*
Burning Bush	Euonymus spp.	Fruit	CAR
Bushman's Poison	Acokanthera spp.	Seeds	CAR
Buttercups	Ranunculus spp.	Sap	GI, CNS, DERM
Buttonbush	Cephalanthus occidentalis	Entire plant	Reputedly TOX
Cabbage	Brassica spp.	Entire plant	Goitrogenic, †
Cactus	Cacti – numerous genera	N/A	Certain species are toxic, *
Caladium	Caladium spp.	Leaves	GI, TOX (**Note:** See also Xanthosoma spp.)
Caladium	Xanthosoma spp.	Leaves	GI, DERM
Caley Pea	Lathyrus spp.	Stems, seeds	CNS
Calico Bush	Kalmia spp.	Leaves, nectar	CAR, CNS, GI
California Chicory	Rafinesquia californica	Entire plant	CARn
Calla Lily	Zantedeschia aethiopica	Leaves	GI
Caltrop	Tribulus terrestris	Entire plant	HEP, CARn, *
Calycanth	Calycanthus spp.	Seeds	CAR, CNS
Canada Thistle	Cirsium arvense	Entire plant	CARn
Canario	Allamanda cathartica	Bark, leaves, fruit, seeds, sap	GI, DERM
Candleberry, Candlenut	Aleurites moluccana	Entire plant	GI
Cardinal Flower	Lobelia spp.	Leaves, stems, fruit	CNS, DERM

Plant	Scientific Name	Poisonous Part	Note
Careless Weed	*Amaranthus hybridus*	Entire plant	CARn; may contain toxic levels of nitrates
Carolina Allspice	*Calycanthus* spp.	Seeds	CAR, CNS
Cassava	*Manihot esculenta*	Entire plant	Cyanide; the root (tuber) is safe when cooked
Castor Bean	*Ricinus communis*	Seeds	GI, DERM
Catclaw	*Acacia greggi*	Foliage	Cyanide
Catclaw, Guajillo	*Acacia* spp.	Foliage	Cyanide
Celandine (also Celandine Poppy)	*Chelidonium majus*	Entire plant	CNS, DERM
Cheeseweed	*Malva parviflora*	Entire plant	CARn
Cherries	*Prunus* spp.	Kernels in pits, plant	Cyanide
Cherry Laurel	*Prunus* spp.	Entire plant	Cyanide
Chickweed	*Stellaria media*	Entire plant	CARn
Chinaberry Tree	*Melia azedarach*	Entire plant	Convulsants
Chinese Lantern	*Physalis* spp.	Unripe berries	GI
Chives	*Allium* spp.	Bulbs, bulblets, flowers, stems	GI, DERM, †
Christmas Berry	*Heteromeles artbutifolia*	Entire plant	Cyanide
Christmas Rose	*Helleborus niger*	Entire plant	CAR, DERM
Clematis	*Clematis* spp.	Entire plant	GI, CNS, DERM
Climbing Lily	*Gloriosa* spp.	Entire plant	GI
Clovers, other	*Trifolium* spp.	N/A	*, †
Coal-Oil Brush	*Teradymia glabrata*	Leaves	HEP

(continued)

Table A-1 *(continued)*

Plant	Scientific Name	Poisonous Part	Note
Coast Goldenbush	*Haplopappus venetus*	Entire plant	CARn
Cocklebur	*Xanthium orientate*	Leaves at sprouted two-leaf stage, germinating seeds	CAR, DERM, TOX, *
Coffeeweed	*Sesbania* spp.	Seeds	GI
Columbine	*Aquilegia vulgaris*	Entire plant	CAR
Common Lantana	*Lantana camara*	Immature berries	CNS, HEP
Coontie	*Zamia pumila*	Trunk, roots	GI, CNS
Copperweed	*Oxytenia acerosa*	Leaves	TOX
Coral Plant	*Jatropha multifida*	Seeds	GI, DERM
Corncockle	*Agrostemma githago*	Seeds	GI
Cowcockle	*Saponaria vaccaria*	Seeds	GI
Cowslip	*Caltha palustris*	Entire plant	GI, DERM
Coyotillo	*Karawinskia humboldtiana*	Fruit	CNS
Crab's Eye	*Abrus precatorius*	Seeds	GI
Creeping Charlie	*Glechoma hederacea*	Entire plant	Volatile oil irritants
Crimson Clover	*Trifolium incarnatum*	N/A	*, sprouts †
Crocus, autumn-blooming	*Colchicum* spp.	Entire plant	GI, DERM
Crowfoots	*Ranunculus* spp.	Entire plant	GI, DERM
Crown Flower	*Calotropis* spp.	Entire plant	CAR
Crownbeard	*Verbesina encelioides*	Entire plant	CARn
Cuckoo-Pint	*Arum maculatum*	Entire plant	GI, DERM
Cultivated Rape	*Brassica napus*	Entire plant	Goitrogenic, HEP, †
Curcas Bean	*Jatropha curcas*	Seeds	GI, DERM
Daffodil	*Narcissus* spp.	Bulbs	GI, DERM

Plant	Scientific Name	Poisonous Part	Note
Day-Blooming Jessamine	*Cestrum diurnum*	Fruit, sap	GI, CNS
Deadly Nightshade	*Atropa belladonna*	Entire plant	CNS
Death Camas	*Zigadenus* spp.	Entire plant	CAR
Desert Rose	*Adenium* spp.	Entire plant	CAR
Devil's Club	*Echinopanax horridum*	Entire plant	DERM
Devil's Trumpet	*Datura stramonium*	Entire plant	CNS, CARn, DERM
Devil's Turnip	*Bryonia dioica*	Entire plant	GI. DERM
Docks	*Rumex* spp.	Leaves	CARn, DERM, oxalates
Dog Hobble	*Leucothoe* spp.	Leaves, nectar	CAR, CNS
Dogbane	*Apocynum cannabinum*	Entire plant	CAR
Doll's Eyes	*Actaea* spp.	Foliage, berries, roots	GI, CNS
Downy Brome-Grass	*Bromus tectorum*	N/A	*
Dumbcane	*Dieffenbachia* spp.	Leaves	GI, DERM
Dutchman's Breeches	*Dicentra cucullaria*	Entire plant	DERM, convulsants
Eagle Fern	*Pteridium* spp.	Fronds	Thiaminase
Elderberry	*Sambucus* spp.	Entire plant	CARn, cyanide
Elephant's Ear	*Alocasia* spp.	Leaves, stems	GI
Elephant's Ear	*Colocasia esculenta*	Leaves	GI
English Ivy	*Hedera helix*	Berries, leaves	GI, DERM
Euphorbia, Milk Bush	*Euphorbia* spp.	Latex	GI, CARn, DERM
European Beech	*Fagus sylvatica*	Seeds	GI
European Mistletoe	*Viscum album*	Leaves, stems	GI

(continued)

Table A-1 *(continued)*

Plant	Scientific Name	Poisonous Part	Note
False Hellebore	*Veratrum* spp.	Entire plant	CAR, DERM
False Jessamine (also Yellow Jessamine)	*Gelsemium sempervirens*	Flowers, leaves, roots	DERM, convulsants
False Sago Palm	*Zamia pumila*	Trunk, roots	GI, CNS
Fanweed	*Thlaspi arvensi*	Seeds	GI
Fetterbush	*Pieris* spp.	Leaves, nectar	CAR, CNS
Fiddleneck	*Amsinckia intermedia*	Seed-like nutlets	CARn; entire plant may contain toxic levels of nitrates
Fireball	*Kochia scoparia*	Entire plant	CARn
Fitweed	*Corydalis* spp.	Entire plant	Convulsants
Flag	*Iris* spp.	Rootstocks	GI, DERM
Flax	*Linum usitatissimus*	Entire plant	CARn, cyanide, goitrogenic
Florestina	*Florestina tripteris*	Entire plant	Cyanide
Florida Arrowroot	*Zamia pumila*	Trunk, roots	GI, CNS
Fly-Poison	*Amianthemum muscaetoxicum*	Leaves, underground parts of plant	RES
Fool's Parsley	*Aethusa cynapium*	Entire plant	GI
Four O'clock	*Mirabilis* sp.	Entire plant	GI
Fowl Mannagrass	*Glyceria striata*	Entire plant	Cyanide
Foxglove	*Digitalis purpurea*	Entire plant	CAR, GI
Foxtail Grass	*Setaria lutescens*	N/A	*
Foxtails	*Equisetum* spp.	Entire plant	TOX, *
Frijolito	*Sephora secundiflora*	Seeds	CNS

Plant	Scientific Name	Poisonous Part	Note
Garlic	*Allium* spp.	Bulbs, bulblets, flowers, stems	GI, DERM, †
Gill-over-the-Ground	*Glechoma hederacea*	Entire plant	Volatile oil irritants
Gloriosa Lily (also Glory Lily)	*Gloriosa* spp.	Entire plant	GI
Goat Weed	*Hypericum perforatum*	Entire plant	PHO, DERM
Goathead	*Tribulus terrestris*	Entire plant	HEP, CARn, *
Golden Ear-Drops	*Dicentra chrysantha*	Entire plant	DERM, convulsants
Golden Shower	*Cassia fistula*	Pulp of pods, leaves, bark	GI
Golden Trumpet Vine	*Allamanda cathartica*	Bark, leaves, fruit, seeds, sap	GI, DERM
Goldenchaintree	*Laburnum x watereri*	Entire plant	CNS
Goldenrods	*Aplopappus* spp.	Leaves	CARn, *
Goldenweeds	*Oonopsis* spp.	Entire plant	May contain toxic levels of selenium
Goosefoot	*Chenopodium glaucum*	Entire plant	CARn
Goosegrass	*Triglochin maritima*	Leaves	Cyanide
Gout Stalk	*Jatropha podagrica*	Seeds	GI, DERM
Greasewood	*Arisaema dracontium*	Entire plant	GI, DERM
Greasewood	*Sarcobatus vermiculatus*	Entire plant	DERM, oxalates
Green Dragon	*Arisaema* spp.	Entire plant	GI, DERM
Ground Cherry	*Physalis* spp.	Unripe berries	GI
Ground Ivy	*Glechoma hederacea*	Entire plant	Volatile oil irritants
Groundsel	*Senecio* spp.	Entire plant	HEP
Guajillo	*Acacia ber landieri*	Foliage	Cyanide

(continued)

Table A-1 *(continued)*

Plant	Scientific Name	Poisonous Part	Note
Heliotrope	*Heliotropium* spp.	Entire plant	HEP
Hellebore	*Helleborus niger*	Entire plant	CAR, DERM
Hellebore	*Ranunculus* spp.	Sap	GI, CNS, DERM
Hemlock, Poison Hemlock	*Conium maculatum*	Entire plant	CNS, DERM, CARn
Henbane	*Hyoscyamus niger*	Seeds	CNS
Higuereta	*Ricinus communis*	Seeds	GI, DERM
Holly	*Ilex* spp.	Berries	GI
Honeysuckle Bush	*Lonicera* spp.	Berries	GI, CAR, CNS
Horse Chestnut	*Aesculus* spp.	Nuts, immature growths	GI
Horse Nettle	*Solanum* sp.	Immature growths	GI, CARn, DERM
Horse Poison	*Hippobroma longiflora*	Entire plant	Convulsants
Horsebean	*Parkinsonia aculeata*	Entire plant	CARn
Horsebrush	*Tetradymia glabrata*	Leaves	HEP
Horsetails	*Equisetum* spp.	Stems	TOX, *
Hyacinth	*Hyacinthus orientalis*	Entire plant	GI, DERM
Hydrangea	*Hydrangea* spp.	Entire plant	DERM, cyanide
India Wheat	*Fagopyrum tataricum*	Entire plant	PHO
Indian Hemp	*Apocynum cannabinum*	Entire plant	CAR
Indian Kale	*Xanthosoma* spp.	Leaves	GI, DERM
Indian Poke	*Veratrum* spp.	Entire plant	CAR, DERM
Indian Tobacco	*Lobelia inflata*	Leaves, stems, fruit	CNS, DERM
Indian Turnip	*Arisaema triphyllum*	Entire plant	GI, DERM
Indigo, Senna, Sickle Pod	*Cassia* spp.	Entire plant	GI
Iris	*Iris* spp.	Rootstocks	GI, DERM
Italian Arum	*Arum italicum*	Entire plant	GI, DERM

Plant	Scientific Name	Poisonous Part	Note
Jack-in-the-Pulpit	*Arisaema triphyllum,* other species	Entire plant	GI, DERM
Japan Plum	*Eriobotrya japonica*	Kernel in pit, entire plant	Cyanide
Japanese Lantern	*Physalis* spp.	Unripe berries	GI
Jasmine	*Cestrum* spp.	Fruit, sap	GI, CNS
Java Bean	*Phaseolus lunatus*	Entire plant	Cyanide (**Note:** cooked beans are †)
Javillo	*Hura crepitans*	Seeds	GI, DERM
Jequirity Bean	*Abrus precatorius*	Seeds	GI
Jerusalem Cherry	*Solanum pseudocapsicum*	Immature growths	GI, CARn, DERM
Jetbead	*Rhodotypos scandens*	Entire plant	Reputedly contains cyanogenic glycoside
Jicamilla	*Jatropha* spp.	Seeds	GI, DERM
Jimmy Weed	*Aplopappus heterophyllus*	Leaves	CARn, *
Jimson Weed, Gysum weed, Gymsom weed	*Datura stramonium*	Entire plant	CNS, CARn, DERM
Joe-Pye Weed	*Eupatorium* spp.	Entire plant	CARn
Johnson Grass	*Sorghum halepense*	Entire plant	CARn, cyanide
Jonquil	*Narcissus* spp.	Bulbs	GI, DERM
Kale	*Brassica* spp.	Leaves	Goitrogenic, †
Karaka nut	*Corynocarpus laevigatus*	Seed	Convulsants; fruit reportedly toxic
Kentucky Coffee Tree	*Gymnocladus dioicus*	Seeds	CNS
Klamath Weed	*Hypericum perforatum*	Entire plant	PHO, DERM

(continued)

Table A-1 *(continued)*

Plant	Scientific Name	Poisonous Part	Note
Knapweed, Starthistle	*Centaurea* spp.	N/A	*
Labrador Tea	*Ledum* spp.	Entire plant	TOX
Laburnum	*Labumum x watereri*	Entire plant	CNS
Lady Slipper	*Cypripedium spectabiles*	Entire plant	DERM
Lady's Thumb	*Polygonum persicaria*	Entire plant	DERM, PHO, CARn
Lambkill	*Kalmia augustifolia*	Leaves, nectar	GI, CAR, CNS
Lamb's Quarters	*Chenopodium album*	Entire plant	CARn
Larkspur	*Delphinium* spp.	Entire plant	CAR, DERM
Laurel	*Rhododendron* spp.	Leaves	CAR
Lechuguilla	*Agave lecheguilla*	Entire plant	HEP
Leek	Allium tricoccum	Bulbs, bulblets, flowers, stems	GI, DERM, †
Lesser Hemlock	*Aethusa cynapium*	Entire plant	GI
Lily-of-the-Fields	*Anemone* spp.	Entire plant	GI, DERM, *
Lily-of-the-Valley	*Convallaria majalis*	Entire plant	CAR
Lima Bean	*Phaseolus lunatus*	Entire plant	Cyanide (**Note:** cooked beans are †)
Linseed	*Linum usitatissimus*	Entire plant	CARn, cyanide, goitrogenic
Lobelia	*Lobelia* spp.	Leaves, stems, fruit	CNS, DERM
Locoweeds	*Astragalus* spp.	Entire plant	Excess selenium
Locoweeds	*Oxytropis* spp.	Entire plant	Reputedly TOX
Loquat	*Eriobotrya japonica*	Kernel in pit, entire plant	Cyanide
Lords & Ladies	*Arum maculatum*	Entire plant	GI, DERM
Lupines	*Lupinus* spp.	Leaves, seeds	TOX

Plant	Scientific Name	Poisonous Part	Note
Madam Fata	*Hippobroma longiflora*	Entire plant	Convulsants
Malanga	*Xanthosoma* spp.	Leaves	GI,DERM
Mallow	*Malva parviflora*	Entire plant	CARn
Manchineel	*Hippomane mancinella*	Latex	GI, DERM
Mandrake	*Mandragora officinarum*	Entire plant	CNS
Mangold	*Beta vulgaris*	Leaves	CARn, may contain toxic levels of oxalates
Marijuana	*Cannabis sativa*	Leaves, flower bracts	HAL
Marsh Marigold	*Caltha palustris*	Entire plant	GI, DERM
Marvel of Peru	*Mirabilis jalapa*	Entire plant	GI, DERM
Matrimony Vine	*Lycium* spp.	Leaves	GI
May Apple	*Podophyllum peltatum*	Entire plant except fruit	CNS, TOX
Meadow Brake	*Onoclea sensibilis*	Leaves	CNS
Meadow	Colchicum autumnale	Entire plant	GI, DERM Saffron
Mescal Bean	*Sephora secundiflora*	Seeds	CNS
Mesquite Grass	*Holcus lanatus*	Entire plant	Cyanide
Mesquite	*Prosopis chilensis*		*
Mexican Firewood	*Kochia scoparia*	Entire plant	CARn
Mexican Poppy, Prickly Poppy	*Argemone* spp.	Entire plant	TOX
Mezereon	*Asclepias* spp.	Entire plant, especially fruit and seeds	CAR, DERM, GI
Mezereon	*Daphne mezereum*	Entire plant	GI, DERM, anticoagulant
Mezereon	*Euphorbia* spp.	Latex	GI, CARn, DERM

(continued)

Table A-1 *(continued)*

Plant	Scientific Name	Poisonous Part	Note
Milk Bush	*Euphorbia* spp.	Latex	GI, CARn, DERM
Milkweeds	*Asclepias* spp.	Entire plant, especially fruit and seeds	CAR, DERM, GI
Miner's Lettuce	*Montia perfoliata*	Entire plant	CARn
Mistletoes	*Phoradendron* spp.	Entire plant	GI, DERM
Moccasin Flower	*Cypripedium spectabiles*	Entire plant	DERM
Mock Azalea	*Adenium* spp.	Entire plant	CAR
Mock Orange	*Poncirus trifoliata*	Fruit	GI
Monkey Pistol	*Hura crepitans*	Seeds	GI
Monkey Pod	*Samonia samon*	Entire plant	GI, DERM
Monkshood, Monkey Pod	*Aconitum* spp.	Entire plant	CAR
Moonseed	*Menispermum canadense*	Fruit	Convulsants
Morning Glories	*Ipomea* spp.	Entire plant	CARn, HAL
Mountain Laurel	*Kalmia latifolia*	Leaves, nectar	GI, CAR, CNS
Mountain-Mahogany	*Cercocarpus montanus*	Wilted leaves and entire plant	Cyanide
Mullein	*Verbascom thapsus*	N/A	*
Mushrooms (many wild varieties)	*Mushrooms (many types)*	Entire plant	Many wild species are toxic, even fatal — see appropriate literature for identification and toxicities
Mustard	*Brassica* spp.	Leaves	CARn, goitrogenic, †
Naked-Lady Lily	Amaryllis spp.	Bulbs	GI

Plant	Scientific Name	Poisonous Part	Note
Needle Grass, Porcupine Grass	*Stipa* sp.	N/A	*
Nettle	*Urtica procera*	Entire plant	CARn
Ngaio Tree	*Myoporum laetum*	Entire plant	Convulsants, TOX
Night-Blooming Jessamine	*Cestrum nocturnum*	Fruit, sap	GI, CNS
Nightshades	*Solanum* spp.	Immature growths	GI, CARn, DERM
No common name in U.S.	*Coriaria myrtifolia*	Entire plant	TOX
No common name in U.S.	*Pernettya* spp.	Leaves, nectar	CAR; genus synonymous with *Gaultheria spp.*
Nux-Vomica Tree	*Strychnos nux-vomica*	Entire plant	CNS
Oaks	*Quercus* spp.	Buds, leaves	GI, KID
Oats	*Avena sativa*	N/A	Safe unless contaminated with smut or fungi
Oleander	*Nerium oleander* and other species	Entire plant	GI, CAR, DERM
Onion	*Allium cepa*	Bulbs, bulblets, flowers, stems	GI, DERM, †
Opium Poppy	*Papaver somniferum*	Seed pods	TOX, HAL
Panic-Grass	*Panicum capillare*	Entire plant	HEP, CARn
Pasque Flower	*Anemone* spp. (includes *Pulsatilla* spp.)	Entire plant	GI, DERM, *
Pea Straw Hay	*Pisum sativum*	N/A	*
Peach	*Prunus* spp.	Seeds, entire plant	Cyanide
Pepper Bush	*Leucothoe* spp.	Leaves, nectar	GI, CNS
Peregrina	*Jatropha integerrima*	Seeds	GI, DERM

(continued)

Table A-1 *(continued)*

Plant	Scientific Name	Poisonous Part	Note
Periwinkle	*Vinca* spp.	Entire plant	HAL
Pheasant's Eye	*Adonis* spp.	Entire plant	CAR
Philodendron	*Philodendron* spp.	Leaves	GI
Physic Nut	*Jatropha curcas*	Seeds	GI, DERM
Pigeonberry	*Phytolacca americans*	Entire plant	GI, DERM
Pig-Lilly	*Zantedeschida* spp.	Leaves	GI
Pigweed	*Chenopodium* spp.	Entire plant	CARn
Pingue	*Helenium* spp.	Entire plant	DERM
Plum	*Prunus* spp.	Seeds	Cyanide
Plumeless Thistle	*Carduus* sp.	Entire plant	CARn
Poha	*Physalis* spp.	Unripe berries	GI
Poinsettia	*Euphorbia pulcherrima*	Latex	GI, CARn, DERM
Point Vetch	*Oxytropis* spp.	Entire plant	Reputedly TOX
Poison Ivy	*Toxicodendron radicans*	Leaves, bark, fruit	DERM
Poison Oak	*Toxicodendron* spp.	Leaves, bark, fruit	DERM
Poison Suckleya	*Suckleya suckleyana*	Leaves	Cyanide
Poison Sumac	*Toxicodendron vernix*	Leaves, bark, fruit	DERM
Poison Wood	*Metopium toxiferum*	Entire plant	DERM
Poison-Vetches	*Astragalus*	Entire plant	Excess selenium
Pokeberry (also Pokeweed)	*Phytolacca americans*	Entire plant	GI, DERM
Polypody Brake	*Onoclea sensibilis*	Leaves	CNS
Popcorn Flower	*Plagiobothrys* sp.	Entire plant	CARn
Potato	*Solanum tuberosum*	Immature growths	GI, CARn, DERM
Poverty Grass, Triple Awn, Wire Grass	*Aristida* spp.	N/A	*

Plant	Scientific Name	Poisonous Part	Note
Precatory Bean	*Abrus precatorius*	Seeds	GI
Prickly Lettuce	*Lactuca sariola*	Entire plant	CARn
Pride-of-India	*Melia azedarach*	Entire plant	Convulsants
Primrose	*Primula* spp.	Leaves	DERM
Princes's Plume	*Stanleya pinnata*	Entire plant	May have toxic levels of selenium
Privet (also Common Privet)	*Ligustrum vulgare*	Entire plant	GI
Puncture Vine	*Tribulus terrestris*	Entire plant	HEP, CARn, *
Purge Nut	*Jatropha* spp.	Seeds	GI, DERM
Purple Allamanda	*Cryptostegia* spp.	Entire plant	CAR
Purple Foxglove	*Digitalis purpurea*	Entire plant	CAR, GI
Purplecockle	*Agrostemma githago*	Seeds	GI
Pursh	*Lupinus* spp.	Entire plant	TOX
Pyracantha	*Pyracantha* sp.	N/A	*
Queen's Delight	*Stillingia treculeana*	Leaves, stems	Cyanide
Ragwort	*Senecio jacobaea*	Entire plant	HEP
Rain Tree	*Samonia samon*	Entire plant	GI, DERM
Raspberry	*Rubus* spp.	N/A	*
Rattlebox	*Crotalaria* spp.	Entire plant	HEP
Rattlebush (also Rattlebox)	*Sesbania* spp.	Seeds	GI
Rayless	*Aplopappus heterophyllus*	Leaves	CARn, *
Red Clover	*Trifolium pratens*	Entire Plant	DERM, PHO, TOX, *
Red Puccoon	*Sanguinaria canadensis*	Juice, sap	DERM

(continued)

Table A-1 *(continued)*

Plant	Scientific Name	Poisonous Part	Note
Rescue Grass	*Bromus* spp.	Entire plant	CARn
Rhododendron	*Rhododendron* spp.	Leaves	CAR
Rhubarb	*Rheum rhaponticum*	Leaf blades	GI, oxalic acid
Ricino	*Ricinus communis*	Seeds	GI, DERM
Rocky Mountain Bee Plant	*Cleome serrulata*	Entire plant	CARn
Rosary Pea	*Abrus precatorius*	Seeds	GI
Rouge Plant	*Rivina humilis*	Leaves, roots	GI
Rubber Vine	*Cryptostegia* spp.	Entire plant	CAR
Rubberweed	*Helenium* spp.	Entire plant	DERM
Rue	*Ruta graveolens*	Entire plant	GI, PHO
Rusty Leaf, Rustyleaf	*Menziesia ferruginea*	Entire plant	TOX
Sacahuista	*Nolina texana*	Foliage	HEP; safe unless contaminated with Ergot fungus (*Claviceps* sp.)
Sage	*Salvia reflexa*	Leaves of certain varieties	CARn
Sandbox Tree	*Hura crepitans*	Seeds	GI, DERM
Sandburs	*Cenchrus* spp.	N/A	*
Scarlet Pimpernel	*Anagallis arvensis*	Leaves	DERM
Scotch Broom	*Cytisus scoparious*	Seeds	TOX
Scouring Rush	*Equisetum* spp.	Stems	TOX, *
Sea Onion	*Urginea maritima*	Bulbs	CAR
Senna (also Coffee Senna)	*Cassia occidentalis*	Entire plant	GI
Sensitive Fern	*Onoclea sensibilis*	Leaves	CNS
Sheep Laurel	*Kalmia augustifolia*	Leaves, nectar	GI, CAR, CNS

Plant	Scientific Name	Poisonous Part	Note
Sheep Sorrel	*Rumex acetosella*	Leaves	CARn, DERM, oxalates
Showy Lady Slipper	*Cypripedium reginae*	Entire plant	DERM
Silky Lupine	*Lupinus* spp.	Entire plant	TOX
Singletary Pea	*Lathyrus* spp.	Stems, seeds	CNS
Skeletonweed	*Lygodesmia juncea*	Entire plant	CARn
Skunk Cabbage	*Symplocarpus foetidus*	Leaves	GI
Slipper Flower	*Pedilanthus tithymaloides*	Latex	GI
Smartweeds	*Polygonum* spp.	Entire plant	CARn, PHO, DERM
Smooth Bromegrass	*Bromus* spp.	Entire plant	CARn
Snake's Head Bulb	*Fritillaria meleagris*	Entire plant	CAR
Sneezeweed	*Helenium* spp.	Entire plant	DERM
Snowberry	*Symphoricarpus albus*	Entire plant	GI, DERM
Snowdrop	*Galanthus nivalis*	Entire plant	GI
Snow-on-the-Mountain	*Euphorbia marginata*	Latex	GI, DERM
Sorghum	*Sorghum* spp.	Leaves	CARn, cyanide
Sorrels	*Oxalis pes-caprae*	Leaves	DERM, oxalates
Sorrels, Sheep Sorrel	*Rumex* spp.	Leaves	CARn, DERM, oxalates
Sourgrass	*Triglochin maritima*	Leaves	Cyanide
Soursob	*Oxalis pes-caprae*	Leaves	Oxalates
Sow Thistle	*Sonchus* spp.	Entire plant	CARn
Soybean	*Glycine* max.	Entire plant	CARn, goitrogenic

(continued)

Table A-1 *(continued)*

Plant	Scientific Name	Poisonous Part	Note
Spanish Needles, Stick-tights	*Bidens* spp.	N/A	*
Spathe Flower	*Spathiphyllum* spp.	Entire plant	GI, DERM
Spindle Tree	*Euonymus europaeus*	Fruit	CAR
Spineless Horsebrush	*Tetradymia canescens*	Leaves, buds	PHO
Spreading Dogbane	*Apocynum androsaemifolium*	Entire plant	CAR
Spring Rabbitbush	*Tetradymia glabrata*	Leaves, buds	HEP
Spurge Laurel	*Daphne laureola*	Entire plant	GI, KID, DERM
Spurge Nettle	*Jatropha* spp.	Seeds	GI, DERM
Spurges	*Euphorbia* spp.	Leaves, stems, latex	GI, DERM
Squill (also Red Squill)	*Urginea maritima*	Bulbs	CAR
Squirrel Corn	*Dicentra cucullaria*	Entire plant	DERM, convulsants
St. Johnswort	*Hypericum perforatum*	Entire plant	PHO, DERM
Stagger Weed	*Dicentra cucullaria*	Entire plant	DERM, convulsants
Staggergrass	*Amianthemum muscaetoxicum*	Leaves, underground parts	RES
Star-of-Bethlehem	*Hippobroma longiflora*	Entire plant	Convulsants
Star-of-Bethlehem	*Ornithogalum umbellatum*	Entire plant	GI
Steer's Head	*Dicentra uniflora*	Entire plant	DERM, convulsants
Strawberry Bush	*Euonymus americanus*	Fruit	CAR
Strychnine	*Strychnos nux-vomica*	Entire plant	CNS
Sudan Grass	*Sorghum* spp.	Leaves	CARn, cyanide

Plant	Scientific Name	Poisonous Part	Note
Sugar Beet	*Beta vulgaris*	Leaves	CARn; may contain toxic levels of oxalates
Summer Cypress	*Kochia scoparia*	Entire plant	CARn
Sweet Bells	*Leucothoe* spp.	Leaves, nectar	CAR, CNS
Sweet Cassava	*Manihot esculenta*	Plant above ground	Cyanide; root (tuber) can be eaten raw
Sweet Pea	*Lathyrus* spp.	Stems, seeds	CNS
Sweet Potato Vines	*Ipomea* spp.	Entire plant	CARn, HAL
Sweetclovers (both white and yellow)	*Melilotus* spp.	Entire plant	CARn
Sycamore	*Platanus occidentalis*	N/A	*
Tall Fescue	*Festuca arundinacea*	Moldy plant	Safe unless contaminated with Ergot fungus (*Claviceps* sp.)
Tansy	*Tanacetum vulgare*	Leaves, stems	GI, DERM, convulsants
Taro	*Alocasis* spp., *Colocasia esculenta*	Leaves, stems	GI
Tarweed	*Amsinckia intermedia*	Seed-like nutlets	CARn; plant may contain toxic levels of nitrates
Thornapple	*Datura stramonium*	Entire plant	CNS, CARn, DERM
Thoroughwort	*Eupatorium* spp.	Entire plant	CARn
Tobacco (also Tree Tobacco)	*Nicotiana* spp.	Leaves	CNS
Tomato	*Lycospersicon (Lycopersicum) esculentum*	Entire plant except for fruit	GI

(continued)

Table A-1 *(continued)*

Plant	Scientific Name	Poisonous Part	Note
Traveler's Joy	*Clematis* spp.	Entire plant	GI, CNS, DERM
Trifoliate Orange	*Poncirus trifoliata*	Fruit	GI
Trumpet Vine	*Campsis* spp.	Leaves, flowers, plant	DERM
Tulips	*Tulipa* spp.	Bulbs	DERM
Tumbleweed	*Amaranthus hibridus*	Entire plant	CARn; may contain toxic levels of nitrates
Tung Nut, Tung Tree	*Aleurites fordii*	Entire plant	GI (**Note:** Fumes from tung oil, found in many paints and wood finishes, are also toxic)
Turkey mullein	*Eremocarpus setegerus*	N/A	*
Variegated Thistle	*Silybum marianum*	Entire plant	CARn
Velvet Grass	*Holcus lanatus*	Entire plant	Cyanide
Venus Flytrap	*Dionaea* spp.	Entire plant	TOX
Vetch (also Common Vetch)	*Vicia* sativa	Entire plant	PHO, Cyanide
Vetchling	*Lathyrus* spp.	Stems, seeds	CNS
Viper's Bugloss	*Echium plantagineum* and *Echium vulgare*	Entire plant	HEP
Virgin's-Bower	*Clematis* spp.	Entire plant	GI, CNS, DERM
Wafer Ash	*Ptelea baldwinii*	Entire plant	PHO, DERM
Wahoo	*Euonymus atropurpureus*	Fruit	CAR
Water Dropwort	*Oenanthe crocata*	Entire plant	Convulsants
Water Hemlock	*Cicuta* spp.	Entire plant	CNS, convulsants
West Indian Pinkroot	*Spigelia* spp.	Entire plant	CNS

Plant	Scientific Name	Poisonous Part	Note
Wheat	*Triticum aestivum*	N/A	Safe unless contaminated with fungi
White Anthurium	*Spathiphyllum* spp.	Entire plant	GI, DERM
White Arum-Lily	*Zantedeschia aethiopica*	Leaves	GI
White Balsam-Apple	*Momordica charantia*	Seeds	GI
White Bryony	*Bryonia dioica*	Entire plant	GI, DERM
White Calla	*Zantedeschia aethiopica*	Leaves	GI
White Clover	*Trifolium repens*	Entire plant	Cyanide, *
White Osier	*Leucothoe* spp.	Leaves, nectar	CAR, CNS
White Snakeroot	*Eupatorium* spp.	Leaves	CARn; plant may contain toxic levels of nitrates
Whorled Butterfly	*Asclepias* spp.	Entire plant, especially fruit and seeds	CAR, DERM, GI
Wild Artichoke	*Helianthus annuus*	Entire plant	CARn
Wild Oats	*Avena fatua*	N/A	*
Wild Parsnip	*Pastinaca sativa*	Entire plant	DERM
Wild Pea	*Lathyrus* spp.	Stems, seeds	CNS
Wild Sunflower	*Helianthus annuus*	Entire plant	CARn
Windflower	*Anemone* spp., (includes *Pulsatilla*)	Entire plant	GI, DERM *
Wintersweet	*Acokanthera* spp.	Seeds	CAR
Wisteria	*Wisteria* spp.	Entire plant	GI
Witchgrass	*Panicum capillare*	Entire plant	HEP, CARn
Wonder Flower	*Ornithogalum thyrsoides*	Entire plant	GI
Wood Laurel	*Daphne* spp.	Entire plant	GI, KID, DERM

(continued)

Table A-1 *(continued)*

Plant	Scientific Name	Poisonous Part	Note
Woody Asters	*Xylorrhiza* spp.	Entire plant	May have toxic levels of selenium
Wormseed	*Chenopodium ambrosioides*	Entire plant	CARn
Yaupon	*Ilex vomitoria*	Berries	GI
Yellow Allamanda	*Allamanda cathartica*	Leaves, bark, fruit, sap, seeds	GI, DERM
Yellow Lady Slipper	*Cypripedium parviflorum*	Leaves, stems	DERM
Yellow Nightshade	*Urechites lutea*	Leaves	CAR
Yellow Oleander	*Thevetia peruviana*	Entire plant	CAR
Yellow Pine Flax	*Linum neomexicanum*	Entire plant	Cyanide
Yellow-Be-Still Tree	*Thevetia peruviana*	Entire plant	CAR
Yews	*Taxus* spp.	Entire plant (except red aril)	GI, CAR, volatile oils

Edible Ornamental Plants

Table A-2 was compiled from several sources, including iguana and other reptile keepers and plant databases, and uses the following symbols:

*   Some or all are high in oxalates; feed only in moderation.

‡   Remove barbed hairs/thorns/prickly spines before feeding.

1   *Plants for a Future* database.

2   Generally considered safe by reptile keepers; saps or resins may be irritants.

3   Anecdotal reports by reptile keepers.

4   University of California, Davis, *Safe Plants* database.

If you feed your iguana any of these plants, keep in mind that a little bit is usually okay, but a lot may not be. Always feed edible ornamentals in moderation and watch your iguana carefully for any signs that the plant has disagreed with him.

Table A-2	Edible Plants		
Plant	**Scientific Name**	**Edible Part(s)**	**Notes**
Astilbe	*Astilbe* spp.	Leaves, flowers	4
Baby's tears	*Soleirolia soleirolii*	Leaves	4
Benjamin Fig	*Ficus benjamina*	Leaves	2
Blue Hibiscus	*Alyogyne huegeli*	Flowers	3
Branched Pencil Cholla	*Opuntia* spp.	Fruit	1‡
Bunny Ears	*Opuntia* spp.	Fruit	1‡
Carnations	*Dianthus*	Petals	1
China Jute	*Abutilon*	Flowers	1
Dahlia	*D. pinnata, D. rosea*	Flowers	1
Dandelion	*Taraxacum officinale*	Leaves, flowerhead	1
Day Lilies (including Coastal Day Lily, Yellow Day Lily, Grassleaf Day Lily)	*Hemerocallis* spp.	Flowers, cooked young leaves	1
Ficus	*Ficus benjamina*	Leaves	2
Geranium (including Lemon Geranium, Apple Geranium, Ivy-Leafed Geranium)	*Pelargonium* spp.	Leaves	1
Geranium (including Wooly Geranium, Sticky Geranium)	*G. bicknelli, G. erianthum, G. viscosissimum* (Not to be confused with *Pelargonium*)	Flowerhead	1
Grape (not ornamental grape — ivys *Cissus* spp.)	*Vitis*	Leaves, fruit	1
Hens and chickens	*Sempervivum tectorum*	Leaves, flowers	4
Hens and chicks	*Echeveria* spp.	Leaves, flowers	4

(continued)

Table A-2 *(continued)*

Plant	Scientific Name	Edible Part(s)	Notes
Hibiscus (including Tropical Hibiscus, Chinese Hibiscus, Shoebackplant)		Leaves, flowers	1
Impatiens	*Impatiens* sp.	Flowers	4
Indian Fig	*Opuntia* spp. and *Opuntia compressa*	Fruit	1‡
Indian Laurel	*Ficus benjamina*	Leaves	2
Japanese Maple	*Acer palmatum*	Leaves	1
Johnny-Jump-Up	*Viola tricolor*	Leaves, flowers	1
Joshua Tree	*Yucca* spp.	Flowers	1
Kudzu	*Pueraria lobata*	Young leaves, shoots	1‡
Lima Beans	*Phaseolus lunatus*	Dried beans that have been cooked only	1
Mesquite	*Prosopis glandulosa torreyana (P. chilensis)*	Leaves	3
Mulberry, Korean	*Morus australis*	Fruit	1
Mulberry, Mongolian	*Morus mongolica*	Fruit	1
Mulberry, White	*Morus alba, M. alba muticaulis*	Leaves, fruit	1
Nasturtium	*Tropaeolum majus, t. minus*	Leaves, flowers, seeds (***Note:*** seeds and seed pods are very spicy hot)	1
Oregon Maple	*Acer macrophyllum*	Leaves	1
Our Lord's Candle	*Yucca* spp.	Flowers	1
Pansies	*V. tricolor hortensis (V. wittrockiana)*	Leaves, flowers	1
Peas (not Sweet Peas), Green Beans	*Pisum sativum* (not *Lathyrus* spp.)	Leaves, seed pods	1
Petunia	*Petunia hybrida*	Flowers	4
Phlox	Phlox paniculata	Flowers	4

Plant	Scientific Name	Edible Part(s)	Notes
Pinks (including Fringed Pinks)	*Dianthus caryophyllus, D. plumarius, D. supberus*	Petals	1
Pothos	*Epipremnum pothos aureus (Epipremnum aureum)*	Leaves	3
Prickly Pear (including Plains Prickly Pear, Twist-Spine Prickly Pear)	*Opuntia* spp.	Fruit	1‡
Red Maple	*Acer rubrum*	Leaves	1
Rock Maple	*Acer macrophyllum*	Leaves	1
Rose (many varieties)	*Rosa* spp.	Petals	1
Small Soapweed	*Yucca* spp.	Flowers	1
Spanish Bayonet	*Yucca* spp.	Flowers	1
Spanish Dagger	*Yucca* spp.	Flowers	1
Spider Plant	*Tradescantia cussonia specata*	Leaves	3
Spiderwort	*Tradescantia virginiana*	Leaves, flowers	1
Split-Leaf Philodendron	*Monstera*	Leaves	3*
Squash	*Cucurbita* spp.	Flowers, fruit	1
Sugar Maple	*Acer saccharinum*	Leaves	1
Sweet William	*Dianthus caryophyllus*	Petals	1
Trailing Abutilon	*Abutilon*	Flowers	1
Tree Chola	*Opuntia* spp.	Fruit	1‡
Violets (not African Violets)	*Viola* spp. (not *Saintpaulia ionantha*)	Leaves, flowers	1
Wandering Jew	*Tradescantia zebrina* and other cultivars	Leaves	3
Yucca (including Datil Yucca, Soaptree Yucca, Soft Tip Yucca, Torrey Yucca)	*Yucca* spp.	Flowers	1
Zucchini	*Cucurbita* spp.	Flowers, fruit	1

Weeds are just plants growing where they aren't wanted. Most of us don't give them any thought. Many, however, are safely edible. To identify weeds and find out whether they're safe to eat, refer to a field guide to edible plants. Several field guides are available. One I like is Thomas S. Elias and Peter A. Dykeman's *Edible Wild Plants: A North American Field Guide* (Sterling Publishing Co., Inc.).

Appendix B

Associations and Veterinary Resources

· ·

*T*wo important resources for iguana keepers are the local herpetological societies and reptile veterinarians. Unfortunately, they can be a bit difficult to find. Herp societies, being volunteer-run organizations, rarely have an office, and the board of directors changes from year to year. They are also rarely listed in the telephone book. By the same token, most reptile veterinarians don't advertise themselves as such, so looking in the phone book is rarely helpful. The information in this chapter can help you locate a herp society if there is one in your area and can help you find vets who are knowledgeable about reptile health care.

Herpetological Societies

My Web site (www.anapsid.org) has a section that includes listings of herpetological societies and reptile veterinarians in the United States, Canada, and, when I've been able to find them, the rest of the world. If you can't find what you're looking for on my Web site, or you don't have access to a computer capable of surfing the Web, check out the following sections.

Local societies

You can search for a local herp society by contacting the following people and places:

- ✔ Departments of biology, ecology, environmental science, vertebrates, veterinary medicine, and/or zoology at junior colleges, colleges, and universities

- ✔ Curators of reptiles, vertebrates, or invertebrates at natural history museums

- ✔ Curators of reptiles, veterinarians, or education departments at zoos

- ✔ Reference librarians at public libraries

✔ Animal shelters, humane societies, departments of animal regulation, or law enforcement agencies that have the primary responsibility for animal regulation in your town or county

✔ Wildlife rehabilitation/rescue centers

✔ Reptile veterinarians

✔ Herpetological societies elsewhere in your state or adjacent states

National and international societies

Here's the contact information for three national and one international herp societies:

American Federation of Herpetoculturists
P.O. Box 300067
Escondido, CA 92030-0067

American Society of Ichthyologists and Herpetologists
Robert Karl Johnson, Secretary
Grice Marine Laboratory
University of Charleston
205 Fort Johnson Road
Charleston, SC 29412
www.utexas.edu/depts/asih/

Society for the Study of Amphibians and Reptiles (SSAR)
George R. Pisani
Division of Biological Sciences
University of Kansas
Lawrence, KS 66045-2106
www.ukans.edu/~ssar/

International Iguana Society (IIS)
P.O. Box 366188
Bonita Springs, FL 34136
www.members.home.net/iis/IISHomePage.html

The International Iguana Society (IIS) focuses more on other iguanid lizards, such as the *Cyclura* (rock and rhino iguanas) and *Ctenosaura* (spiny-tailed iguanas). The IIS does occasionally have articles on green iguanas in its quarterly journal, but *all* articles are appealing if you're interested in iguanas and the areas they come from.

Finding a Reptile Vet

If you can't find a veterinarian through the listings at my Web site or through your local herp society (or there's no herp society in your area), check out the following resource:

Association of Reptilian and Amphibian Veterinarians
P.O. Box 605
Chester Heights, PA 19017
Phone: 610-358-9530
Fax: 610-892-4813
www.arav.org

Your county and state veterinary societies are listed in your phone book (look in the county and state listings). Specify that you're looking for a veterinarian who is experienced in treating reptiles. Note that a veterinarian who advertises that he or she is a reptile specialist may or may not be.

Publications and Booksellers

• •

*A*t this time, there aren't any green iguana–specific periodicals besides the journal of the International Iguana Society (see Appendix B) — and even that journal focuses mostly on other iguanid lizards. But there are several herpetocultural magazines published in the United States and Europe. They all seem to run green iguana–related articles at least once a year. The information in the articles may vary, though, depending on the author's expertise and research.

Publications and Other Resources

This section lists English-language herp magazines published in North America and Europe. You can find herpetocultural magazines in other languages through the herp societies in other countries and at the Herp Magazine page at my Web site, http://www.sonic.net/melissk/herpmagazines.html.

Magazines

Herp magazines publish a variety of articles on all species of herps and many invertebrates, such as tarantulas. You will find articles on captive care, herps in the wild, herp health, herp-related news from around the world, and information on such things as new products, herp expos, and other reptile-related products.

International Reptilian (in the United States)
Zoo Med Laboratories, Inc.
3100 McMillan Road
San Luis Obispo, CA 93401
Phone: 805-542-9988
Fax: 805-542-9295
http://www.zoomed.com

International Reptilian (in Europe)
Zoo Med Europe
Wnketkaai 16, B2800
Mechelen, Belgium
Phone: 32 0 15 202086
Fax: 32 0 15 209433
http://www.reptilian.co.uk/

Reptile & Amphibian Hobbyist
TFH Publishing, Inc.
One TFH Plaza
Third and Union Avenues
Neptune City, NJ 07743
1-800-631-2188
http://www.tfh.com

TFH recently acquired one of the oldest and best herp magazines, *Reptile & Amphibian Magazine*. TFH may have back issues of *R&AM* available for individual purchase.

Reptiles
Subscription Dept.
P.O. Box 58700
Boulder, CO 80322-8700
http://www.animalnetwork.com/reptiles/

Fancy Publications, publisher of *Reptiles* magazine, recently purchased *The Vivarum*, the second oldest and best herp magazine. Contact *Reptiles* to see if it has any back issues of *The Vivarium*.

Journals

For those with an interest in the natural history — biology and behavior — of the green iguana, several herpetology journals sometimes have research articles on various aspects of the life of the green iguana. Here are a few of those journals:

Contemporary Herpetology (an online journal)
University of Louisiana
http://eagle.cc.ukans.edu/~cnaar/CH/

Copeia
American Society of Ichthyologists and Herpetologists
Robert Karl Johnson, Secretary
Grice Marine Laboratory

University of Charleston
205 Fort Johnson Road
Charleston, SC 29412
http://www.utexas.edu/depts/asih/

Herpetology Review and ***Journal of Herpetology***
Society for the Study of Amphibians and Reptiles (SSAR)
George R. Pisani
Division of Biological Sciences
University of Kansas
Lawrence, KS 66045-2106
http://www.ukans.edu/~ssar/

A video

Are you one of those folks who'd get more out of *watching* how to take care of
an iguana than reading about it? I can help. I co-wrote (with colleague Adam
Britton) a video called *Captive Care of the Green Iguana*. Here's a review about
it that was published in *Iguana Times*, 6(1):14-15, the journal of the
International Iguana Society:

> "The quality of the video is apparent throughout. The photography is
> superb, the writing excellent, and the graphics and special effects well
> done. Experts are interviewed throughout the video, with careful atten-
> tion given to every detail. Although somewhat lengthy at 70 minutes, the
> production is a pleasure to watch. Most important of all, the authors who
> wrote most of the text are exceptionally well-informed and provide an
> abundance of interesting and accurate information."

The video is available in the United States through Tiger Netorder's Web site,
at http://www.tigernetorder.com/film/docu/green_iguana.htm).

In Canada, you can order it through Burgham Sales Ltd., Toronto,
416-293-8080.

In the United Kingdom and Europe, you can order it through the producer,
Howard Rockliffe, Scimitar Productions, at hr@scimitarprods.com.

In Belgium, you can find it in two pet stores:

Jungle Shop, Jozef II straat 4, 9000 Gent, +32(0)92243600

De ark, St Jansplein 32, 2060 Antwerp

Herp Booksellers

The widest assortment of books relating to the natural history of wild reptiles and the care of captive reptiles is sold by booksellers specializing in herp books. Some advertise in the various reptile magazines. Many do sales through their Web sites. Here are some of the more notable ones:

Fazo-Corp. Products
Box 69007
RAM, Laval,
Quebec H7X 3M2 Canada

Herpetological Booksellers
P.O. Box 49686
Athens, GA 30604
Phone/Fax: 706-5434-564
http://www.herpbooks.com/

Herpetological Search Service & Exchange
117 East Santa Barbara Road
Lindenhurst, NY 11757
516-957-3624

Herpmed
Steve Grenard
57 Clay Pit Road
Staten Island, NY 10309
718-227-6234
http://www.xmission.com/~gastown/herpmed/phibia.htm
grenard@con2.com

Krieger Publishing Company
Herpetology and Veterinary Medicine
P.O. Box 9542
Melbourne, FL 32902-9542
407-724-9542
http://www.web4u.com/krieger-publishing/

Zoo Book Sales
P.O. Box 405
403 Parkway Avenue North
Lanesboro, MN 55949
Phone: 507-467-8733
Fax: 507-467-8735
http://www.zoobooksales.com/
zoobooks@means.net

Appendix D

Supply Sources

• •

*I*guanas are spreading around the world faster than the supplies they need to survive and thrive. As an iguana keeper, you need to access a wide range of supply sources to provide your iguana with all the things he needs. How difficult that is depends on where you live. This appendix lists various mail-order suppliers for a wide range of herp products as well as other stuff useful to many iguana keepers.

Mail-Order Herp Product Supplies

Along with UVB lights, heat lights, branches, and such, some of these suppliers also carry Nolvasan (a disinfectant), veterinary Betadine (povidone-iodine), and feeding tubes and syringes suitable for reptiles.

For a wide range of captive environment supplies:

The Bean Farm
32514 NE 77th Street
Carnation, WA 98014-6701
Phone: 425-861-7964
Fax: 206-333-4205
www.beanfarm.com

Big Apple Herpetological
90-1 Colin Drive
Holbrook, NY 11741
Phone: 800-92-APPLE; 516-419-1050,
Fax: 516-419-1058
www.bigappleherp.com

David Blair's Critter Corner, Inc.
3410 Del Lago Boulevard, Suite A334
Escondido, CA 92029
Phone (for more info): 760-746-5422
Phone (for orders or a catalog): 800-HERP-NUT
Fax: 760-746-1732
www.herpnut.com

Pondside Herp Supply
516 Townsend Road
Mason, NH 03048-4804 USA
Phone: 603-878-9848
www.herpsupplies.com/

For a wide range of captive environment and health supplies:

Jeffers
310 W. Saunders Road
Dothen, AL 36301
Phone: 800-633-7592
www.1800jefferes.com

UPCO
3705 Pear Street
P.O. Box 969
Street Joseph, MO 64502
Phone: 800-254-8726
www.upco.com/

Valentine, Inc.
Reptile Supply Catalog
4259 S. Western Boulevard
Chicago, IL 60609
Phone: 800-GET-STUF

For rubber and metal feeding tubes, feeding syringes, disinfectants, and candling lights:

Feeding Tech
1935 Dinsmore Road
Clarksville, TN 37040
Order line: 800-688-0850
Info line: 615-647-0273
Fax: 615-647-2829

General captive environment and herp suppliers for Canadians:

The Canadian Zoological Supply Company
P.O. Box 46054
Edmonton, AB
Canada T5K 2S3
Phone: 403-488-1305

Send $2 for a price list.

Pondside Herp Supply
516 Townsend Road
Mason, NH 03048-4804 USA
Phone: 603-878-9848
www.herpsupplies.com/

Outdoor Enclosure Supplies

The following companies sell rigid plastic mesh that's useful for outdoor and indoor enclosures, connectors to simplify the making of frames, and free-standing aviaries.

For rigid plastic mesh:

InterNet, Inc.
7300 49th Avenue North
Minneapolis, MN 55428
Phone: 800-328-8456
Fax: 612-971-0872
http://info@internetplasticnet.com

Norplanet Plastic Nets
Gran V Ia 48 1º Izq.
Bilbao
48011 Bizkaia, Spain
Phone: +34 94 423 09 39
Fax: +34 94 425 70 29
Norplanet@mundivia.es
www.mundivia.com/norplanet/

For connectors to construct enclosures:

Rectangular Connectors
Plow and Hearth
P.O. Box 6000
Madison, VA 22727
Phone: 800-627-1712
www.plowhearth.com

Starplate Connectors
Stromberg's Chicks and Gamebirds
P.O. Box 400
Pine River, MN USA 56474-0400
Phone: 800-720-1134 and 218-587-2222

For free-standing wire aviaries and aviary materials:

Swelland's Cage & Supply Co.
P.O. Box 1619
Ramona, CA 92065
Phone: 760-789-3572 and 800-662-2089
Fax: 760-789-2994
www.swellands.com

Caging Plans and Photos

For caging plans and photos, visit these Web sites:

Catherine Rigby-Burdette's Knock-Down PVC/Mesh Enclosure
www.geocities.com/RainForest/9008/pvccage.html

Jennifer Swofford's Caging Page
www.baskingspot.com/iguanas/cagepage/index.html

This site includes a photo of an outdoor enclosure made with starplate connectors.

Donna Lindeman's Iguana Condo
ourworld.compuserve.com/homepages/ANAUGI/igcondo.htm

George Buce's Water Dragon Enclosures
www.wco.com/~gbuce/html/dragons/cagemain.htm

If you use the enclosures here as a model, be sure to make them bigger for green iguanas.

Enclosure Designers and Makers

Many companies make and sell enclosures, including enclosures made and marketed specifically for reptiles, but few of the enclosures are actually large enough and designed appropriately for the needs of iguanas — and fewer still are reasonably priced. Here are a couple of designers/makers who do both — make well-designed enclosures that are large enough for most iguanas and reasonably priced:

Cages By Design
Rustin Keller
2005 Parkside Drive
Oshkosh, WI 54901
Phone: 920-426-3074
www.cagesbydesign.com/

Cages By Design designs and builds enclosures.

Custom Cages
4 Dry Run Road
River Falls, WI 54022
Order Catalog: 800-766-6354
Fax: 715-425-9998
Orders: 800-766-6354
www.customcages.com/

Custom Cages can produce custom sizes and plans for custom enclosures
outside of its regular product line.

Plant and Veggie Seed Supplies

Many leafy green and vegetable staples can be difficult to find all the time —
or even seasonally, depending on where you live. An alternative is to start
growing your own. You can get all the plants in seed form, and some may be
available as seedlings.

Note that some plants, like chard, may become somewhat invasive, growing
all year long — which isn't necessarily a bad thing if you're looking to provide
some variety in your own salads and soup pot as well as in your iguana's diet.

In the United States:

Park Seed Company
1 Parkton Avenue
Greenwood, SC 29647-0001
Phone: 800-845-3369
Fax: 800-275-9941
www.parkseed.com/

Shepherd's Garden Seeds
30 Irene Street
Torrington, CT 06790
Phone: 860-482-8926
Fax: 860-482-0532
www.shepherdseeds.com/

Territorial Seed Company
P.O. Box 157
Cottage Grove, OR 97424-0061
Phone: 541-942-9547
Fax: 888-657-3131
www.territorial-seed.com/

W. Atlee Burpee Company
300 Park Avenue
Warminster, PA 18974
Phone: 800-333-5808
www.burpee.com/

In the United Kingdom/EEC:

Chiltern Seeds
Bortree Stile, Ulverston
Cumbria, LA12 7PB, England
Phone within the UK: 01229 581137
Phone outside of the UK: 44 1229 581137
www.chilternseeds.co.uk/

Exhibition Seeds
Garden Cottage, Mulgrave Castle
Lythe, Whitby
North Yorkshire, YO21 3RJ, United Kingdom
Phone: 44 (0) 1947 893315
www.exhibition-seeds.co.uk/

In Canada:

McKenzie Seeds
30 - 9th Street
Brandon, Manitoba
Canada, R7A 6E1
Phone: 204-571-7500
www.mckenzieseeds.com/

Territorial Seeds Ltd.
206-8475 Ontario Street
Vancouver, BC, Canada V5X 3E8
Phone: 541-482-8800

Vesey's Seeds
York
Prince Edward Island, Canada - C0A 1P0
Phone: 902-368-7333
Fax: 800-686-0329
Order Desk: 800-363-7333
www.veseys.com/

E-mail Discussion Lists

Many iguana e-mail discussion lists now exist. Some have international memberships; others are more localized by country or regions within a country.

The original Iguanas Mailing List (IML) was started several years ago. The IML is now housed at Onelist.com and has over 800 members worldwide. To find out how to join this list, access the general information page:

www.egroups.com/group/IguanaMail

You can find other e-mail discussion lists by checking through the following Web sites:

E-Groups
www.egroups.com

Escribe
www.escribe.com/

Liszt
www.liszt.com

Topica
www.topica.com

Vivian Neou's List Finder
www.catalog.com/vivian/interest-group-search.html

Index

• B •

baby iguanas. *See also* hatchlings
  feeding, 150, 156–157
  holding, 23
  scales on, 58
  tails of, intentional breaking of, 59
babysitters
  basic description of, 164–167
  difficult behavior and, 170
  introducing iguanas to, 168, 169
  recruiting, 164–167
  trial runs with, 169
bacteria, 64, 95
  air flow and, 114
  bites and, 244–245
  black spots and, 221–222
  E. coli bacteria, 138, 160, 243
  feeding and, 160
  gram negative, 245
  gram positive, 245
  mites and, 236
  types of, 245
baseline assessments, 36
basilisks, 51
basking, 33, 37
  areas, importance of, 44
  areas, setting up, 105–106
  branches for, 28, 31
  enclosure size and, 86
  free-roaming and, 105–106
  photoperiods and, 69
  social groups and, 40
  thermoregulation and, 68
bathing
  basic description of, 131–134
  daily routines and, 194
  getting rid of stubborn dirt when,
    133–134
  insuring complete shedding through, 231
  povidone-iodine baths, 214, 222, 233,
    237–238, 245
  tips, 132–133
  treating constipation with, 223

  treating dermatitis with, 233
  treating mites with, 227–238
  treating prolapses with, 229
Baytril, 232
Bean Farm, 331
Betadine, 29
Big Apple Herpetological, 331
biting, 13, 24, 77, 244–245. *See also*
    aggression
black spots, 221–222
blackening skin syndrome, 222
bladder, 64
bleach, 135, 138, 160
bleeding, 288
blisters, 214, 233–234
blood, 60, 64, 66, 68
blood-stop powder, 29
blotched lizards, 51
blue-belly lizards, 51
boarding iguanas, 167–168, 170
bodyguarding iguanas, 195–196
bones. *See also* metabolic bone disease
    (MBD)
  broken, 24
  disease, 25, 63, 147, 166
  prominent, 25
booksellers, 330
boredom, 164
branches, for basking, 28, 31
breathing, heavy, 60–61
breeding, 38, 62–63. *See also* eggs
  aggression and, 174–175
  basic description of, 249–258
  behavioral changes related to, 252–256,
    261–262
  constipation and, 223
  feeding and, 159, 262–264
  physical changes related to, 250–252
  tympanum and, 56
brewer's yeast, 151
Britton, Adam, 329
Buce, George, 334

• I •

• J •

• T •

Notes

Notes

Notes

IDG BOOKS WORLDWIDE
BOOK REGISTRATION

Register This Book and Win!

We want to hear from you!

Visit **http://my2cents.dummies.com** to register this book and tell us how you liked it!

- Get entered in our monthly prize giveaway.
- Give us feedback about this book — tell us what you like best, what you like least, or maybe what you'd like to ask the author and us to change!
- Let us know any other *For Dummies®* topics that interest you.

Your feedback helps us determine what books to publish, tells us what coverage to add as we revise our books, and lets us know whether we're meeting your needs as a *For Dummies* reader. You're our most valuable resource, and what you have to say is important to us!

Not on the Web yet? It's easy to get started with *Dummies 101®: The Internet For Windows® 98* or *The Internet For Dummies®* at local retailers everywhere.

Or let us know what you think by sending us a letter at the following address:

For Dummies Book Registration
Dummies Press
10475 Crosspoint Blvd.
Indianapolis, IN 46256

™
...FOR DUMMIES

BESTSELLING BOOK SERIES